Versatile VIZSLA

MARION I. COFFMAN

Alpine
Blue Ribbon Books
Loveland, Colorado

Versatile Vizsla
Copyright © 1991, 2004 by Marion I. Coffman

Library of Congress Cataloging-in-Publication Data

Coffman, Marion I., 1928-
    Versatile vizsla / Marion I. Coffman--2nd ed.
        p. cm.
    Includes bibliographical references and index.
    ISBN 1-57779-056-1
        1. Vizsla. I. Title.

SF429.V5C64 2004
636.75--dc22   2004047716

The information contained in this book is complete and accurate to the best of our knowledge. All recommendations are made without guarantee on the part of the author or Alpine Publications, Inc. The author and publisher disclaim any liability with the use of this information.

For the sake of simplicity, the terms "he" or "she" are sometimes used to identify an animal or person. These are used in the generic sense only. No discrimination of any kind is intended toward either sex.

Many manufacturers secure trademark rights for their products. When Alpine Publications is aware of a trademark claim, we identify the product name by using initial capital letters.

This book is available at special quantity discounts for breeders and for club promotions, premiums, or educational use. Write for details.

Cover Design: Laura Newport
Front Cover Photo © Christina M. Freitag
Back Cover Photos: (top) © Pet Portraits by Pam and Sherry; (bottom) © Sharon Malnar
Editing: Deborah Helmers
Layout: Laura Newport

First printing of Second Edition, May 2004

2 3 4 5 6 7 8 9 0

Printed in the United States of America.

Contents

This one is for you, Sanyi.
My sweet, gentle, happy friend.
You never met a person you
didn't like. You were my teacher.
And I —listened

There is a special place in life,
A goal I must attain.
A dream that I must follow,
For I won't be back again.
There is a mark that I must leave,
However small it be.
A legacy of love for those,
Who follow after me.

—Author unknown

Preface

The history of today's Vizsla is a composite of fact and fiction, legend and conjecture, which often lacks specific dates and description. However, by closely studying the history of Hungary and its people, one is able to combine the development of the country with the use and type of dog desired for specific conditions. What we do know is that in feudal times, hunting was the exclusive privilege of wealthy landowners, and they demanded high standards in everything associated with hunting. We owe them much for developing the wonderful Vizsla.

In my thirty-six years of breeding, raising, training, and exhibiting innumerable Vizslas, I have learned and accumulated a wealth of practical experience and knowledge that I hope, by putting it down in this book, will interest all Vizsla owners, whether first-time owners or experienced breeders or exhibitors. I hope I am able to help you gain some insight into the wonderful world of Vizslas.

My treatment of genetics and its application to the breeding of Vizslas has been simplified so as to reach the beginning breeder, but it is only with some knowledge of how the genes function that we can have control over the results of any breeding program. My principal advice to every breeder is never to compromise—aim for quality from the first litter to the last, and do not settle for anything less than the best, not only with your brood bitch, but with your stud dog.

All puppies are appealing; it is how they grow up that makes the difference. Hopefully, the photographs of young puppies will help beginning owners make a wise choice when selecting their first puppy. I cannot emphasize enough that the Vizsla has to be a close family member to be truly appreciated. His intelligence, affection, and wonderful personality put him on a level far above most breeds.

The whelping chapter should be able to guide not only the experienced breeder, but the owner who is facing the scary situation of whelping a first litter. If it is any consolation, whelping my twentieth litter was just as frightening as the first. Each birth can present a new situation.

My last chapter on the aging dog was written with tears in my eyes. I have lost a lot of Viszlas over the years, since I always owned multiple ones at the same time. I know all too well what it is like to put a part of yourself into the grave with one of your favorites.

I hope readers enjoy going through this book as much as I enjoyed putting it together. It is not just an up-to-date version of my previous one. It is a whole new story.

Marion I. Coffman

Acknowledgements

Thanks to all those who provided photographs for this book, and for those breeders and owners whose support of the first edition made this second edition possible. Thanks also to the staff of Alpine Publications for believing in The Versatile Vizsla and for editorial and publishing expertise.

I owe so many special thanks to a very dear friend who is no longer with us, Elizabeth Mihalyi. I met Elizabeth years ago in California and spent several trips flying back to visit and collect a part of her story. She was the strongest, bravest woman I have ever met, even though she looked upon her flight from Hungary as an adventure in a covered wagon, like the American pioneers. She brought the same indomitable spirit to America to start a new life that had supported her during the six years as a refugee

She came East to Connecticut for a month to paint a picture of my Vizsla and we spent our dinner hours over wine and food while she fascinated me with stories of her life. I promised her I would go to Hungary some day to see the land she had left behind, and I got my chance in 1999. I walked the hills and streets in Budapest and saw damage from bombings and tanks. I saw the immense mansions that had belonged to the wealthy, now turned into beautiful museums and monuments. And I saw the small towns, beautiful horses, thatched roofs, farms . . . and Vizslas. I thanked Elizabeth every minute I was there for her inspiring story.

A welcome rest in the sun. Photo © Christina M. Freitag.

CHAPTER ONE

Meet the Vizsla

Owning a Vizsla will change your life forever. The Vizsla standard calls for the breed to be "demonstratively affectionate," and whether he is jumping up to lick your face, grabbing your wrist in his mouth, sharing your bed, dinner, chair, or lap, or just bringing a favorite toy, he is impossible to ignore.

The Hungarian Vizsla represents the best in both sporting dog and loving, loyal companion. He is the smallest of the all-round pointer-retriever breeds and size is undoubtedly one of his most attractive characteristics.

A Vizsla holds a unique position for a sporting dog—that of both house companion and family dog, and a close-working personal gundog in the field. He does not make a good kennel dog and only reaches full capacity as an enjoyable companion when he is a member of the family. Bred and owned originally by wealthy Hungarian landowners, Vizslas were always very privileged canines, holding a high place in the Hungarian sporting circles but not expected to sleep outside at the end of a day in the fields. The Vizsla always lived and traveled with his family and was as much a family member as a child.

A Vizsla is striking in appearance. His beautiful golden-rust color never fails to attract attention. He is a joy to watch in motion and he is just as enthusiastic about chasing a

Am. Int'l Ch. BISS CMF Leitz, Camera, Action. Photo © Christina M. Freitag.

ball as a butterfly, leaf, or squirrel. Still, he can freeze to a perfect pointing statue when he has quartered a birdfield and found game.

A Vizsla is highly intelligent—do not ever underestimate the learning potential of a ten-week-old puppy. He is obedient and ever strives to please, but he gets bored without a challenge and something active to do. Because of his highly developed sense of humor and intelligence he not only can be taught easily, but can think up things to do on his own. A Vizsla can use his front feet or mouth to figure out how to turn a doorknob or open a refrigerator, or even get out of his crate. He has been known to climb a ladder and sit on a roof. He can ring bells, collect shoes, empty wastebaskets, and be an official greeter and a guardian.

A comfort seeker, a Vizsla would rather sleep on your bed than on the floor. He thinks sofas were made especially for him and, if allowed, will remain a lap dog for life. He will follow you around the house from room to room rather than be left alone for even a minute. If you put your Vizsla out-side, he will sit on the doorstep begging for you to come out with him.

In the field, a Vizsla combines all the attributes of the Pointer, Setter, and Retriever. He points by instinct, and is a very close-working dog, making him an ideal weekend companion gundog. He is fast, extremely birdy, enthusiastic, with a good nose. He has a soft mouth, retrieving game without damage or marring, and is a diligent worker on upland game, with discriminating bird sense. His striking color in the field and quick, graceful movement make for an enjoyable combination.

The Vizsla has become more popular in the show ring as his aristocratic appearance, dignified and balanced bearing, intelligence, animation, graceful carriage, and love of attention has attracted new enthusiasts. Once you own a Vizsla, you are hooked for life. Each new owner finds a new and different way to incorporate his dog into his own life.

A Vizsla can cheerfully go backpacking, hiking, and camping and can accompany his owner to the office. He enjoys tobogganing

Life can't get much better than this.

Off for a successful find in the bird field. Photo © Christina M. Freitag.

in the snow and he loves water. A perfect companion on a boat trip or in a swimming pool at home, a Vizsla will be happy to swim or retrieve balls all day. He will even be content just to stand for hours in a shallow stream and silently watch small fish swim around him. As long as he is with his owner, he is a happy dog.

As a trained obedience dog, a Vizsla can be used to educate and entertain at civic centers, county fairs, schools and nursing and retirement homes. He has been employed as a drug sniffer, a guide dog for the blind, and a hearing-impaired service dog. His easy care and willingness makes him an ideal choice for these tasks.

Obedience and agility competition enthusiasts will tell you that these are where the Vizsla excels. He is a natural showman, and is never happier than when he has been given something to do. He is easily bored

Ch. Russet Leather Warrior's Mark, JH. Owned by S. Samuels and B. Wanjon. Photo © Kit Rodwell.

Koppertone's Casey Baratom, UD, AX, AXJ, Intense, with ears flying, clears the agility bars jump. Owned by Marianne Megna. Photo by S. Surfman.

Ch. Dorratz Diamond Tiara at twelve years of age, still enjoys a kiss from a young friend. Photo by Doris Ratzlaff.

with the repetition of the beginning classes and training but will find his element in jumping and retrieving exercises. It comes as no surprise to Vizsla owners that the first dog in American Kennel Club history to earn a Triple Championship title for completing field, show, and obedience championships was a Vizsla. History repeated itself when the Vizsla was the first dog of any breed to earn a Quintuple Championship. The breed is truly versatile.

For an emotionally disturbed or handicapped child, a Vizsla can be sensitive and loving. In many cases a child has been able to relate closely to a dog when every other contact has failed. A Vizsla will bond easily to someone who needs him in a special way.

A Vizsla teaches so much about love because he has so much to give, His affection is always there. He is a joy to know and happiness to own. He is full of strength, vitality, elegance, and beauty. A Vizsla is a 365-days-a-year companion, accepting the role of protector, friend, and hunter. A Vizsla is truly a dog to be proud of owning, and he is forgiving in case, in a moment of forgetfulness, you call him a dog—he is a *Vizsla*.

Early History of the Vizsla

The history of Hungary, including information about its Magyar nomads who had hounds that may have been the ancestors of the Vizsla, first appeared in writings around 890 A.D. Before that date, there is little to be found in history books that is not guesswork. Language researchers have been able to establish the nomads as descendents of Ugrians and Finns. Included in that group were people from areas ranging from Turkey to Manchuria and Mongolia. There have been many attempts through the years to find the original home of the Magyars, but all without success.

While it has been established that most of the nomads raised reindeer, cattle, and horses, it is doubtful that there was any set pattern of breeding dogs for a specific use during the years wandering. Their "camp dogs" were yellow-colored descendents of the Mastiff and hound-type dogs encountered along the way.

When the Great Wall of China restrained the nomads in their search for new grazing lands, it diverted them to the west, and out of that melee of footloose tribes the Hungarians began to emerge. Climbing the Carpathian Mountains, they crossed the Vereke Pass, and in 890 A.D. moved into the area that came to be known as Hungary. Primitive carvings in stone found in the Carpathian regions and estimated to be 1,000 years old show the early Magyar hunter with dogs closely resembling the early Vizsla.

The Magyars elected Stephen I (969-1038) as their first king and settled down to periods of farming between wars with invading hordes. It was during King Stephen's rule that the country was centralized. He organized Hungary into counties, each headed by a count. Conveying land titles to these major nobles assured Stephen of their aid during times of need. This form of feudalism kept its grip longer in Hungary than in almost any other country in Europe.

This organization of tillable lands then entered a peak period that would last almost three centuries. With the landowners settled down to peaceful farming, producing grain and raising horses, cattle, and pigs, there was time to develop a breed of dog related to these landowners' needs and the type of hunting they pursued.

A Mastiff-hound strain of dogs was originally found in the great mountain spine stretching east to west across Asia and Europe and comprised of the Himalayas and the mountains of Tibet—the very area that the Magyars had traversed in their nomadic search for farmland. The Magyars' yellow dogs, closely allied with this type of dog, were then selectively bred until the hunter had dogs with specialized abilities. The breeds that resulted, despite their diversity in size and color, resembled each other in the acuteness of their sense of smell, a pronounced stop, large ears, and a short muzzle.

5

At this point the sporting element was secondary to necessity. Birds were hunted using these scenting dogs to search for game and falcons to retrieve it. Thus it was that the pointer type evolved as a suitable dog. The quiet movements and deliberate action of these dogs made them especially useful to the Magyars. This pointer type could also drive the pheasants and partridge they located into nets, or serve as useful retrievers of the dead birds, although at that time they probably lacked the soft mouth of the later dog.

In 1526 the Turks invaded Hungary, occupying and ruling it for the next 150 years. The Turks brought their own dogs, which were subsequently bred to the Magyars' yellow pointers. Since the Magyars were supposed to have come from that part of Asia which was the land of the Turk, the crossbreeding of these dogs could be considered as a sort of "linebreeding." The name *Vizsla* in Turkish means *seek* and in Hungarian *point*. The Vizsla obviously did both at this stage of development.

With the end of Turkish occupation, Hungary was ruled by the German Hapsburgs and, under this new rule, inheritance of land was limited to the upper class and its descendents. These were the people who played an important part in the early development of the Vizsla as we know it today. The breed became a favorite of those early barons and war lords who, either deliberately or by accident, preserved its purity. Even then the reason for the Vizsla's continued existence lay in the fact that his innate hunting ability was fostered and developed by the terrain in which he lived, namely the plains of Hungary.

Here was a section of the country almost entirely agricultural, where grains were raised in abundance, where the growing season was lengthy, the summers hot, and the winters tempered by the proximity of water. Wheat, corn, rye, and barley

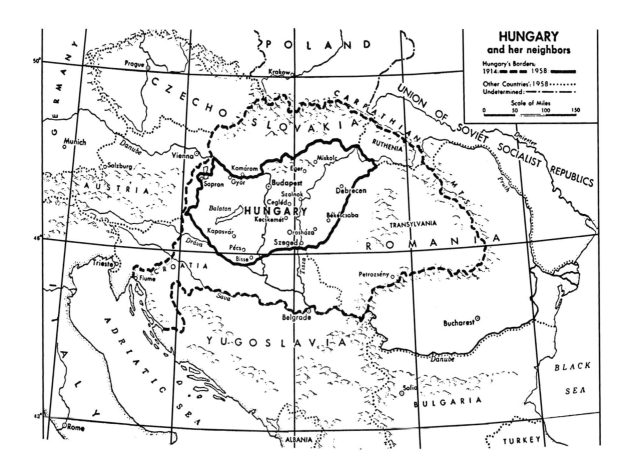

attracted partridge and other game birds, and so it was inevitable that a hunting dog suited to that climate and the available game would be popular. What the huntsmen had was a dog swift of foot, yet cautious so as not to alert quarry, a dog of superior nose and high-class hunting ability.

During this period in history, firearms were developed. In order to use this new weapon, the sportsman had to get it ready by seeing that the priming was right and lifting the lid of the pan holding the powder before advancing to shoot game. He needed a close-working dog that combined the duties of both a pointer and a retriever; a dog that could stand still during this preparation. At that time such a dog could be found all over Eastern Europe—one developed by many German and English hunters, mainly from the early hound types brought in by the Normans.

Small shoots were organized by the aristocratic landowners, and hunters from other countries were invited to bring the pointing dogs they had developed. These dogs were eventually crossed with the yellow-colored dogs of the Hungarians. The Vizsla became versatile in the hunting of both birds and small game. A dog would show he had found game by freezing into position with his head held low, one forefoot raised, and his tail held straight out. As better guns were invented, the Vizsla grew into the pointer-retriever type that brought the game back from a distance. They were also used as tracking dogs to find the large hares and small deer prevalent in the area.

Once the Hungarian hunters had developed the Vizsla into the type of dog needed for their specific hunting areas, they kept the breed pure for many generations to come. As sportsmen came from other countries and saw how the yellow pointer blended into the wheat fields, making it easy to stalk game, they wanted him crossbred with their own dogs.

German hunters took male Vizslas back to their own country to improve their stock, as did sportsmen from Austria and England, where they crossbred them to their own Pointers and Irish Setters. Vizslas occupied a position between the extremely fast English Pointer and the slower German Shorthair, combining some of the known qualities of both breeds together with a very distinctive color, type, and aristocratic bearing that set him apart.

When the first field trial was held for Vizslas in 1882 near Budapest, these same sportsmen brought their dogs back to compete. However, the island where the trial was held was not felt to have the same hunting conditions as the dogs were exposed to inland, and the following year it had little support and interest.

At this point the aristocratic landowners realized they had remaining only a few of what they had originally bred and called the Vizsla. They set about rebuilding the breed, and it is believed that they may have used the Schweizhund—a solid red hound with powers of scent said to be equal to those of the Bloodhound—to bring the desired coat color back to the Vizsla. They may also have used a Pointer from Transylvania to re-establish the pointer ability. Since this Pointer had as his ancestor a black, tan, and white hound from the same area, the white markings on his chest and feet also appeared on the Vizsla.

Whatever breeds were used, once the Vizsla was re-established, dedicated owners joined forces to keep the breed from extinction. Hubertus, an organization formed by Hungarian hunters in 1917, established a hunting dog's division which greatly helped in preserving the breed. This organization selected a dozen Vizslas which it felt represented the true breed as it was depicted in the early historic drawings, and all the registered Vizslas in Hungary descend from this foundation stock of three males and nine females.

The re-establishment of the breed was drastically affected after the end of World War I when, in 1920, the Hungarian Peace Treaty was signed at the Grand Trianon

Palace in Versailles. Hungarians had traditionally considered themselves to be an integral part of Western Europe and the eastern outpost of Western civilization in Europe. A monarchy for almost 1,000 years, it now had a brief, four-year Communist dictatorship, during which time much land was taken away the wealthy. Hungary had 125,000 square miles of which sixty-one percent was farmland. Rumania was given most of the Transylvania area; Czechoslovakia got all of Northern Hungary; Yugoslavia got most of the south of Hungary; and Austria was awarded part of the west. Some three million Hungarians were transferred to foreign soil. Hungary, reduced to the size of the state of Indiana, could not decide on a king and so a dictator, Admiral Horthy, ruled for the next twenty-five years.

The kingdom that had withstood the Turk, the Hapsburg Empire, and great power jealousies now underwent a gigantic land reform. The Vizslas, personal gundogs to the large aristocratic estate owners, were now living in parts of Hungary that had become other countries. This, however, did not deter the dedicated owners, and late in 1920 the Magyar Vizsla Breeding Association was formed with the help of Dr. Kalman Polgar, Count Laslo Esterhazy, and Elemer Petocz. The heads of the organization were Dr. Polgar, Andre Felix, Karoly Baba, and Balazs Otvos. When this group held their first field trial in the fall of 1922, they drew tremendous support.

The Association drew up the first Vizsla standard at this time and kept separate stud books for both the show and the field dogs. The standard was revised in 1935, at which time the Federation Cynologique Internationale (FCI), a worldwide federation of national dog clubs, gave recognition to the breed.

Hungary had suffered political battles and armed aggression through hundreds of years of history, but the next battle changed the world. It also took the Vizsla out of his native land and eventually to America.

Although Hungary entered and fought in the World War II as a German ally, it fell under German military occupation, during which time the Horthy regime was swept away by a pro-Nazi dictatorship in October 1943.

When Soviet planes dropped bombs on North Hungarian towns, Hungary was forced into the war against the Allies by German pressure from within. The German forces were driven out by advancing Soviet armies in a hard-fought campaign ending in April 1944. Just ahead of the invading communist armies, the wealthy landowners fled the country, taking with them what they could carry and seeking sanctuary in Austria, Italy, Czechoslovakia, and Turkey. Many emigrants managed to take their Vizslas with them but in the ensuing flights, most pedigrees and registrations were lost or left behind. The Vizslas left behind and protected by loyal Hungarians were used to establish new breeding programs in Hungary.

Before the war 5,000 Vizslas had been registered in Hungary, but with the Soviet invasion and occupation, eighty to ninety percent were destroyed or lost. Hundreds of Vizslas were destroyed by the Communists, who resented the breed as a symbol of

Photo of oil painting done by Elizabeth Mihalyi of her Panni XV while a refugee in Austria in 1948.

1942 photo of Hevizi Lurko at the Festeviches' kennel in Toponar, Hungary.

Elizabeth Mihalyi shown at a hunt in 1944 in Hungary with the dam of Panni XV, Csitri.

wealth. Many emigrants were able to take their Vizslas with them when they fled, but most of the dogs had to be left behind in other countries when the owners immigrated to America.

Elizabeth Mihalyi was one of the Vizsla breeders to flee Hungary. She took with her eleven loaded farm carts, forty-four horses, two carriages, and her Vizsla, Panni XV. Panni was pregnant with her third litter, but when she whelped the puppies during the flight, it was impossible to care for them and they had to be destroyed. Elizabeth arrived in Austria six weeks later and was able to keep Panni with her by performing menial jobs that allowed her to remain outside the refugee camps. An accomplished artist, she also painted portraits for American army officers in exchange for food for herself, her relatives, and Panni.

During the six years she spent in Austria awaiting passage to America, Elizabeth

located a male Vizsla owned by a Mr. Hofbauer of Vienna. The dog had been born at the kennels owned by the Festeviches in Hungary and rescued by their gamekeeper. The Hofbauers had named him Betyar and registered him as the first Vizsla in the Austrian International Dog Registry. Panni was registered as the second Vizsla in this book, and when she gave birth to Betyar's puppies, the litter was registered as the first Vizsla litter born in Austria. Born January 19, 1949, there were seven puppies that all carried a name beginning with a "C." Several of these puppies went to people living in Italy and Germany, and they were the foundation stock for Vizsla breeders in those countries.

Elizabeth Mihalyi had to leave both Panni and Panni's daughter with the Hofbauers in Austria when she finally emigrated to America. However, several years later she was able to have a granddaughter of Panni's (Freda Von Schloss Loosdorf) sent to her and she continued breeding Vizslas in her new country. Panni lived past seventeen years of age.

The combination of Betyar and Panni is in back of many of our pedigrees today if we search far enough. Importers brought second-generation Betyar-Panni Vizslas which were eventually bred to other Vizslas in this country to establish a three-generation pedigree for registrations.

Vizslas that had to be left behind in Hungary when the aristocratic landowners were forced to flee in 1944 were impossible to identify. It is probable that in future breedings brother and sister were unknowingly bred to each other. Without identifying pictures or pedigree backgrounds, new litters were finally registered as "of unknown breeding" in the Hungarian stud books that were compiled in 1955.

During the post-war years when the Communist government was established, purebred dogs and activities related to them were discouraged, especially breeds that had belonged to the aristocracy. Dog breeding and canine pursuits became more and more difficult as the Hungarian people struggled to survive and rebuild. In 1956, after a revolt against the regime, living became easier in Hungary, and dog activities again began to flourish. In that year Mike Kende was appointed Director of the Magyar Dog

Breeders' Association, and he started to register dogs that fit the Vizsla standard. These registered dogs were then able to be bred to those that had identifiable pedigrees, but if any questionable characteristic appeared in the litter, it was culled. It was only by means of this careful culling that the breed was finally re-established in its homeland.

With the government's bare tolerance for dog shows and breeding, difficulties again surfaced in 1973 when the license tax for a dog was raised to an amount similar to what most workers earned in a month. This action did more damage to the breed than both World Wars. Dogs became too costly to own and had to be abandoned; breeding came to a standstill. It was several years before the Hungarian Kennel Club was able to persuade the government to change this luxury tax on dogs, but when it was finally resolved, the hunting breeds were given a tax break.

All field training and hunting in Hungary fell under the province of the Ministry of Agriculture and Food. The Forestry and Woods Industrial Office regulated the hunting seasons, hunting grounds, and licenses.

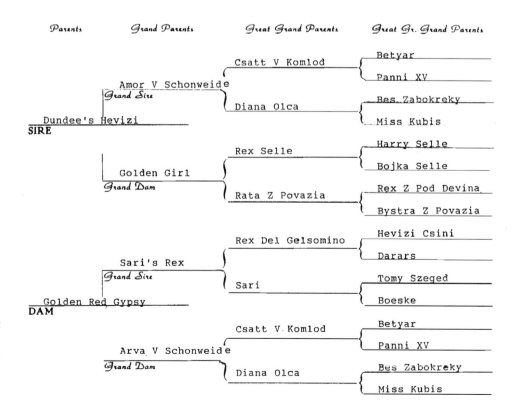

An early pedigree of a litter born in this country going back to the original Panni and Betyar breeding.

Parents	Grand Parents	Great Grand Parents	Great Gr. Grand Parents
		Csatt V Komlod	Betyar
			Panni XV
	Amor V Schonweide *Grand Sire*	Diana Olca	Bes Zabokreky
			Miss Kubis
Dundee's Hevizi **SIRE**		Rex Selle	Harry Selle
			Bojka Selle
	Golden Girl *Grand Dam*	Rata Z Povazia	Rex Z Pod Devina
			Bystra Z Povazia
		Rex Del Gelsomino	Hevizi Csini
			Darars
	Sari's Rex *Grand Sire*	Sari	Tomy Szeged
			Boeske
Golden Red Gypsy **DAM**		Csatt V Komlod	Betyar
			Panni XV
	Arva V Schonweide *Grand Dam*	Diana Olca	Bes Zabokreky
			Miss Kubis

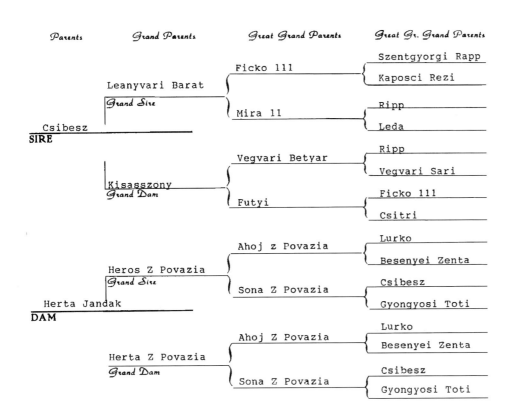

Parents	Grand Parents	Great Grand Parents	Great Gr. Grand Parents

Csibesz
SIRE

Leanyvari Barat
Grand Sire

Ficko 111
- Szentgyorgi Rapp
- Kaposci Rezi

Mira 11
- Ripp
- Leda

Kisasszony
Grand Dam

Vegvari Betyar
- Ripp
- Vegvari Sari

Futyi
- Ficko 111
- Csitri

Herta Jandak
DAM

Heros Z Povazia
Grand Sire

Ahoj z Povazia
- Lurko
- Besenyei Zenta

Sona Z Povazia
- Csibesz
- Gyongyosi Toti

Herta Z Povazia
Grand Dam

Ahoj Z Povazia
- Lurko
- Besenyei Zenta

Sona Z Povazia
- Csibesz
- Gyongyosi Toti

Note the strong inbreeding of brother and sister in this Hungarian pedigree.

Field trials are held by the National Association of Hungarian Dogbreeders under the FCI regulations.

The standards for the Vizsla, like other European versatile breeds, are high, and the dogs are expected to perform superbly. They are used for hunting deer and wild boar, along with the native partridge, pheasant, fox, and hare. The dog has to possess a keen nose, and retrieving and tracking instincts.

In the early 1930s Hungarian foresters and gamekeepers interbred the Vizsla with the Wirehaired German Pointer to get a dog with a heavier coat, suitable for work during the colder periods. The result, known as the Wirehaired Vizsla, is everything the shorthaired Vizsla is, except for the rough coat. Greater emphasis is laid on their hunting performance than on an elegant appearance. With this weatherproof coat they are able to lie quietly in wait on foggy, frosty autumn dawns or to sit for hours in a boat. This new breed was accepted by the FCI as an independent breed in 1966. Wirehaired Vizslas are usually excellent all-round gun-

dogs and great care is being taken to ensure that the existing dogs being bred are purebred with pedigrees that can be traced back in order to increase the gene pool.

The Wirehaired Vizsla has slowly gained popularity in Canada where the Vizsla has two classifications: smooth and wire coats. However, to date, the dog has never created much interest with American hunters.

In Hungary today, Vizslas have regained their early popularity, being proudly held by the Hungarian people as their national dog. From the early differences in color, size, bone and body type, the present-day Vizsla has finally evolved. The breed's many excellent attributes not only bring him appreciation by the hunters, but make him loved and valued as a family dog.

THE VIZSLA IN AMERICA

In the 1940s the Vizslas were virtually unknown in the United States. Although dog lovers returning from a visit to Europe and Europeans emigrating to the United

A Vizsla met on the streets of Budapest. Note the dewclaws and long tail.

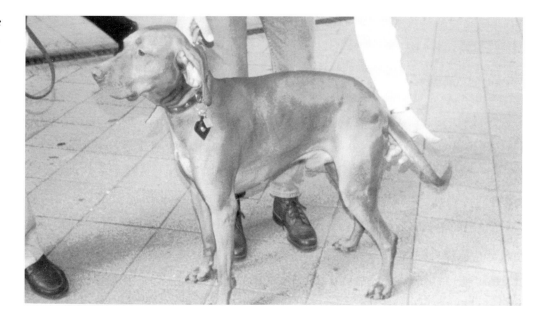

A Vizsla met on the streets of Budapest. Note the dewclaws and long tail.

A Vizsla being worked in the fields near Budapest.

States had brought Vizslas with them, these dogs were family pets and companions. Herbert Pulitzer became one of the first documented American owners when he brought a Vizsla back from Europe in 1938. When Baron Mile Kende in Hungary invited the Pulitzers on a hunting trip, they became very attached to Baron Kende's bitch, Zsoka of Sashegy, and persuaded him to sell her to them. They brought Zsoka with them when they returned to the United States, and a short time later sent for a two-year-old male, Dendi. Although records show that Zsoka won a field trial in Manitoba in 1940, there is no record of her ever being bred.

In 1945, a Jewish family by the name of Amuli was ordered to leave Budapest on short notice and resettle in Yugoslavia. They took with them their one-year-old Vizsla bitch, Sari, but lost her registration papers in their flight. In November 1948, the Amuli family was expatriated from Yugoslavia and decided to settle in Israel. Traveling by train, they smuggled Sari with them wrapped in a sack, but when they stopped in Rome they were in a quandary as to Sari's future. They took their problems to a British foreign service staff officer there by the name of John Shattack, who offered to give Sari a home.

When Shattack was transferred to South Africa two years later, he appealed to Emmett Scanlon, a young lawyer stationed in Rome as a representative of the Department of State, to provide a home for Sari. Scanlon could not, but he had a friend in the United States, Frank Tallman, who liked dogs and would care for Sari if they could get her out of Rome. Scanlon experienced numerous difficulties in clearing Sari for export, and while waiting for all this red tape to clear, Sari was bred. When she was finally shipped to Kansas City, Missouri,

Photo taken in 1952 shows possibly the first litter of Vizsla puppies born in America. Breeder, Frank Tallman. Photo courtesy of E. Mihalyi.

Broc Olca, imported from Czechoslovakia by Dr. Osborn, was considered to be one of the most valuable stud dogs in both Europe and the U.S. Photo courtesy of Joan Hunt.

on October 7, 1950, two of her eight-week-old puppies, Tito and Shasta, accompanied her.

When the crates were first opened at the Kansas City airport, no one before had seen a breed that looked like this and at first it was thought that an off-color Weimaraner had been sent. Tallman liked the Hungarian pointers and the interest they created. The next year he had a male, Rex del Gelsomino, sent secretly out of Hungary into Yugoslavia and eventually to Rome, and from there the dog was shipped to Kansas City, arriving on July 14, 1951.

From Sari and Rex, and from Sari's daughter Shasta and Rex, Tallman produced several litters of puppies which were true to the breed in all respects. The first American-born litter from Sari and Rex was whelped on April 2, 1952, and from then on, Frank Tallman spent his time promoting the breed in every state, firmly establishing the Vizsla, especially in the Midwest. He sold some of the puppies, gave some to friends, field trained, exhibited, and generally was responsible for the beginning of, and demand for, the breed in America. From Hungary to Yugoslavia, to Rome and then America, the "golden pointer" can trace its ancestry directly to Kansas City and Frank Tallman.

As interest in the breed grew, a Minnesota veterinarian, Dr. Ivan Osborn, began making plans to import several of the breed and was determined to find influential and reputable breeders and turned for help to Czechoslovakian contacts. The breed masters of that country consented to let foundation stock leave there to insure the future of the breed in case the Russians should rule the dogs out of existence. By working through the veterinarian college, Osborn was able to select outstanding specimens of the best strains from behind the Iron Curtain. One of the advantages of the various Iron Curtain strains was the existence of established specialized characteristics within the breed itself, such as dark coats, medium-range quartering, pointing and retrieving gundogs, very sharp field instincts, short-coupling, strong musculature, elegant conformation, and extremely aggressive hunting qualities.

The Czech breeders furnished complete breeding records and in the spring of 1953, Dr. Osborn was able to get his first five-generation Vizsla stud, Broc Olca. He also imported a Czech bitch, Rata Z Povazia. When she and Broc were bred, Dr. Osborn had the first known litter of complete six-generation pedigreed Vizslas to be born outside the Iron Curtain.

Broc Olca was a dominant sire and considered to be the most valuable stud dog outside the Iron Curtain and many breeders in the United States can trace their lines

Diana Olca, owned by Alexia Manner in Austria, was the top producing bitch there in 1954. Several early imports to this country came from Diana.

Early import Fritz V Auskia, son of Rex Selle, is the grandsire of Bobo Buck Selle.

Nine-month-old Red Ryder, son of Brilliant, an English import, owned by Charles Hunt.

directly back to him. He produced Field Ch. Ripp Barat, thought to be the finest field dog ever.

Dr. Osborn imported over fifty Vizslas from different bloodlines, mostly from behind the Iron Curtain. With his decision to firmly establish and promote the Vizsla in this country, he imported the best he could, and started breeding as a business. He felt that any specialized attempt to breed the Vizsla strictly for show type would eventually invite degeneration in character, strength, and hunting ability. His careful selection of breeding stock from only the best certainly had a lot to do with where the Vizsla breed is today in America.

In the early 1950s, Hungarian refugees were coming to America in large numbers, many of them bringing their own Vizslas with them. In most cases, pedigrees and registrations had been lost along the way and there was no way to claim ancestry. One of the immigrants was Jeno Dus, who had been the last director of the Vizsla Club of Hungary. Before he had fled, Dus buried the original stud books, leaving them forever unclaimed. With the loss of these documents, the only complete stud book for the Vizsla was Czechoslovakian registration.

Jeno Dus settled in northern New York State soon after arriving in this country and had one of the first litters born in the East when he bred his bitch Jutka, from the Rex and Sari breeding, to his own male, Pic, in 1954. From that combination came Csisckas of Goncoltanya, one of the foundation stud dogs for the Hunts in Tennessee. The

Csillan V Hunt, sired by Csisckas of Goncoltanya, from dam Annavolgy Arany.

Imported from Czechoslovakia by the Hunts, Morho Z Povazia was the sire of Adalyn Hunt, the first American-born Vizsla imported into England by the Hunts.

Hunts had also imported dogs from Czechoslovakia and they were to become a leading force in breeding and promoting the Vizsla over the next twenty years.

MAGYAR VIZSLA CLUB OF AMERICA

After several delays and postponements, a representative group of Vizsla owners gathered in Des Moines, Iowa, on January 16, 1954, in a meeting that was to decide the future of the breed in America. Those owners had a single determination—to protect and improve the Vizsla, that the breed might truly become one of America's respected and loved companion gundogs. Great emphasis was placed on the work that had been accomplished in the last two years by Frank Tallman, Charles Hunt, and other importers regarding the correspondence with the American Kennel Club (the AKC) and the American Field about recognition of the breed. The first elected officers were: President Jack Hatfield, Vice-President

Harry Holt, Secretary Charles Hunt, and Treasurer Roy Hawkinson.

The AKC was interested in the distribution of Vizslas across the country, the responsibility of the club, its conduct of affairs and discharge of duties, care in breeding, and publicity of the breed. With recognition closer at hand, word went out around the country on the requirements: with imports, a three-generation pedigree certified by a foreign club was needed. With imports without certified pedigrees, the Field Dog Stud Book required a sworn statement and a list of as many sires and dams as possible that were believed to be true and accurate.

By then most of the early importers knew the problems they faced in getting certified information from foreign countries on their Vizslas. Many people had left Hungary with their dogs, but the papers were lost. Owners remembered the call names of parents but not the registered names on the pedigrees. Some requests for information were answered, but many went unanswered for fear of getting involved. But through the

Rakk Selle showing excellent style on point. Rakk was the winner of the Derby stakes at the first field trial held by the Magyar Vizsla Club.

strong beliefs of the Vizsla owners, ten months later the Magyar Vizsla Club of America had progressed from obscurity to recognition and the breed was accepted for registration in the American Field, leading the way to charter membership in the National German Pointing association. This group was formed to establish field rules and regulations under which all breeders could compete in official regional and national trials. Their breeds included the German Shorthair, Weimaraner, and the Drathaar.

At that time the fledgling club was the only Vizsla club in existence in the world, and was responsible for discovering and preserving all historical documents for future generations. The Club had made surprising growth from the sixteen interested men and women who met in Des Moines to eighty-five members only fourteen months later, and new applications were being received daily. Constant letters were received from Vizsla owners in America who had a desire to know more about the breed they had come to love. Fanciers of an unknown breed had helped an unknown club to become an organization that was international in character and activity.

In 1960 the club met the requirements of the AKC by submitting 500 three-generation Vizsla pedigrees, and on November 25, 1960, the Vizsla was officially the 115th breed to be recognized by the AKC and was accepted into the Sporting Group. At that time the club dropped the "Magyar" from its name and became the Vizsla Club of America (VCA). A new standard for the breed was approved in December 1961 and remained the same until it was revised in 1983 and again in 1996.

EARLY VIZSLAS IN COMPETITION

Vizsla breeders have always been determined to keep the true heritage of the breed in mind. The years following AKC acceptance were crucial in setting standards for the Vizsla breed. With their first appearance at AKC dog shows and field trials, their popularity grew. The first Vizsla to gain a show championship title was Miklos Schloss Loosdorf, owned by the Warholms in California, in 1961. Miklos followed that with several group placings and was the top-winning Vizsla in 1962.

Csisckas of Goncoltanya, owned by the Hunts, was the second Vizsla to finish his championship title and the first to earn a Sporting Group placing. He was the top-winning Vizsla in 1961, lived to the age of seventeen years and had an impressive record as a stud dog. His son, Csopi V Hunt, was the top-winning Vizsla in 1967.

The Hunt's bitch, Annavolgi Arany, imported from Hungary in 1957, was the third Vizsla to finish a bench championship, and the first bitch to do so, when she earned her title in 1961. The fourth champion was also a bitch, Duchess of Shirbob, owned by Walter Campbell.

Only nine Vizslas finished their championship titles in the year following AKC recognition, and only twelve gained titles in 1962, but the breed was rapidly attracting attention in the show ring, and more dogs were being brought into the United States and more dogs were being bred. The next few years saw an increase in registrations and activity in obedience and field competition.

The Vizsla enjoyed several years in the obedience trials even before gaining AKC recognition. One of the earliest to gain a title was Georgia's Auburn Heidi, owned by the Philips in Georgia. Heidi, three generations down from the Betyar and Panni breeding, earned her Companion Dog (CD) title in August 1958.

In November 1962 the AKC granted a license to the VCA to hold their first field trial, granting points towards a field championship. Open to other breeds in the Open Limited All-Age stakes, the trial drew a total of fourteen entries with Vizslas making an exceptional showing. Ripp Barat, owned by Betty Kenly of Arizona, and handled by Paul Sabo, placed first in both the Open All-Age stakes for Vizslas only, and the Open Limited All-Age stakes. Ripp Barat is considered by many to have been the best field trial Vizsla on record, having had over seventy wins and placements in all types of competition. He was voted into the VCA Hall of Fame in 1981 for his outstanding contribution to the breed.

Vizslas had to compete in field trials against other pointing breeds in those early years of trialing and, unfortunately, it took considerable effort before judges were willing to recognize the Vizsla as a breed apart. After a slow acceptance, the Vizsla began to build a reputation in field trial circles. All who worked with the breed—handlers and owners alike—were impressed by their easy trainability, intelligence, great driving power, stamina, and tremendous desire to hunt. The Vizsla's sensitivity and desire for praise and affection along with his close-working tendencies led to an increase in owner-handlers who enjoyed having a companion gundog.

The first Vizsla Field Champion was Broc Selle, bred by Dr. Osborn and owned by Don Anderson of Colorado. Broc earned his title in 1964.

Count Bela Hadik of New Hampshire was one of the strongest promoters of the Vizsla as a Dual dog. His Futaki Darocz gained a show championship in July 1965,

Gingo V Schloss Loosdorf, an early import owned by Vern Halmrest, is shown after a day of duck hunting. Gingo is the sire of the first AKC Vizsla champion, Micklos Schloss Loosdorf.

Am. Can. FCh. Ripp Barat. Sire: Broc Olca. Dam: Rata Z Povazia. Owned by Betty Kenly. Photo courtesy of Joan Hunt.

Dual Ch. Futaki Darocz, the first Vizsla to gain a Dual Championship. Sire: Ch. Hunor. Dam: Piri. Owned by Bela Hadik.

two months after earning a field championship, making him the first Dual Champion for the breed. Darocz was also the sire of two Dual Champions, Bobo Buck Selle and Szekeres Kis Szereto, the first Vizsla bitch to earn the title. At present there are at least fifty Vizslas with Dual Championships.

In the forty years since AKC recognition, the Vizsla has gained a respected place as an all-round sporting dog, adaptable and comfortable in a variety of tasks. Vizsla owners and breeders have kept the heritage foremost. The courage and loyalty to the breed shown by displaced people from a war-torn country make us continuously grateful for the affection, companionship, beauty, and enjoyment of our Vizslas.

CHAPTER THREE

The Vizsla Standard

A breed standard is a set of qualifications and detailed descriptions covering the ideal example of a breed. The purpose of the standard is to provide a blueprint with which to work in order to have uniformity. However, any standard is subject to individual interpretation and variations within each breed, depending on the country and conditions.

Standards should require few changes and, when well written in the beginning, should last for many years. In most cases the original dog was more representative than the current one, but breeders today feel the changes in the standard should be made to conform to what they are breeding now, not the dogs of yesterday. Standards are criticized, analyzed, and altered. Most have definitive descriptions that should make it easy for a judge to understand. Each standard should describe elements that are so fundamental to the correct type that they should be easy to identify while still outlining that which is correct.

All breeders should consider themselves to be guardians of the breed. They should look at the standard and consider where it came from, where it is today, and in which direction it will head tomorrow.

The first Hungarian Vizsla standard was drawn up in 1922 by Hungarian breeders. These early standards were not written by people who lacked sufficient knowledge of the breed, but instead, were written by those hunters and breeders who knew the breed well and wanted and needed ideal and consistent specimens. They put together a "blueprint" and description as a guide to other breeders. As more people participated in the development of the Magyar Vizsla without detailed knowledge and firsthand experience, the early standard needed to change into a more explicit one. With each revision through the years, the language of the standard changed to describe angulation, shoulder lay-back, and correct movement.

The first standard was revised in 1938 and again in 1956. After a modification request was solicited by the Hungarian Kennel Club in 1999, the current Hungarian standard was adopted in 2000.

The VCA drew up its first breed standard in 1960 when it was given recognition by the American Kennel Club. It was revised in 1983 with the most outstanding changes being in size, general appearance, eye color, and defining body descriptions. The next revision was in 1996 with the emphasis being on the amount of white allowed.

HUNGARIAN SHORT-HAIRED POINTER (VIZSLA) STANDARD
(June 4, 2000)

UTILIZATION: A versatile gun dog that must be able to work in the field, forest and water. Having the following typical qualities: an excellent nose, firmness on point, excellent retrieves and determination to remain on the scent even when swimming, which he manifestly enjoys. He copes with difficult terrain as well as extreme weather conditions. As he is intended to be an efficient hunting dog, gun and game shyness, unwillingness to point and retrieve, as well as a dislike of water are undesirable. Because of his easygoing nature and his adaptability, he can easily be kept as a companion dog in the house.

GENERAL APPEARANCE: Medium sized, elegant gun dog of noble appearance with short russet gold coat. His rather light, dry, lean structure embodies the harmony of beauty and strength.

IMPORTANT PROPORTIONS: The body length slightly exceeds the height at the withers. The depth of the brisket is slightly less than half the height at the withers. The muzzle is slightly shorter than half the length of the head.

BEHAVIOR/TEMPERAMENT: Lively, friendly, evenly tempered, to be trained easily. His outstanding willingness to keep contact with his master while working is one of his essential qualities. He cannot bear rough treatment and must be neither aggressive nor shy.

HEAD: Dry, noble, well proportioned.
CRANIAL REGION:
Skull: Moderately wide, slightly domed. A slightly pronounced groove runs from the moderately developed occiput towards the stop. The superciliary ridges are moderately developed.
Stop: Moderate.
FACIAL REGION:
Nose: Well developed and broad nostrils as wide as possible. The color of the nose harmonizes in a dark shading with the coat color.
Muzzle: Blunt, not pointed, with strong jaws, strongly muscled. The bridge of the nose is straight.
Lips: Tightly fitting, no pendulous flews.
Jaws/Teeth: Powerful jaws with a perfect, regular and complete scissors bite; the upper teeth closely overlapping the lower teeth and set square to the jaws, with 42 healthy teeth according to the dentition formula.
Cheeks: Strong, well muscled.
Eyes: Slightly oval, of medium size. Well fitting eyelids. Intelligent and lively expression. The brown eye harmonizing with the coat color, as dark as possible preferred.
Leathers: Set on at medium height, a little backwards. Fine leathers hanging closely to the cheeks, ending in a rounded V shape. The length is about three quarters of the length of the head.

NECK: Medium length, harmonizing with the overall appearance. The nape very muscular and slightly arched. Tightly fitting skin at the throat.

BODY:
Withers: Pronounced and muscular.
Back: Solid, strong, well muscled, taut and straight. The vertebral spines should be hidden by the muscles.
Loin: Short, broad, tight, muscular, straight or slightly arched. The portion from back to loin is well coupled.
Croup: Broad and of sufficient length, not cut off short. Sloping slightly to the tail. Well muscled.
Chest: Deep and broad and well developed, well muscled, moderately arched forechest, sternum extending as far back as possible. The sternum and the elbow should be at the same level. Ribs moderately arched. Last ribs carried well back.
Underline: Elegant, tight, arching line towards the rear, slightly tucked up.

TAIL: Set on slightly low, strong at the base, then tapering. In countries where tail docking is not prohibited by law, the tail may be shortened by one quarter to avoid hunting hazards. If tail docking is prohibited, the tail reaches down to the hock joint and is carried straight or slightly saber like. On the move, it is raised up to the horizontal. It is well covered by dense coat.

LIMBS:
FOREQUARTERS: Viewed from the front, straight and parallel. Viewed from the side, legs are vertical and placed well under the body. Good bones, strongly muscled.
Shoulders: Long, sloping and flat, well attached shoulder blade. Flexible, strong, dry musculature. Well angulated between shoulder blade and upper arm.
Upper arm: As long as possible. Well muscled.
Elbows: Fitting close to the body, however, not tied in, turning neither in nor out. Well angulated between upper arm and forearm.
Forearm: Long, straight, sufficiently muscled. Bone strong, but not coarse.
Pastern joint: Strong, tight.
Pastern: Short, only very slightly sloping.
Forefeet: Slightly oval, with well knit, sufficiently arched, strong toes. Strong brown nails. Tough, resistant, slate grey pads. The feet are parallel when standing or moving.
HINDQUARTERS: Viewed from behind, straight and parallel. Well angulated. Strong bone.
Upper thigh: Long and muscular. Good angulation between pelvis and upper thigh.
Stifle: Well angulated.
Lower thigh: Long, well muscled and sinewy. Its length is almost equal to that of the upper thigh. Good angulation between lower thigh and metatarsus.
Hock joint: Strong, dry and sinewy. Rather well let down.
Metatarsus: Vertical, short and dry.
Hind feet: Similar to forefeet.

GAIT/MOVEMENT: The typical gait is an animated, light-footed trot, elegant and far reaching, with much drive and corresponding reach. Not exhausting gallop when working in the field. The back is firm and the topline remains level. Good, upright carriage. Pacing undesirable.

SKIN: Tightly fitting, without folds. The skin is well pigmented.

COAT:
HAIR: Short and dense, should be coarse and hard at the touch. On the head and the leathers, it should be silkier and shorter. The hair underneath the tail should be slightly, but not noticeably longer. It should cover all of the body; the underside of the belly is a little lighter coated. No undercoat.
COLOR: Various shades of russet gold and dark sandy gold. The leathers may be a little darker, otherwise uniform in color. Red, brownish or lightened color is undesirable. A little white patch on the chest or at the throat, not more than 5 cm in diameter, as well as white markings on the toes are not considered faulty. The color of the lips and the eye rims corresponds to the color of the nose.

SIZE/WEIGHT:
HEIGHT AT WITHERS
Dogs: 58-64 cm
Bitches: 54-60 cm
It is ineffective to increase the height at the withers. A medium size should be aimed at. Overall balance and symmetry are much more important than the mere measurable size.

FAULTS: Any departure from the foregoing points should be considered a fault and the seriousness with which the fault should be regarded should be in exact proportions to its degree.

ELIMINATING FAULTS:

- Distinct deviations from the characteristics of the breed.
- Strong deviation from the sexual characteristics.
- Atypical head.
- Spotted nose.
- Pendulous or dribbling flews.
- Under or overshot mouth. Wry mouth, including all intermediate forms.
- One or more missing incisors and/or canine and/or premolars 2-4 and/or molars 1-2. More than two missing PM1; the M3 are disregarded. Non-visible teeth are assessed as missing ones. Supernumerary teeth not in line with the others.
- Cleft palate.
- Light yellow eyes. Very loose eyelids; ectropion, entropion.
- Pronounced dewlap.
- Dewclaws.
- Very faulty movement.
- Atypical coat.
- Dark brown or pale yellow color.
- Parti-colored, not uniformly colored.
- White chest patch larger than 5 cm.
- White feet.
- Lacking pigmentation either on the skin or on the lips and eye rims.
- Any type of weakness in temperament.
- Deviation of more than 2 cm from the above-mentioned heights at the withers.

NB: Male animals must have two apparently normal testicles fully descended into the scrotum.

1. Muzzle
2. Flews
3. Stop
4. Occiput
5. Neck
6. Withers
7. Loin
8. Croup
9. Hock
10. Pastern
11. Lower thigh
12. Stifle
13. Thigh
14. Flank
15. Chest
16. Forearm
17. Elbow
18. Upper arm
19. Shoulder
20. Back

VIZSLA CLUB OF AMERICA STANDARD
Approved January 31, 1996

GENERAL APPEARANCE:

That of medium-sized, short-coated, hunting dog of distinguished appearance and bearing. Robust but rather lightly built. The coat is an attractive solid golden rust. This is a dog of power and drive in the field, yet a tractable and affectionate companion in the home. It is strongly emphasized that field conditioned coats, as well as brawny or sinewy muscular condition and honorable scars indicating a working and hunting dog are never to be penalized in this dog. The qualities that make a "Dual dog" are always to be appreciated, not depreciated.

HEAD:

Lean and muscular. Skull moderately wide between the ears with a median line down forehead. Stop between skull and foreface is moderate, not deep. Foreface, or muzzle, is of equal length or slightly shorter than skull when viewed in profile. It should taper gradually from stop to tip of nose. Muzzle square and deep. It must not turn up as in a "dish" face nor should it turn down. Whiskers serve a functional purpose; their removal is permitted but not preferred. Nostrils slightly open. Nose brown. Any other color is faulty. *A totally black nose is a disqualification.* Ears thin, silky, and proportionally long, with rounded leather ends, set fairly low and hanging close to cheeks. Jaws are strong with well-developed white teeth meeting in a scissors bite. Eyes medium in size and depth of setting, their surrounding tissue covering the whites. Color of the iris should blend with color of coat. Yellow or any other color is faulty. Prominent pop eyes are faulty. Lower eyelids should neither turn in nor out since both conditions allow seeds and dust to irritate the eye. Lips cover the jaws completely but are neither loose nor pendulous.

NECK AND BODY:

The neck is strong, smooth, muscular, moderately long, arched, and devoid of dewlap, broadening nicely into shoulders which are moderately laid back. This is mandatory to maintain balance with the moderately angulated hindquarters. Body is strong and well proportioned. Back short. Withers high and the topline slightly rounded over the loin to the set on of the tail. Chest moderately broad and deep, reaching down to the elbows. Ribs well sprung; underline exhibiting a slight tuck-up beneath the loin. Tail set just below the level of the croup, thicker at the root and docked one-third off. Ideally, it should reach to the back of the stifle joint and be carried at, or near, the horizontal. An undocked tail is faulty.

FOREQUARTERS:

Shoulder blades proportionately long and wide, sloping moderately back and fairly close at the top. Forelegs straight and muscular with elbows close. Feet cat-like, round and compact with toes close. Nails brown and short. Pads thick and tough. Dewclaws, if any, to be removed on front and rear feet. Hare feet are faulty.

HINDQUARTERS:

The hind legs have well-developed thighs with moderately angulated stifles and hocks in balance with the moderately laid back shoulders. They must be straight as viewed from behind. Too much angulation at the hocks is as faulty as too little. The hocks are let down and parallel to each other.

COAT:

Short, smooth, dense and close-lying, without wooly undercoat. *A distinctly long coat is a disqualification.*

COLOR:

Solid golden rust in different shadings. Solid dark mahogany red, and pale yellow, are faulty. White on the forechest, preferably as small as possible, and white on the toes are permissible. *Solid white extending above the toes, or white anywhere else on the dog except the forechest is a disqualification.* When viewing the dog from the front, white markings on the forechest must be confined to an area from the top of the sternum to a point between the elbows when the dog is standing naturally. *White extending on the shoulders or neck is a disqualification.* White due to aging shall not be faulted. Any noticeable area of black in the coat is a serious fault.

GAIT:
   Far-reaching, light-footed, graceful and smooth. When moving at a fast trot, a properly built dog single-tracks.

SIZE:
   The ideal male is 22-24 in at the highest point over the shoulder blades. The ideal female is 21-23 in. Because the Vizsla is meant to be a medium-sized hunter, any dog measuring more than 1 1/2 in over or under these limits must be disqualified.

TEMPERAMENT:
   A natural hunter endowed with a good nose and above-average ability to take training. Lively, gentle-mannered, demonstratively affectionate and sensitive though fearless with a well developed protective instinct. Shyness, timidity or nervousness should be penalized.

DISQUALIFICATIONS:
1. Completely black nose.
2. Solid white extending above the toes or white anywhere else on the dog except the forechest.
3. White extending on the shoulders or neck.
4. A distinctly long coat.
5. Any male over 25 1/2 inches, or under 20 1/2 inches; and any female over 24 1/2 inches or under 19 1/2 inches at the highest point over the shoulder blades.

ANALYSIS OF THE VCA STANDARD

Extreme departures from the breed standard do not occur very often and newcomers to the breed should realize that even though opinions and interpretations are bound to vary somewhat among breeders, most Vizslas do fit the standard. The standard describes, trait by trait, those features which make up type and soundness, with each minor trait considered in relation to the whole dog.

Head

A good head is essential for true type. It should be well-proportioned without being heavy or coarse, and even though both males and females have a lean, smooth look to their heads, the male head is slightly larger and wider. The skull is fairly flat on top without the occipital bone being conspicuous. The median line, formed by a furrow of bone formation, should start on the top of the skull and run down the center of the nose. The step between the eyes, called the stop, should be moderate and never as abrupt as in the Cocker Spaniel or the Pointer. It should lend definition to the sculpture around the eye without being a deep groove. Without that step between the eyes, a Vizsla has what is called a "roman nose." The length of the nose is slightly shorter than the skull.

The muzzle ends squarely instead of tapering to a point. The flews, or upper lips, should not be pendulous but should end cleanly at the bottom of the jaw. The breed standard says nothing about the reverse layer of hair growing on the top of the nose, but quite a few Vizslas have what looks like velvet rubbed the wrong way. Brown pigmentation of the nose is called for in the standard, but it is actually closer to the color of the dog's coat, as in the area around the mouth and eyes.

The eyes are medium-sized and more almond-shaped than round, and although their color should be in harmony with the coat color, a dark eye is always preferred. The eyes should have an expression of intelligence,

The male head should be fuller and heavier and not leave any doubt that you are looking at a male.

The female Vizsla has a more feminine head.

alertness, and trustworthiness. A light eye lacks this and often appears hard instead of soft and gentle. The lower eyelids should fit tightly and not droop, so as not to allow in irritating dust and dirt particles.

The ears are fairly large and long, set slightly lower than most sporting breeds, lying close to the side of the head. Correct ear-set contributes to an alert expression, and too low an ear-set ruins the look of even the prettiest dog. The ears should be thin with rounded ends, reaching no longer than the canine teeth.

A lot of the early Vizslas were unique in that they had small appendages on the upper front parts of their ears. Since so many dogs bred from Count Bela Hadik's Futaki Kennels sported these growths they were called Futaki horns, and it was rumored at one time that dogs sporting these growths were superior hunters. The horns, or growths, can occur on one ear or both and in different sizes from an almost indistinguishable bump to a half-inch appendage covered with hair. Since the Vizsla breed was at one time

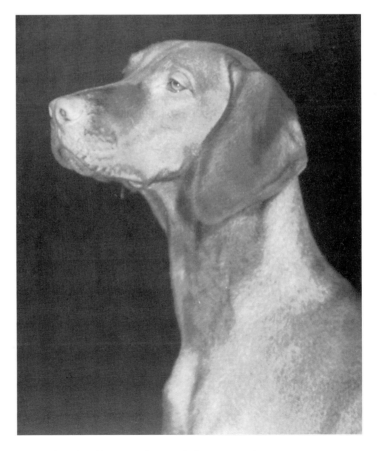

The median line between the eyes defines expression.

Minor faults include pendulous flews.

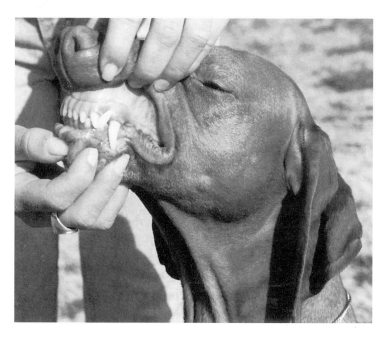

The correct bite is a scissors bite.

joined with the Hungarian Agar hound that passed on, among other characteristics, the distinctive "horns," these growths are well accounted for.

The teeth should meet in a scissors bite, the front surfaces of the lower incisors touching the inside of the uppers. While an even bite, in which the teeth meet end-to-end, is often allowed, this type of bite causes considerable wearing of the teeth and so the correct scissors bite is preferred.

Neck and Forequarters

The neck should be well-muscled with tight-fitting skin. There should not be any excessive dewlap, which is loose skin on the neck and throat area. The length of the neck should be in proportion to the length of the back and they should balance each other. If a dog is in balance, a longer neck and back, along with correct angulation, will give a longer reach and smoother gait. There is a slight arch to the neck and it should flow smoothly into the shoulder area without any obvious flatness at the withers, which are located directly behind the base of the neck, at the junction of the neck and back.

The neck plays a big part in movement. The area around the arch of the neck is the anchor point for many muscles, tendons, and ligaments, including some that aid in moving the front forward. A longer neck permits longer muscles, contributing to better movement.

The Vizsla standard calls for moderate angulation both in forequarters and hindquarters. Angulation is the angle created by two bones meeting at various joints. One of these junctures is where the shoulder blade, or scapula, meets the upper arm, or humerus. The most desirable angulation is ninety degrees.

Along with correct shoulder blade angulation, a strong muscular development in that area is also necessary or good movement will suffer. The shoulder blade is attached to the rib cage by means of muscles both on top of and under the shoulder blade. If the outer muscles are heavy and coarse, the ones under the shoulder blade will also be that way. This mass of muscles will cause the shoulder blades to be pushed too far from the rib cage and will give the dogs "loaded shoulders." This, in turn, leads to a dog being "out at the elbows," and results in tiring movement. It is the shoulder blade, more than any other individual body part, that will determine what kind of movement your Vizsla will have. Wrong interpretation of the standard by breeders is perhaps the reason we are seeing

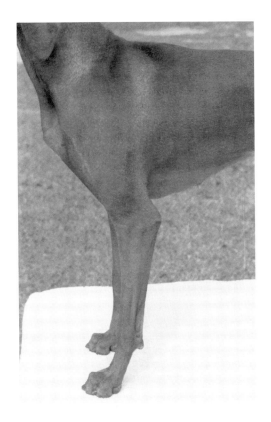

At two years of age, the chest is fully developed.

Shoulder blades are proportionately long, sloping moderately back. Forelegs are straight and muscular.

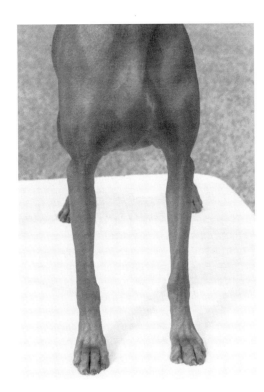

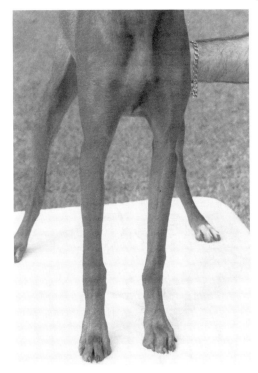

The correct chest is moderately broad with a fairly prominent breastbone.

Faulty front, too narrow, with the chest not reaching to the elbows.

Height Measurement

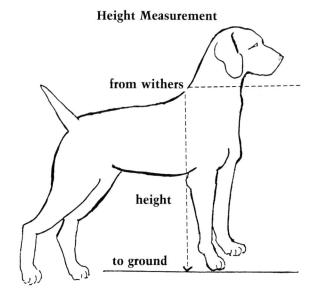

from withers

height

to ground

The ribs are well-sprung and the underline exhibits a slight tuck-up beneath the loins.

upright shoulders in the breed. If the shoulders are straight, the legs will not be able to extend fully with forward motion. The leg will pound into the ground and an extra shock must then be absorbed by the front.

Correct shoulder placement is also necessary, not only to improve the profile, but to support the ribs and back. A forward shoulder blade fails to offer that support and reveals itself as a dip behind the top of the shoulder blades.

The lower arm must also be strong with good muscles. Lack of exercise can weaken the muscles to the point of loose elbows and weak pasterns.

The chest is deep, reaching down to the elbows. The forechest bone, the prosternum, is prominent. A too narrow or under-developed chest will restrict lung capacity, but a too broad or round rib cage will interfere with front movement and cause a dog to be out at the elbows, or to toe-in.

Back and Body

Balance always must be the first consideration. If the back is short and coupled with a short neck, it would be hard to get the long reach or a ground-gaining gallop. The object of good movement is efficiency and the total dog must be considered.

The back must be straight and strong without any signs of a weak or sagging topline or a roached back. There is a slight rise over the croup with the tail set on slightly lower than the back.

The abdomen should have a moderate tuck-up beneath the loin. Exercise keeps the area tight and strong.

Tail

Since the Vizsla does not have the high tail-set that is usual in most sporting breeds, many judges in the conformation

Topline slightly rounded over the loin to the set of the tail.

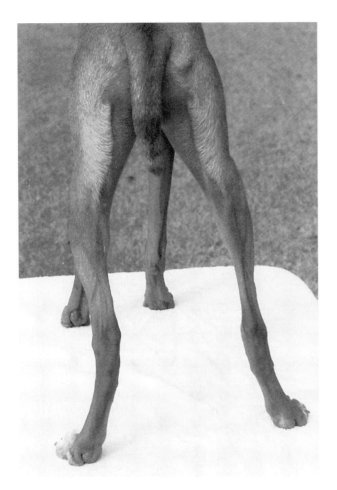

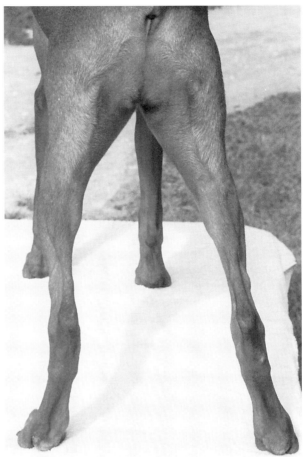

Faulty rear, slightly cow-hocked, with poorly developed thigh muscles.

Upper and lower thighs should be strong and well muscled.

ring fault the breed incorrectly. The tail should be carried outstretched above the level of the back and should not drastically bend towards the back in a curve, as in a "gay" tail. The tail is usually in motion as evidence of the happy nature of the breed. Docked to the correct length, it should reach down to just opposite the stifle joint when measured.

Hindquarters

The pelvic bones should be strong and wide, covered with well-developed muscles. The angles at the junctures of the hip socket where the hip bone, or femur, attaches to the pelvic girdle should be equal to the angle of the shoulder blades in order to have good freedom of movement and a good length of stride.

Hocks should be strong and turning neither inward nor outward.

The lower thigh area should also be well muscled. When viewed from the side, a properly angulated dog will stand naturally with his rear pasterns perpendicular to the ground on a line just behind the point of his buttocks. With a short lower thigh, the legs will be under the rear too much; if the lower thigh bone is too long, the dog will appear to be over-angulated and give the impression of standing too far behind himself.

The hocks should be strong and turning neither inward or outward. Unless it is a genetic fault, weak hocks can often be corrected and strengthened with exercise.

The hindquarter angulation should be in balance with the angulation of the forequarters. Most of the angulation begins with the upper thigh and pelvis. An extremely flat croup on your Vizsla can mean virtually little angulation in that area. The correct slope of the croup is an indication of the correct pelvis attachment to the spinal column. It permits longer muscles to run from it to the stifle. Since the major portion of the dog's power is derived from the leg during the backward sweep, these muscles are important as they draw the leg back into a long back stroke, adding power to the drive.

Feet

Really good feet are genetic, although exercise can strengthen the muscles and improve poor ones. Feet are often overlooked in the makeup of the complete Vizsla but are extremely important. The feet should have thick pads not only to protect them from injury, but to cushion effectively the impact on the forequarters. The toes should be close together and well knuckled. Flat feet are splayed, causing fatigue in an otherwise well-moving dog.

The nails should be cut short so they do not touch the ground. Long nails can rapidly break down the foot structure and take away its shock-absorbing effectiveness.

Coat

The coat is short, smooth, and a golden rust color. In some lines a slightly lighter or darker overall shade predominates, but most Vizslas have the lighter shadings over the sides of the neck and shoulder. In some very dark lines this "saddle" may be missing. A thicker undercoat will be present in cold weather but is easily stripped out in the spring. Good health assures a glossy sheen to the coat, making

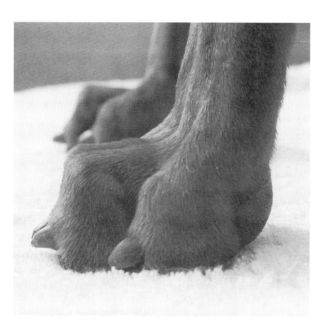

Feet are cat-like, round, and compact with toes close. Nails are brown and short.

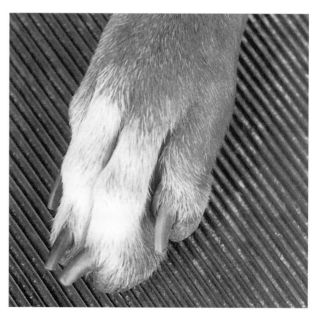

White extending above the first knuckle of the toes is a disqualification.

Rear Movement

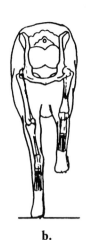

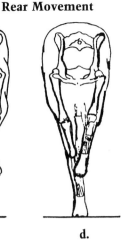

a.   b.   c.   d.

a. moving correctly
b. moving close
c. moving cow-hocked
d. crossing over

the Vizsla an attractive breed in any circumstance.

A small amount of white is permissible on the chest. Each breeder may differ when interpreting how much white is allowed on the chest but a massive area is unacceptable. White is permitted on the toes but not above the first knuckle, at which point it is considered to be on the foot.

The pigmentation of the nose, eyelids, and around the mouth is close to flesh-colored. Any black shades would be considered a sign of crossbreeding. Pads of the feet and nails are a darker shade of flesh. Eye color should harmonize with the coat color.

Rears

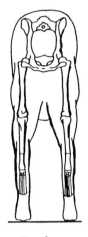
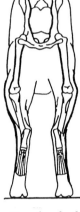

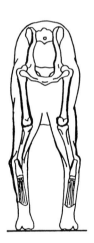

Good rear   Cow-hocked   Toeing in

Gait

The Vizsla needs to have a long-reaching, smooth gait. A correct gait is dependent on correct angulation at both ends. If the front fails to match the rear, gaiting defects will show up in the form of crabbing, hackneying, or overreach.

Crabbing occurs when the rear legs track to one side to avoid interference with the front feet. This action is usually caused by the dog having less angulation in the front than in the rear, in combination with a short back.

A hackneyed gait is apparent in a dog that is trying to avoid the pounding his shoulders may take when a poorly angulated front restricts reach. In order to lessen the strain of pounding some dogs will compensate by using the abductor muscles, which bend the elbow and lift the lower leg. By using these muscles, the dog is able to lift his feet higher than normal and hold them there just for a fraction. This hesitation action helps him to reduce the shock the pounding gives. This gait is quite pretty to look at, but is a severe fault in movement for the Vizsla because of its tiring effect and waste of energy in the field.

The trot is the easiest gait in which to judge correct angulation. The diagonally opposite legs move back and forth at the same time, each taking equal portions of the stress on the joints, with the front feet leaving the

This Vizsla shows the correct extension and drive typical of the breed. Photo © Christina M. Freitag.

ground just ahead of the hind feet. When viewed from the front or the rear, the dog's legs should tend to angle in toward a central line beneath his body, seeming to converge on one track as the speed increases. When this action, called single-tracking, is correct, the rear legs travel on the same planes as the front without any extra twisting or turning out at the various joints.

Size

The Vizsla is a medium-sized, robust, but lightly built hunting dog. A large, rangy appearance detracts from the aristocratic bearing that has long been associated with the breed. Certainly, too small a male may lack bone and substance, and too large a female may have too much. The desirable size has always differed with breeders, governed only by the disqualifying heights in the standard. Overall appearance, balance, gait, and above all, purpose and attitude must be given more emphasis as long as the dog is within the required limits.

Temperament

Not many breed standards describe a dog as "demonstratively affectionate" as does the Vizsla standard. Any shyness or nervousness in the breed should be penalized, as should aggressiveness. The Vizsla is always willing to please, but training and corrections must be done gently, as a strong reprimand will make a Vizsla unsure of himself. He will accept discipline in an intelligent manner if it is not meted out with a heavy hand. He will be an eager, happy worker in the field or in the home, and always sensitive to the environment around him.

Ch. Rheingold Loge Anton Dvorak, SH, is owned by Steve Shlyen and Stan Miller.

Ch. Stonepoint's Thunderheart, owned by Ute and Christopher Plass, receives the Award of Merit at the 2002 Nationals.

Ch. Rheingold Loge Anton Dvorak, SH. Photo © Mitchell Photography.

Ch. Prairie Heartsong is owned by Jan Cox and F. Bushnell. Photo © Garden Studio, Inc.

Ch. Elgin's Cariad Anaztazia is owned by Meg and Mike Farmer and Ed Foster. Photo © Garden Studio, Inc.

Ch. Russet Leather Sacajawea, JH, MX, AXJ, owned by J. Walton, C. Dosta and B. Wanjon. Photo © MyDogPhoto.com.

CHAPTER FOUR

Selecting a Vizsla Puppy

Photo by Luellen Hart.

Most dog behaviorists agree that the forty-ninth day in a puppy's life is the optimal time to go to his new home. However, several states in the United States have laws prohibiting the sale of puppies under the age of eight weeks. Even if this is not a law where you are, do not accept a puppy under the recommended forty-ninth day. If a puppy is removed from his littermates and dam at too early an age, he will relate poorly to other dogs as an adult and will become overdependent on his human owners. A puppy needs the interaction with littermates and the corrections his mother gives for his first seven weeks of life in order to establish behavior patterns for life.

The young puppy that you select is going to be a member of your family for the next fourteen or fifteen years. Choosing him should be an enjoyable experience, and a reliable and dependable breeder will gladly help you with your decision. Do not consider getting two puppies at once even if they are not littermates. It is extremely important that your new puppy bond with you and not imprint on another dog.

In your search for a puppy, be prepared to answer all kinds of questions as to your lifestyle, family, home, job, and future plans and expectations for your Vizsla. Many breeders will not let a new puppy go to a home with small children or an unfenced yard. They will also want to know how much time each day you will be spending with a new puppy. Hopefully, this breeder will become your mentor and help you understand and know the breed, so that a close connection can form between you and your dog, thus preventing your Vizsla from ending up in a rescue situation later on.

WHERE TO FIND YOUR PUPPY

A good puppy that is a pleasure to live with is the result of much planning by the owner of the bitch. Thought, and care of both the dam and her puppies, should be evident whether you are picking your Vizsla for field training, show, obedience or agility competition, or a pet. The puppy you choose must be healthy, happy, exuberant, friendly, and raised in a clean environment. It is virtually impossible to have confidence in a breeder whose young puppies are too dirty and smelly to pick up and hug.

It is wiser to not give in to impulse buying after falling for that Vizsla puppy in the window or cage at a pet store. A reliable or well-known breeder will not deal with pet stores. The puppies you see in those circumstances have mostly been supplied by multiple-breed puppy farms and dealers. Quite often they are raised in deplorable conditions, taken away from their dams too young and sold to suppliers who deal with pet shop sales. These puppies face an uncertain future since they have not had the socialization and care needed to reach their genetic potential as a companion.

Finding a reputable Vizsla breeder may require a little research on your part. If there

This little eight-week-old puppy grew up to become Ch. Cariad's Classic Mariah, ROM. Owned by Marcia Folley.

is a local all-breed club, someone should be able to give you information on Vizsla area clubs, exhibitors, or breeders. Attend dog shows, field trials, and training classes in your area to learn more of what it is like to work and train a Vizsla. Owners and exhibitors have a good communications network and hear of litters or planned breedings in other parts of the country.

The best references will be from the Vizsla Club of America's membership list. Contacting its secretary will give you a choice of breeders; keep in mind, however, that none of these referrals are recommendations, but merely contacts. It will be up to you to locate the right puppy for your needs. You will probably have to put your name on a waiting list, since most of the well-known breeders have people waiting for one of their puppies. You could actually spend a year waiting for the right dog, but the wait will be worth it.

You will find that, through the years, established breeders have developed certain characteristics in their dogs for easy recognition of particular lines. These include a darker or lighter coat, a dark or light eye, and a certain-shaped head and muzzle,

topline or tail-set. All of these Vizslas fit the interpretation of the standard; however, you may personally find one "type" more acceptable than another. Learn to read and understand pedigrees. "Champion lines" do not necessarily mean that your new puppy will have a champion sire or dam. Look for some consistency in the pedigree, which shows desirable linebreeding. And look for titles at the end of the parents' names which indicate attention to developing both mental and physical conditioning and competition by the breeders.

If you are visiting breeders, you should be able to see the dam and get an idea of how her puppies will look at maturity. Look at pictures of the sire if he is not present and determine how his personality and characteristics are going to develop in your choice of a puppy. No honest breeder can guarantee that an eight-week-old puppy is going to be a top-winning field or show dog, only that the potential is there based on the breeding behind him.

In the process of checking breeder and litter availability, you may even see an older Vizsla puppy already trained with basics and ready for the show or agility ring. Be prepared to pay a high price and sign a contract agreeing to continue the showing or training. If you do not want an active puppy, consider asking the breeders you visit if they have an older dog that they would part with to a good, quiet home. There are many Vizslas who would love that one-on-one relationship.

Unfortunately, sometimes a puppy does not live up to his new owners' expectations. And at any age, Vizslas are turned in to humane societies and shelters to be either euthanized or placed in a new home, perhaps due to changed family situations or to behavior problems with an untrained dog. It is always amazing how many of the Vizsla rescue cases are the result of the owners not knowing what living with a Vizsla entails.

The Vizsla breed is lucky in that there are numerous rescue groups across the country ready to step in, take these Vizslas from the shelter, evaluate health and behavior

Seven weeks of age is a good time to evaluate a puppy.

Always look at the puppy's parents if they are available. Ch. Cariad's Classic Mariah, owned by Marcia Folley, is shown with her four-month-old daughter, Classic Call The Wind Mariah.

problems, and care for them in a foster home before placing them in their "forever" home with a new family. Some of these rescue dogs may not be suitable in a home with children or other dogs—in many cases, the dogs have been abused, starved, neglected, and abandoned. Some are white-faced veterans that deserve a kinder, gentler life in their old age. While it may be hard to understand how an older dog can be given up after being a family member for many years, it is important to recognize that unfortunate events may have forced their owners to give their dogs up. Adoption can put their Vizsla into a new loving home. Any VCA member can give you the name of the person in charge of rescue in your state.

While educating breeders about placing a puppy in the right home is the first step, there will still be people who breed who fail to communicate with a new owner when the owner needs help with the new puppy. If you are going to be waiting for a considerable length of time for your new puppy, spend that time learning. Be prepared—owning a Vizsla changes your life and your lifestyle.

MALE OR FEMALE?

The choice of sex is usually a decision based on your future plans for a puppy, but it will also involve personal preference. The male is usually larger than the female, and if size is a consideration, this may influence your decision. Both sexes are happy, healthy, friendly, outgoing, and intelligent. Both are also demonstratively affectionate, but the male demands and needs more attention. Males are sweet, soft dogs that need more reassurance than females. If a male stubs his toe, he will be a bigger baby about it and will need to be comforted.

Both male and female are mischievous diggers. They are lovable, intelligent, and exuberant but tractable dogs that take training easily, yet both sexes are sensitive when corrected as they have a strong desire to please.

If a bitch's twice-yearly seasons are likely to bother you and there are no plans for future breeding, she can be spayed around eight months of age. If you are worried about a male's tendency to question authority when he reaches puberty, neutering may help reduce that risk. Male or female—either will make a wonderful companion and friend.

Mother and twelve-week-old son enjoy a quiet time after playing.

PICKING A FIELD PUPPY

The Vizsla is born with a natural instinct to stalk and point everything from a lizard to a grasshopper. The majority can be easily trained to be excellent companion gundogs but if you want one to eventually go into field trial competition, selecting the right puppy is going to be more demanding than finding the best available show or obedience puppy.

Aim for litters from sires and dams that work as field dogs, or at least that come from hunting and field stock. It would be nice if, because a puppy's sire or dam were top field trial champions, each puppy in a litter would be automatically good at trialing. Unfortunately, that is not always the case. Do remember, when you are considering a puppy, to look for a breeder who has raised his litter with an eye toward developing naturally, from an early age, their curiosity and sense of adventure.

Try to attend field trials and watch dogs in competition to get a clear view of what you are after. Do not hesitate to ask owners about the trial records of their dogs.

Most breeders are striving to breed Vizslas of true trial caliber with Dual title potential. You should be looking for a puppy from parents that not only have proven their working ability under actual field conditions, but that also meet the Vizsla standard. The qualities to look for in both the parents and offspring are physical soundness, intelligence, correct size and conformation, a stable temperament, and a tremendous desire to hunt.

When looking at a litter, there are many ways to test puppies for intelligence and alertness. One way is to take a tennis ball, roll it past all the puppies, and see which one is the most interested in the movement. Then separate those puppies that indicated a quick mind and, one at a time, roll the ball past each one. (Puppies who function well with littermates are sometimes insecure when by themselves). Lastly, fasten a bird wing to the end of a pole, wave it back and forth in front of each puppy, and look for the puppy that shows aggressive interest and desire. When you are down to final selections, have a friend drop a book or clap his

Puppy Aptitude Testing

Quite a few veterinarians and animal trainers will tell you that it is environment that will mostly influence your puppy after he is in a new home. However, there is also a train of thought that aptitude testing is the best way to place a young puppy in the right home. Since the breeder has had the opportunity to watch the litter as it grows, she will have seen the difference in personalities and attitudes. She may also rely on a series of aptitude tests designed to show how the puppy will adapt to his future training. Score the following tests 1 through 6, with 1 being the highest and strongest degree of acceptance and 6 being the lowest.

Restraint: This tests the degree of dominance or submission tendencies and how he accepts restraint. Crouch down and gently roll the puppy on his back and hold him with one hand for a full thirty seconds. Score the reaction on whether he struggled, bit, or settled down.

1

Following: Stand up and walk away from the puppy. Make sure he sees you walk away. This tests the puppy on how willingly he will follow you. Unwillingness to follow indicates independence.

2

Retrieving: Crouch beside the puppy and attract his attention with a toy or ball. When he starts to show interest, toss it about four feet in front of the puppy. There is a high correlation between the willingness and desire to retrieve as a puppy to his willingness to work in obedience and the field in the future and to work with a person. Vizslas are born with a natural retrieving instinct and it should be very apparent in the young puppy.

3

Sound Sensitivity: This test shows the reaction to loud noises. Place the puppy by himself and hit a metal spoon against a metal pan and watch the response. His reaction may indicate whether the puppy will have a potential problem in the field because of gun-shyness.

4

Sight Sensitivity: Place several strange objects in different areas of the room and watch how the puppy approaches them. Note whether he runs or shies away from the objects or investigates them.

5

Conformation: This test is important if you are looking for a puppy for the show ring. Stand the puppy on a grooming table in a natural stance and go over the shoulders, croup, front, and hocks and feet. Consider which will change for the better or worse, and which minor faults you can accept and live with.

6

Evaluating Scores—Scoring can be interpreted in different ways by different people, and you can probably spend hours trying to pre-judge a puppy. For that reason alone, go on your own instinct. Some puppies will show a degree of independence but that does not mean they will not accept human leadership. It may show that a pup has the potential to become a wonderful working dog, providing the owner knows what he is doing.

A puppy that tests with an extremely submissive attitude will work out best in a structured and predictable environment and may not have the attitude for accepting strange situations. If not handled correctly, this puppy may remain shy and fearful but, on the other hand, obedience, agility training and a lot of encouragement may give him the confidence to accept new situations. He has the ability to bond very strongly if his owner is not overly demanding.

A puppy that is outgoing and friendly, accepting of humans and different environments, will do well in any future plans. His flexible temperament will help him adapt well to different types of training.

A puppy that shows an extremely dominant and aggressive nature during these tests could easily grow up to be one that is constantly testing authority. He should go to a home without children and only to an individual who knows how to handle a dominant dog. An active, structured life based on obedience will work best for him.

hands to see which puppy has natural curiosity about the source of the sound.

Because unethical breeders have been known to breed their Vizslas with Pointers to give them a far-ranging dog in the field, avoid any litter with a dog that has a questionable large area of white. Remember that the Vizsla has always been bred to be a close-working dog in the field.

PICKING A SHOW PUPPY

There are numerous breeders across the country whose Vizslas have made outstanding achievements in the show ring. These breeders have established a reputation for breeding very closely to the Vizsla standard. That is not to say that these show dogs are incapable of winning at field trials—they are, as is evidenced by the long list of Dual Champions, and NAVHDA (North American Versatile Hunting Dog Association) and hunting titles. But if you have established that you are interested in show ring competition, a good breeder will help pick your new Vizsla puppy with that future in mind.

A seven- to eight-week-old puppy will go through a lot of physical changes as he grows, but if he closely resembles one of his parents, you will be able to make an educated guess as to his appearance at maturity. You will want to choose a puppy with a nice blunt, or square, muzzle, not snipey. The muzzle should have moderate flews without being excessive. The eyes should be an amber color or darker, never yellow. The teeth must come together in a correct "scissors bite." (An incorrect bite in puppy teeth seldom corrects itself in the adult mouth.) The neck must be smooth and clean with little throatiness or loose folds of skin under the throat. The front legs must be straight, with strong pasterns. The feet should be rounded and tight, with the toes close together. At this age the feet may point out a little, but as the puppy grows and his chest spreads, his front legs will straighten.

Look for a nice length of neck, even in an eight-week-old puppy, and a length of back in balance with the neck. A longer-backed dog should have a longer reach and stride than one with a short back. The rib cage should be nicely oval. Too round a rib cage at this point will interfere with the front movement and will cause your puppy to be out at the elbows.

A balanced puppy is characterized not only by the proportion of head size, neck, chest depth, and the ratio of body to legs, but also by the angulation of the fore- and hindquarters. Angulation refers to the bend in the joints and their influence on mechanical function and efficiency. The Vizsla should have moderate angulation, which strongly influences the length of stride and freedom of movement. In picking a puppy—not only for show potential, but also for work in obedience, agility and the field—consideration must be given as to how well he will be able to perform at maturity. If he has correct angulation as a puppy, he will have it as an adult. Angulation does not change with growth.

In an ideal front, the upper arm should slope down and back at approximately the same degree of angulation—preferably not less than ninety degrees. The same should apply to the rear where the thigh bone

There are different head types, all within the standard. A narrow, snipey look is the least attractive. Look for a nicely rounded head with a deep muzzle.

Four-month-old puppy training for the show ring.

Five-month-old Storm already knows how to pose for a winning photo.

meets the lower thigh. Do not expect to be able to recognize correct angulation and movement in a puppy. Many experienced breeders are unable to do it. They do, however, have an eye for a good puppy that just seems to put it all together.

The back should be strong and level with a slight rise in the croup area before it slopes down into a tail-set a little lower than most sporting breeds. The correct tail length should measure even with the knee joint and the tail should be carried in a horizontal line, not in a curve over the back. A "gay tail," as it is called, has been a problem with many breeders for a long time as it is hard to breed out.

The hocks should be strong and turn neither in nor out at this point. They will strengthen considerably with correct exercise as the puppy grows.

There should be no evidence of temperament problems in a puppy. If you have been able to see the parents, you can judge for yourself from their behavior how their puppies will develop. If the dam, in particular, is a happy, outgoing, friendly dog, there is a good chance that her puppies also will be that way. She is the parent with the greatest environmental influence on the puppies.

If you do not have the time or interest to pursue any "career choices" for a Vizsla puppy, inform the breeder that your puppy will not be going that route and also will

not be used for breeding. Most breeders like their first-choice puppies to go to exhibitors and breeders, if possible, in order to maintain their reputation for producing top-quality dogs. However, a puppy bought as a pet has had the same thoughtful care that went into each puppy in that litter, and your future plans may very well change when you get involved with the active, happy Vizsla.

Many breeders keep the pick of their litters for themselves to evaluate for future use. However, a choice show potential at eight weeks can have a misplaced tooth at sixteen weeks, or an undescended testicle, or he may just not live up to expectations for that particular breeder. Do not hesitate to ask the breeder if he has an older puppy available for a pet or even obedience or agility training. This dog probably has had the best of care and all his vaccinations, and he likely is housebroken and partially trained. The hard part has been done for you and you will be getting a wonderful puppy.

PICKING AN OBEDIENCE OR AGILITY PUPPY

Picking a Vizsla puppy for potential obedience or agility competition is a harder job than any of the other fields. This puppy has to be intelligent, quick to bond with owner/handler, and adaptable. Time has changed our style of living and we no longer have to accept untrained dogs to live with. The benefit of obedience competition is that it also gives a person a dog that will fit into their busy, complicated life more easily. Every Vizsla puppy should have the basics in order to keep his owner sane and happy, and now the training goes even further with active competition in agility.

Many trainers consider the initial trainability window for a puppy to be from twelve weeks to nine months. The bonding that obedience people go through with their dogs during that period of time is far more intense than that of the owners with dogs in the breed ring. For that reason, you don't want to pick a dominant puppy from the litter that might exhibit the tendency to do everything on his own. With his dominant nature he may attempt to resist human leadership, although in the right experienced hands he may have the potential to become a good working obedience or agility dog.

Look for the puppy easily controlled but self-confident, friendly, and outgoing, one that has the Vizsla willingness that makes him

A four-week-old puppy with a lovely head.

continually look to an owner who is a firm, consistent, and knowledgeable leader. He should have a flexible temperament that adapts well to different places, people, and training. Ahead of you are years of very active fun and competition and you need to pick a puppy that will enjoy it wholeheartedly.

REGISTRATION AND GUARANTEE

When you buy your puppy, you are entitled to receive from his breeder an individual form to register him with the AKC in your name. If the breeder has not yet received this paperwork back from the AKC, he is required to give you information identifying the puppy in the meantime. This should include the name of the sire and dam, their registration numbers, and the date of your puppy's birth. Whenever you get the registration, fill out your choice of names, sign it and send it in with your check to the AKC. The registration is only valid for a period of twelve months from the date of issue. When the registration comes back in your name, make a copy of it for future reference and put the original in a safe place.

Most breeders will also include a four- or five-generation pedigree for your puppy, feeding instructions, a bill of sale, and vaccination and worming records. Make sure you get, and understand, a written guarantee concerning the health of your new puppy. A reputable breeder will stand behind a guarantee to take the puppy back if he does not work out in his new home or if he eventually shows a fault such as size, bad bite, hip dysplasia, or any other health problems which would eliminate him from showing or breeding. The breeder should then either offer a refund or replacement puppy.

It is up to you to take your new puppy to your veterinarian to be checked over within a few days of purchase. Take along the vaccination and worming records and follow the veterinarian's recommendations for a schedule of care.

CHAPTER FIVE

Your Vizsla's First Year: Care and Development

The first year in your Vizsla's life is an exciting period of development, adjustment, and physical and mental change as he leaves his littermates and dam and bonds with his new family. How he is cared for in the first few months will establish the behavior pattern for later in his life.

HOMECOMING

Bringing a new puppy into your home is a wonderful time for the people involved but it can be a frightening experience for the puppy. Try to bring him into a quiet house without a lot of friends and family crowding him. New smells, voices, and surroundings are going to confuse him. Let him explore each room on his own and make the first approach to all the "strangers."

Try not to alarm the new puppy with a lot of new commands all at once. Cuddle and hug him and save strong corrections for a later time. However, if he climbs on furniture which you have no intention of allowing him on, remove him gently and distract him with a toy.

Having decided on a call name for your puppy, start using it immediately and often. Do not use a name that will rhyme with, or sound like, an obedience command you intend to use later. Puppies respond more quickly to two-syllable names, especially when used in a happy tone of voice. Use your puppy's name when giving praise, calling him to eat, or encouraging him to come to you.

CHILDREN AND PUPPIES

If there are small children in the home, explain to them that a puppy is not a new toy, but a living creature that must be handled gently and correctly at all times. This puppy will grow up to be their friend and protector, but in the meantime he and the children of the house need to get to know each other.

Have the children sit on the floor when they want to hold the puppy. Young children make strange noises and movements which will alarm the puppy if he came from a breeder without children. Instruct the children to be quiet and calm to help him adjust to his many new experiences. They should let the puppy come to them instead of them chasing after him. Remember that puppies' teeth are like sharp needles that can unknowingly cut into a child's thin skin. Supervise constantly.

Instruct everyone that the correct way to pick up a puppy is by firmly supporting both his front and his rear. The sensitive jaw of a young puppy can be severely injured by a fall. For the same reason do not ever leave him sitting alone in a chair.

Just like a small child, a young Vizsla needs frequent naps. Explain this to your

Children must be shown how to safely hold and handle a small puppy.

Always a perfect combination—a boy and his puppy.

children and make sure they understand that the puppy cannot be handled constantly. A Vizsla takes on the personality of his family and environment. If there is noise and a great deal of activity around him, his rest periods will be shortened and he may become stressed, tense, anxious, nervous, and overactive. This can lead to complaints that the Vizsla is a "hyper" breed. It may simply be that his owner has a "hyper" household.

A parent should never stand by and allow a child to hurt or tease a puppy in any way. A good many breeders will not even consider selling a puppy to a home with young children. As the puppy has to learn control in all things, so does a child. Teasing a young puppy will teach him defensive biting and aggressiveness. A puppy should be able to learn that human hands and actions are associated with pleasure and comfort rather than pain. A child who slaps or hits at the puppy is going to make him

hand-shy and nervous. From that point on he may become overly submissive or defensive and turn into a "fear biter."

A child should be made to understand that the puppy's crate or bed belongs only to the puppy. It is his place to run to when he wants to escape the noise and confusion around him. Children should also be instructed to leave a puppy alone while he is eating. A puppy has a short attention span and can easily get distracted from finishing his food, or he may become defensive about protecting his dish.

Do not allow a small child to give the puppy an unsafe toy, an old shoe, or even a cookie. Your puppy is closer to the level of a youngster, and hand-feeding will encourage him to grab food from the child.

A Vizsla is like a child in many ways but you are not going to be able to ask him to mind. You will have to tell him, and in no uncertain terms either. You have to be the boss, the pack leader, the alpha and a disciplinary figure. Both children and puppies are in a constant state of learning, the difference being that children grow up trying to reinforce and establish their position in society, while the puppy grows up to accept his part in it.

There are many aspects of caring for your Vizsla that should be left to adults, but some can be shared with children who are at least four years of age or older. A young puppy just leash-broken will follow after a child sooner than an adult, and is still small enough to be controlled. A young child can take part in the grooming, even if it is only running a brush down the puppy's back. Letting a child share the responsibility of a simple job, such as keeping the water bowl filled, will make the child aware of the dog's need for attention and care. On shopping days your child can help select dog food and put it away when you get home. A new toy selected by your child with special thoughts for his pet will give him a learning experience on safe toys. Having your child accompany you to the veterinarian's office will teach him about the puppy's need for good health and care.

Adolescence can be a trying and emotional time for a child. Unable to relate to adults, the adolescent often turns to his dog as confidant and friend. Always tuned to the emotional state of his owner, a Vizsla easily fills the need for understanding in a young teenager.

It is going to be hard bringing a young puppy into a home with children and then putting all kinds of restrictions on both of them. If you have small children, it will mean constant supervision of both, and a lot of patience. Vizslas adore children and naturally gravitate to them. As they both grow, the bond they form will be a joy to remember.

OLDER PETS AND PUPPIES

A resident older dog should never have to feel threatened by a new puppy if you are

Four-month-old Bowie wants his friends to come out and play with him.

considerate and do not ignore the older. For some older dogs life takes on new excitement with a companion to keep them company, but it may take some time.

A young puppy can be rough and annoying to an older dog that has had your individual attention for a long time, and until the new addition has been accepted, supervision may be necessary. After the initial trial period is over, you may find that the older dog takes the place of the puppy's mother, disciplining him if he gets rough. The young puppy learns by imitation and a "come" obeyed by the older dog teaches the younger basic obedience. A puppy being taught to walk on a leash will readily follow along with the older dog.

You will have to make sure that your puppy learns to respect your older dog's food dish in particular. Feeding the new puppy in his crate will eliminate the need for your older dog to protect his food. Crating a new puppy will also give you time to give individual attention to the older dog, thus avoiding a jealousy problem. Although the new puppy is going to need a lot of your time, it is never fair to push the older dog into the background and forget that he has been your wonderful companion for many years.

A cat is a territorial creature and may object strongly to another animal brought into the home, especially a busy puppy that refuses to leave him alone. The puppy will gravitate to your cat, not only out of curiosity, but because he cannot believe that another animal would not want to play with him. Luckily, a cat can easily get out of reach of a puppy by jumping up on the top of a cabinet or refrigerator, but you will have to supervise and correct your new puppy for a long time.

Some cats and dogs adjust quite well and can even play and romp together, but care must always be taken that a cat does not get cornered and threatened to the point of using his nails for protection. An eye injury can become serious and possibly blind a dog.

FEEDING PROGRAM

From now on the person who is feeding and caring for the puppy will, in effect, take the place of his mother. A bond is being established that will have a permanent influence on him. At no other period in his life will your puppy have the ability to achieve as strong a bond or rapport with humans as he will at this age.

If you have brought your puppy home at seven or eight weeks of age, he will be staying on a schedule of four meals a day for at least the next two weeks. Try not to make any changes in his schedule until he has become comfortable in his new surroundings. This is a period of stress for your puppy and it takes time to get over his separation from his littermates.

Your puppy should be on a good kibble meal, made especially for puppies, with a high protein content for good bone and tissue growth. This dry meal will be the basis of his feeding for the rest of his life, even when you later switch to an adult product that meets his needs. Use the same product, if possible, that the breeder has been feeding since any sudden change in diet can cause diarrhea.

Soak the kibble in a small amount of warm water to soften it a bit, and add a small amount of boiled hamburger or canned dog meat. Good occasional additives can be cooked egg, cottage cheese, juice from vegetables, oils from canned tuna or sardines, but table scraps should be discouraged to prevent a fussy eater.

When you are unable to be home to feed the puppy his midday meal, you should make arrangements for someone else to come in and exercise and feed him. By the time your puppy is ten weeks old, the night meal can be discontinued. He should stay on three meals a day until he is four months old, with the amounts being increased as he grows.

Too much activity around your puppy at mealtime may distract him from eating, and if that is the case try feeding him in a quieter area or even in his crate. He may miss the competition of littermates around the feeding dish, and for that reason it may take a few days for him to get accustomed to eating alone. It may even be that his food is a little cooler or warmer than that which he was in the habit of eating. Anything can put off a slightly fussy eater but as soon as he adjusts to his new routine he will gain self-confidence.

If your puppy is too fat (being fat is not an indication of good health) decrease the amounts being fed. Too much weight on young bones and cartilage can cause problems later.

If, for the sake of convenience, you have to change your puppy's kibble, make a choice of which commercial food you prefer and he likes, and then stay with it. Change the food gradually, mixing it in with the older variety, to avoid digestive upset.

Your puppy will be confused if you keep changing diets every week. If he looks good and eats well, do not make any major changes. A Vizsla thrives on consistency even though serving him the same food day in and out may become boring to you.

Your Vizsla will get his adult teeth between four and six months of age and may go through a period of not eating. If so, keep him on three meals rather than cutting down to two. Do not try to entice him with table scraps or special cooking as it will be easy to turn him into a fussy eater. Continue to give sensible additives to his food instead.

Because your puppy's rapid growth rate starts to slow down during the latter part of his first year, adjust the food amount to keep him in good weight, but not overweight. The growing puppy needs amounts sufficient in quantity and quality to maintain him in good condition during this very active time. Use common sense to adjust the food given according to his growth spurts, activities, and weather. Any dog will eat less in hot, uncomfortable weather.

Make sure he is on a high-quality, nutritionally balanced, dry meal made especially for growing puppies, one that includes a higher protein and vitamin content. It is usually safer, with regard to bloat or gas, not to use a self-feeder. Instead, moisten the dry food with water and boiled hamburger before serving to eliminate the high consumption of water after eating dry meal. Keep fresh water available at all times. The use of vitamins and calcium supplements should not be necessary if your Vizsla is already eating a meal with sufficient amounts added, as most of them are. Such supplements can sometimes be toxic if given in too high a dose. If you are concerned about your Vizsla's coat being dull and dry, you may want to consult your veterinarian about adding some type of oil to his food.

Your Vizsla should remain on two meals a day for life, adjusting the amounts needed. The Vizsla is a very mouth-oriented breed and loves to carry things around.

Some quiet time in the sun.

On an empty stomach he may be tempted to chew and eat things he shouldn't. Like humans, he is probably more comfortable with something in his stomach.

The dog being trained or running in the field should never be fed before any type of exercise. He should be left to rest after he has finished working and should not be fed until his entire system has had a chance to slow down. If he is fed only once a day, that one meal has to be of sufficient quantity to maintain him in good condition and supply the extra energy needed. Because of all the energy he is expending, the working field dog's diet should be of utmost concern.

It is important to your Vizsla's regimen that a schedule is adhered to whenever possible. Not only will it keep his bowel movements regular but it will relieve any stress on his part.

SAFE TOYS

From the time that a Vizsla puppy is five weeks old, he will enjoy carrying small toys around in his mouth. He is a natural retriever and if he cannot find anything to bring to you, he will take your wrist in his mouth to show affection. Giving your

Sarah prefers to have two toys in her mouth much of the time.

Giving young dogs a lot of quality exercise will keep them out of mischief.

young puppy a soft, washable stuffed animal to carry will encourage the desired soft mouth, but if he starts destructively chewing it, he must be corrected.

The need for toys to be available at all times is particularly important. A young puppy has a short attention span and needs things to do to keep him out of mischief. Playing with toys will keep his interest and help prevent boredom. Select toys carefully for safety to make sure they cannot be torn into small parts that your puppy can swallow. Rawhide chews are often recommended but pieces chewed off and swallowed can expand in the stomach and intestines, causing blockage.

A tennis ball is safer than a rubber ball with a bell inside and will provide self-exercise for a young puppy. Rubber squeaky toys should never be bought for a Vizsla, as they will be quickly destroyed and eaten, showing up in the stools as bright-colored pieces of vinyl.

Nylon products are a better choice for safety and give hours of chewing enjoyment. They come in a variety of shapes and sizes and are very safe toys, made of indestruc-

tible nylon. There is also a variety made of a softer nylon; these also give hours of entertainment and help puppies through their teething stages.

A fairly large marrow bone from the meat market is always enjoyed. Boil it to remove the marrow and it will stay clean while still retaining its flavor and odor.

Toys designed for tug-of-war games should be discouraged as they could cause a misalignment of the teeth or encourage aggressive behavior unless your puppy is taught to relinquish on command. Do not give your puppy an old sock or shoe to play with and then punish him when he chews new ones; he cannot be expected to know the difference. A Vizsla puppy will proudly carry a stick in his mouth, but if he stops to chew, take it away and give him a safe toy instead.

A puppy gets bored with the same old toy, just as a young child does. You will be surprised at how happy your Vizsla puppy will be when he receives a new toy. Give him a toy box, fill it full of toys, and let him pick the one he wants. If you can teach him to put the toys away when he is done with them you are far ahead of the game.

Every Vizsla needs a place of his own.

By the time a puppy is five months old, she should be able to share quiet times on your bed.

SLEEPING ARRANGEMENTS

For the first few nights, bedtime will be a time during which you will have to harden your heart against your puppy's loneliness and resist the urge to bring him into your own bed to keep him from crying. He has had a lot of excitement and experienced sudden changes and should be tired; hopefully, if you ignore his cries, he will soon fall asleep.

Putting your Vizsla puppy in a crate placed alongside your bed should go a long way towards comforting him and may smooth the adjustment. Remember that Vizslas do not like to be alone, so if you do not use a crate give your puppy some other form of bed near you, with a clean, folded blanket and a toy for comfort.

Take your puppy out to eliminate for the last time just before you are ready to go to bed yourself. If he does wake up during the night and is only whimpering a little, reassure him quietly that you are nearby. As soon as he realizes he is not alone he will probably drift back to sleep. But if he starts to sound desperate, no amount of hushing is going to work. You are going to have to take him out to eliminate before either of you can sleep.

If you are not a "morning person," your life is in for a big change. Do not expect your young Vizsla to sleep late into the mornings. When he wakes he will be ready to start his day—and yours.

By the time your puppy is past five months of age, has been completely housebroken, and has had some basic training and is communicating well with you, he will also be wanting to spend a good deal of his time with you. The old adage, "If you don't want a dog that follows you to the toilet all day, don't get a Vizsla," is true. He will also be graduating to sleeping on your bed at night. Most Vizslas do. It is not spoiling your dog to allow it; it is part of the bonding process. If you are away from home a good part of the day, this is a time for contact and attention with your Vizsla. Do not play or wrestle with him on the bed. He must understand that the bed is for sleeping or quiet communication. Letting him sleep on your bed provides extended but undemanding contact between you and him and builds trust and confidence.

IMMUNIZATIONS

Your puppy's breeder should have included your dog's feeding and care instructions, the health certificate from the veterinarian, types of vaccine given, and the dates when the next are due. The immunity your puppy received from his dam at birth will have been diminishing and the vaccines he is injected with will stimulate his own antibodies.

Infectious diseases can be contracted by your Vizsla in various ways, depending on the disease. For most of them, prevention is the only option but recent reviews of the vaccinations have led to questions as to the duration of immunity conferred by the currently used protocol. Too often they can be the cause of lowering the autoimmune system of the dog.

Vaccinations can overwhelm the system that is also stressed from a new environment, new diets, and viral exposure.

As combination vaccines contain antigens other than those of the most important infectious disease agents, some may be unnecessary and their use may increase the risk of adverse reactions. Adverse reactions to conventional vaccinations can be immediate (anaphylactic) or can occur twenty-four to forty-eight hours later. Adverse reactions include fever, stiffness, jaundice, sore joints, inflammation, even seizures, liver and kidney problems, and bone marrow suppression and collapse.

Some vaccines, such as the one for Lyme disease, may not be needed because the disease is limited to certain geographic areas with a high tick incidence. Leptospirosis vaccines give little protection against most of the strains of lepto and only last a few months. Rabies, while required in many areas to be given every year, has a three-year duration. The overall risk and benefit of using certain vaccines or multiple vaccines given simultaneously must be examined. Antibody titers can be performed annually before revaccinations.

The new protocols are quite a different way of thinking after so many years of following a certain schedule, so it is advisable to follow your veterinarian's recommendations for the young puppy and consider alternative protocols for the older dog that will include titers.

Veterinarian vaccinologists have recommended the following new schedules. These include the puppy series followed by a booster at one year and further boosters in a combination vaccine every three years until the dog reaches geriatric age, at which time boosters are unnecessary and may be unadvisable for those with aging and immunologic disorders.

Relatively little information has been published about the duration of immunity following vaccinations, but by following a schedule of annual titering, your dog will have less chance of his immune response falling below the levels of adequate protection.

Dr. Jean Dodds, president of HEMOPET (a canine blood bank), has advised that except where vaccination is required by law, all animals that previously experienced an adverse reaction to vaccination can have serum antibody titers measured annually instead of revaccinations. If adequate titers are found, your dog should not need revaccination until some future date.

Suggested Vaccine Schedule

7 weeks—distemper/measles
8 weeks—parvo (killed)
12 weeks—parvo (killed)
15 weeks—DA2P*+ killed parvo (separate sites)
18–20 weeks—DA2P+ killed parvo (separate sites)
6 months—rabies
18 months—rabies for your state requirements
20–24 months—booster for parvo

*Distemper, adenovirus-2, parainfluenza

GROWTH AND DEVELOPMENT

The eight- to sixteen-week-old Vizsla develops both mentally and physically at a faster rate than at any other time in his life. By four months of age, your puppy will be about sixteen inches at the shoulder. The growth rate then slows considerably over the next few months and by six months a male will be at least twenty-two inches tall. A Vizsla does not reach his adult height until around one year of age.

Your puppy will gain at least one and a half pounds a week. His body and head will lengthen, and by the time he is sixteen weeks of age, you should have some idea of body proportions at maturity.

The thirteenth, or floating, rib that was in evidence until the twelfth week rounds out as your puppy's rib cage spreads. The ribs should be covered with enough fat under the skin so that they barely show. The ribs will continue to spread with the chest, reaching almost to the elbows, although body development will not be complete until he is well past two years of age.

The shape and length of the rib cage is important in a sporting dog as it affects the heart and lung capacity, which determines the endurance of the dog in the field. A chest that reaches down to the elbows is essential to provide space for the expanding heart and lungs. Even with the adequate depth of chest, a narrow-fronted dog would lack the necessary width. However, the rib cage must expand without becoming barrel-chested, which would restrict correct movement.

Your puppy's legs will seem to grow faster than any other part of him and he may go through several gawky stages during his first year. Some puppies stay perfectly balanced, however, and never experience those stages.

The majority of puppies will go through a period, usually around seven or eight months of age, when the rear is higher than the front. Amazingly, in just a few weeks after hitting this fast growth spurt, they will even out nicely as if it never happened.

Cariad's Surfstone Szuka, eight months old, starting her show career by winning the Sweepstakes. Owned by Paul Gornoski. Photo © Gilbert.

At eight weeks of age, a male puppy should have both of his testicles down into the scrotum. Sometimes one of them will "float" up and down but when the puppy is relaxed you should be able to feel both of them, and they should stay in place. The testicles should feel rather firm, and be of similar size and shape. By twelve weeks of age, both of them should have descended into place and stayed there. If one of them is completely retained in the abdomen, the dog is described as being monorchid, or unilateral cryptorchid. If both testicles are retained, it is called bilateral cryptorchidism. Either condition will eventually require surgery to remove the possibility of problems with the retained testicle. Since a male only needs one testicle to sire a litter, a neutering is usually recommended to avoid the continuance of what could be a genetic problem. The presence of both testicles in the scrotum is necessary for competition in the breed ring at an AKC show.

Your Vizsla puppy may show a darker line of color in his coat, mainly going down his back, which is an indication of the shade

A young puppy exploring on her own.

his hair will be at maturity. There should lighter shades of color on the sides of his neck and shoulders which form an area called the saddle. He will retain these lighter areas throughout his life.

Eyes should darken by ten weeks of age, although in some breeder's lines a Vizsla may have a lighter eye until he has finished cutting his teeth at six months of age. The eye color should blend with the coat color. Yellow eyes are faulty and undesirable.

Teeth

By twelve weeks of age, the sharp, needle-like points of your puppy's deciduous teeth will be worn down and will not be as painful if you inadvertently connect with them. Remember to refrain from tug-of-war games that may change the normal position of the teeth as his jaw grows.

By sixteen weeks of age, your Vizsla will start losing some of those baby teeth and replacing them with the permanent set. The first ones lost will be the incisors, which are the six top and bottom teeth between the large corner canines. Next to go are the large canines. One of the baby canines may be retained as the new one grows alongside

it. Since the canines have longer roots that are slower to be absorbed, try giving your puppy marrow bones or nylon chew toys to loosen these teeth before consulting the veterinarian about pulling them. However, if the baby teeth do not loosen, causing the adult canine teeth to come in at an angle, they will have to be extracted surgically. The premolars and molars come in last. The total adult set numbers forty-two teeth, with twenty on the top and twenty-two on the bottom. It is rare for a Vizsla to have any teeth missing unless as a result of an injury.

Your puppy's gums and mouth may be tender for several weeks while he is cutting teeth and he may refrain from finishing his meals. Since the last molar does not come in until he is almost six months old, he may experience some weight loss. Be patient. Keep him on a good, high-protein puppy meal, and he will gain back any loss as soon as his teeth are no longer a problem.

Gait and Movement

Vizsla puppies are great exponents of the bouncing gallop, never walking into a room, but bouncing into it. In fact, this movement continues well into their adulthood as their actions show the exuberant happiness so characteristic of this breed. A developing five-month-old puppy will not yet have reached the clumsy stage and so that is a good age to observe his movement and gait.

Basic mechanics of movement can be observed in the walking puppy, as his legs travel slowly with action staggered in a four-beat gait. At a walk he needs and uses only part of his potential front and rear extension and reach, but as he begins to put on speed his legs will begin to move farther forward, momentum will increase, and with his longer steps, an easygoing, trotting stride will become evident. He should be light-footed and graceful and a joy to watch.

Even at this early age, a Vizsla puppy should pick up his feet purposefully and cleanly, never shuffling them. Faulty front quarters with over-angulated shoulders show up in a puppy moving forward from his elbows instead of swinging from his lower shoulder blades. A puppy with this problem will appear to have his back half moving faster than the front to keep from stepping on his front feet.

At the other extreme, a "mincer" will take short, stilted steps. Such a dog usually lacks the correct front angulation. He will move out from the shoulders with flashy, fast steps, appearing to cover a lot of ground, but having to work harder at it.

Stand directly in front of your puppy and watch him coming to you in a straight line. As he increases to a trot, his legs should tend to converge under the midpoint of his body. This convergence, if seen by paw prints, would be evidenced by a single line, referred to as single tracking, which is the correct action for a sporting dog. Correct movement on a puppy will not change as he grows, unless influenced by lack of exercise and muscle tone.

GROOMING

A young puppy's coat requires minimal attention, but he should be groomed or brushed weekly. The prime function of this attention is to train the active puppy to accept and submit to necessary restraints while he is still mentally flexible and can be easily managed. Vizslas love the attention of brushing but they must be taught to stay still for it. Getting your Vizsla into the habit of being placed on a grooming table, or any other raised surface, while still a young puppy will prevent backaches for you, his groomer. Besides the weekly coat brushing, his nails will need trimming, his teeth must be checked for any accumulation of tartar, and his ears will require special attention to prevent wax or yeast buildup.

Several times a week, place him up on the grooming table. Do not let any part of his grooming become a punishment, but use this time to enforce some basic obedience commands such as sit and stay. Never leave your dog unsupervised on a grooming table.

At eight weeks of age, this puppy shows the excellent reach of correct movement.

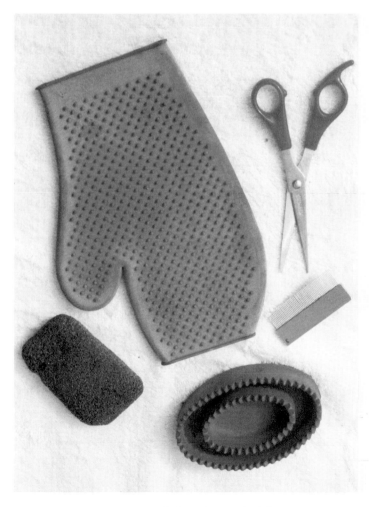

Basic grooming equipment includes a fine-toothed flea comb, rubber curry brush, pumice stone, rubber grooming glove, and scissors.

Teaching a puppy to accept grooming on a table will also aid in stacking and baiting.

With a dog that stays as close to your side as a Vizsla does, it will be easy to notice if your dog is a little down. Maybe all he will need is a little attention to make it right, or he may not be feeling well due to an upset stomach or diarrhea. Stay tuned to your Vizsla's emotional state as well as his physical one. It can be an indication of something serious.

Coat Care

Accustom your Vizsla puppy to grooming by running a rubber curry brush over him weekly. This will also give you the chance to check his skin for any dandruff, burrs, injuries, or allergy or mange problems. Running your hand over his coat against the hair, or using a small, fine-toothed flea comb, will disclose any external parasite problem.

A good digestive system and intestines free of parasites are the first requisite for healthy hair, since any clogging of the system with poisons will inevitably work to the detriment of your Vizsla's coat. Your Vizsla should always have a shiny, clean coat, nourished from the inside.

Depending on the time of year, your Vizsla will shed his puppy coat around the end of his first year when he reaches puberty or, in the case of a bitch, her first season. The new coat usually comes in darker and will be his true color. A rubber brush or pumice stone is the easiest way to get the short, stiff, dead hairs out of his coat and hasten new growth.

In cold weather climates, the Vizsla will grow a thicker undercoat, especially on the neck and shoulders, that will need special attention in the spring. A dry coat from a heated house can benefit from wheat germ capsules or peanut oil added daily to the diet.

The Vizsla standard allows for whisker trimming, and if you decide that you would like your dog's face clean, it will be easier to start trimming while he is still a puppy to get him used to having them snipped. A Vizsla has a lovely face and the whiskers do not really enhance it. It is still debatable whether the whiskers actually serve a functional purpose.

Bathing

Vizslas love water, whether they are swimming or playing in it, and they enjoy baths or showers as soon as they become accustomed to them. Start while your puppy is young—in fact, most puppies need bathing more than adults since they tend to roll on the ground when playing.

Bathe your Vizsla whenever you think he needs it. You are the one holding and hugging him, and if you think he needs a bath once a week, then do it. Do remember, however, that too many baths will rob his coat of natural oils, so unless he is really dirty or smelly, it might be better to hold off.

Use a shampoo especially formulated for either your puppy or your adult, whether it is a flea shampoo or merely a cleansing shampoo. Rinse well and dry him, remembering the inside of his ears. Do not leave him in an air-conditioned room or in a draft while he is still damp.

Nail Care

Nail cutting is the one aspect of grooming with which most dog owners have difficulties. Nails will have to be clipped regularly for the rest of your Vizsla's life so the earlier you get him to accept it, the easier the job will be.

The guillotine type of nail cutter is the best tool to start out with in cutting a puppy's nails, but as the care of the nails gets easier for both you and him, an electric nail grinder tool is faster. There are two types: a regular electric grinder and a battery-operated one. The latter does not seem to cause as much vibration, is quieter, and may be more easily accepted by your dog. The Vizsla should have well-arched toes, close together, and short nails will keep both the feet and the pastern area strong. A weekly trimming will be enough to keep the nails from touching the floor.

Make sure that your puppy has had plenty of exercise, as the best time to get him to settle down to having nails trimmed is when he is tired. Sometimes it is possible to do the job on a very young puppy as he sleeps on your lap.

The secret of successful nail trimming is knowing how far to go without cutting into the quick, causing bleeding. The quick is the line running through the center of the nail, and you can see it easily if you hold the foot up in a good light.

If you are worried about cutting into the quick, cut off only a small amount of the nail at a time. If you accidentally cut the nail too short and the quick bleeds, do not panic. It will bleed quite a bit but press a cold wet cloth tightly against the end of the nail until the blood clots, or apply some styptic in the form of powdered ammonium alum. After cutting the nail, follow up by smoothing the edges with a grooved file if necessary. Bleeding seldom occurs when you use the powered nail grinder since the heat from the friction cauterizes as you go. A light touch is needed with this type of nail grinder, so be careful not to bear down. Take only a little off at once.

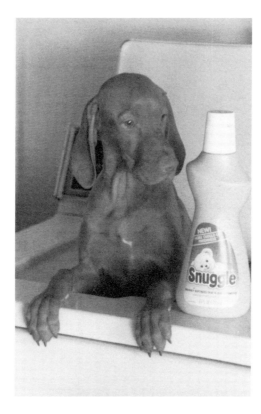

There are better places to get a bath.

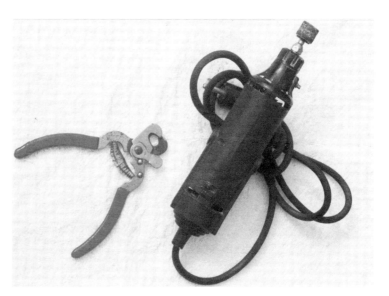

Nail grooming equipment can be either a nail clipper, or an electric or battery-powered nail sander.

If your young dog protests too much about having his nails cut, do one foot at a time, brushing his coat for a few minutes in between. Progress like this until all toes are done. Doing the rear feet first may give you an easier start. You may need someone to

Nail Trimming Guide

As the nail grows, the quick (blood supply) lengthens. If you cut into the quick, the nail will bleed profusely.

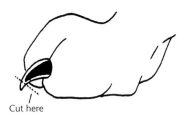

Cut here

Trim as shown and avoid cutting into the blood supply. The quick will begin to recede.

Trim or file a small portion of the nail tip every few days. The quick will continue to recede.

A properly trimmed nail. When kept short, the nail can be maintained without bleeding or discomfort to the dog.

hold the puppy the first few times, or you can try a biscuit to distract him. However hard it is, do not tolerate any protests. Long nails are easily snagged on crates, fences, or brush and can be severely painful when torn.

Your puppy is like a young child and he will learn to accept nail trimming as a part of discipline and training if you keep at it. But if you find, for any reason, that you are not able to keep his nails cut, make regular visits to a groomer.

IDENTIFICATION

Besides a collar holding immediate identification information, your Vizsla should have a permanent form of identification such as a tattoo or microchip. No matter how careful you may be, the unexpected can occur. For example, in the case of an auto accident, your frightened dog could escape the car, running very far very quickly. If found by strangers and taken to a shelter, your uncollared dog still can be identified through a tattoo on his inner thigh or a microchip in his shoulder area, saving both you and him much anxiety.

There are several "lost dog" registries that use different forms of tattoo identification. Check with your local kennel club or veterinarian since they often know of someone who does the tattooing. Tattooing is painless, takes only a few minutes, and requires no anesthesia. Make sure you register the number with a registry—it won't do any good if the tattooed number cannot be traced.

A second method of permanent identification is having a tiny microchip implanted in the shoulder area of your dog. Using a syringe and taking no more effort or pain than that of a regular vaccine shot, this has now become the system used in rescue shelters to identify a "found" dog. With the use of a small hand-held scanner that reads the number and registry on the chip, a shelter can contact frantic owners that their lost dog has been found. Like the tattoo, the microchip with your name and address has to be registered with the company whose system you are using.

CHAPTER SIX

Your Vizsla's First Year: Behavior and Training

The average Vizsla puppy displays friendliness, gaiety, and an overwhelming demonstration of affection both to his owners and to strangers, especially in a home environment where he always feels secure and comfortable. No matter what the future plans for your puppy include, you should deliberately widen his exposure, from puppyhood on, to include strange places, sounds, situations, and people.

SOCIALIZATION

Trips to your veterinarian should be counteracted by joyful excursions elsewhere so that your puppy does not associate auto rides with unpleasant experiences. Vizslas thrive on trips to shopping centers or parks. People are always curious about the breed, gravitating to the aristocratic style and attractive color. Owners should always welcome these encounters with strangers and allow their dog to greet them. Ask a stranger to pet your puppy by scratching him under the chin or behind the ears. This will teach the puppy to lift his head for attention. Patting a puppy on the top of his head will give him the idea to approach strangers with his head down.

At the same time that you are getting your puppy used to the big wide world, try to expose him to other breeds and encourage short play sessions with friendly dogs that will accept a puppy. Your young Vizsla will gain confidence in himself when he finds that nothing he is exposed to poses a threat. A puppy will learn through his imitation of another dog. If your Vizsla is being brought up by an older, shy, retiring companion, chances are that he will also behave in this manner. The older dog that gives a happy enthusiastic welcome to everyone will be your greatest asset in teaching your young puppy. Confidence will make him a better all-round companion no matter what is asked of him

During the socialization period, your Vizsla puppy will go through a fear period, and any frightening or painful experience can have a lasting impact on him. The puppy may perceive something as a bad experience even though you do not realize that it scared or worried him. He may react to little things, like a stranger walking towards him with a cane or umbrella, an upset garbage can, a broken branch blowing across the ground, or even something so small that you do not even see it. Great care must be taken not to reinforce negative behavior. Being forced to face the situation can frighten the young dog, and soothing tones serve to encourage his fear. His fear should be handled with patience and kindness. Any kind of obedience training during the fear periods puts the dog in a position of success, allowing him to

Vizslas are wonderful companions, they are never far from your side.

Cricket and her granddaughter Eve (four months old) have a quiet time in the sun. A young puppy can learn a lot from an older, quieter dog.

work things out while building self-confidence. Sometimes all you have to do is walk up to what is scaring him, touch it, and tell your puppy it is all right. Let him check it out and see for himself what the strange object actually is.

CRITICAL PERIODS IN YOUR PUPPY'S FIRST YEAR

If your new puppy comes into your home at eight weeks of age, he will be in the midst of a critical period of development. During seven to twelve weeks of age, he is in the canine socialization period. He has the brain waves of an adult dog and has the ability to learn respect and simple behavior responses such as sit and come. His housebreaking begins during this period and he is bonding to his new owner, learning by association and able to accept gentle discipline and gain confidence. This period is also part of the first fear impact period, and children and other animals should not be allowed to hurt or scare him—either accidentally or deliberately. Learning at this age is permanent.

Between the ages of thirteen and sixteen weeks, your Vizsla puppy comes to the age not only of cutting teeth but of testing dominance and leadership. Biting and mouthing are a normal behavior for a puppy, and your puppy's ability to control the force of his bite is called "bite inhibition." It is a critical skill that every puppy needs to learn from you, although his dam probably began the corrections when he was with her. The first time your puppy bites you, scream "Ow!" in a loud voice. Then refuse to pay any attention to him for a few minutes. If your puppy tries it a second time, take him by the scruff of the neck, give him a gentle shake, and scold him in a threatening voice. If he still doesn't get the message, flip him over on his back and scold him, holding him in that position until he stops struggling. Biting behavior must be completely discouraged.

Between the ages of four to eight months, your puppy will test his wings and turn a deaf ear when called. This period may last from a few days to several weeks, and how you give corrections can minimize negative behavior. Since this period also corresponds to the time your puppy is cutting new teeth, behavioral problems become compounded by the physiological development of chewing. The second fear period starts during this time, usually around six months of age and corresponding to growth spurts. Great care must be taken on handling any negative behavior since any force can scare the dog, but soothing tones can serve to encourage his fear. Again, obedience training during this critical time can put the dog in a position of success while building self-confidence.

Your Vizsla will continue to grow during his first year, and the closer a male gets to puberty, the more likely that you will see an increase in renewed testing for leadership. A Vizsla never needs a heavy hand for any type of corrections. All he needs is the displeasure in your voice and firm gentleness in corrections and training. But give him no opportunity to affirm his leadership. The key to successfully rearing your puppy is to establish yourself as the pack leader and then to maintain that position for the life of your dog.

EXERCISE

Vizslas are adaptable; many living in high-rise apartments get their daily exercise from riding up and down in an elevator and walking around the block. Even in most situations of this kind, however, the owner usually finds some way to take his Vizsla to a park or a field on a weekend to really let him run. Many cities have set aside fenced areas where owners can take their dogs off-leash and let them run and play with other friendly dogs.

Exercise is important to both the mental and the physical well-being of your Vizsla. Quite often a young dog will get sudden bursts of energy, tearing wildly through the house, around the dining room table and over the sofa, simply enjoying himself until he gets it out of his system. He even may, without warning, start racing around and around the yard with no discernable purpose. Whether this is just boredom or a sudden need for more exercise is uncertain, but for a dog to develop properly, he must have a chance to blow off steam, whether in an enclosed yard or an enclosed park. He may not necessarily be unhappy in a limited space, but rarely is a Vizsla well-muscled or a good mover under those conditions.

Muscle development is a continuous process, beginning the moment the puppy is

Young puppies need exercise to keep them out of mischief and build muscles and stamina.

Four-month-old puppies love romping in the snow.

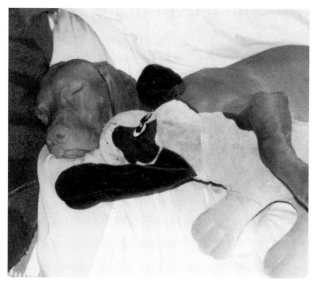

Vizslas at every age LOVE to play in water.

This young Vizsla snuggles with his oversized toy.

Time out from exercising to pose for a lovely picture.

The young dog being trained in field work will always be getting exercise, but he should never be encouraged to go off and hunt on his own or he may develop the habit of working for himself and not for his owner. The dog in agility or obedience training will get his exercise from each training session that includes jumping.

The importance of powerful musculature on a show dog is often overlooked. The Vizsla, like most sporting breeds, should be shown in working condition. Many dogs that look like first-place winners when standing still drop right out of contention as soon as they move across the ring. Unfortunately, many Vizslas are unsound in movement because of underdeveloped muscles from sedentary lives. Vizslas do need exercise to present a healthy appearance and relieve their boredom. Short, regular bouts of activity are generally more beneficial than longer but infrequent ones.

The dog whose hindquarters need an extra bit of tightening up may benefit from trotting up and down a hill, across a beach, or over uneven ground. Romping or swimming in a lake or pool will also tighten these muscles. It is the consistent push that develops the power—so essential to a sporting dog—in the legs, lungs, and back.

born and progressing throughout his life. Getting your Vizsla outside regularly for walks, play, training, or even jogging sessions is essential. A young puppy can be taught to retrieve a tennis ball in his own yard and get exercise that way. Rarely does a Vizsla get bored with retrieving anything. Another canine companion can give him added incentive to exercise. The Vizsla with a big yard or field to roam in will quite often be found sitting on the doorstep wanting someone to keep him company, and this may also be the incentive for the owner to get out more too.

EARLY TRAINING

The sooner your puppy is taught to behave and "mind his manners," the easier he will be to live with and the fewer bad habits he will develop. There is no one way to train a dog, nor is there any set age at which formal training should begin, but after a few days of letting your new puppy settle in, he should be secure enough in his new surroundings to be ready for early basic lessons and training.

Puppies grow so fast that they cover in one year what most children cover in eight to ten. During your puppy's first few months you should outline, in your mind, a few basic plans for habit patterns you wish to set up and then adhere closely to a training program to instill them.

Whether the plans include field training, hunt tests, the show ring, or even obedience, agility, or a companion that you can live with, the close contact during this early period will do much to give your Vizsla courage, confidence, and knowledge that he could not gain if he were in a kennel environment. It is essential that a good rapport with people—especially with you, his owner—be established during this time, as his emotional development is linked with his physical and mental growth. In this first year, your Vizsla puppy will form a strong bond with you that will last for life.

Since a Vizsla puppy is so cute and smart, it is easy for the new owner to tend to allow him to do anything he wants when he is small, and then correct problems when he is older. To take the extra work out of training, teach your dog good habits from the beginning instead of having to break bad habits you could easily have prevented. A dog is actually capable of learning anytime after the age of three weeks. At twelve weeks, with a series of vaccinations behind him, your Vizsla can be started in a puppy kindergarten class, and at six months, formal obedience and agility lessons can be undertaken. His learning begins the day he comes home with you and continues throughout his life.

This young bitch shows a natural tendency to point.

Crate Training

The cage, or crate, is a sanctuary for your Vizsla. From the day you bring him into your home, give him a place he knows is his. It is important for his peace of mind and well-being and can make the difference in whether he adjusts well to his new home and environment or not. The crate should never be used as a form of punishment but should be viewed by your young Vizsla as a place where he can escape in order to rest or nap in peace away from family activities. Most Vizslas love a crate and adapt easily to its use. It should not take more than a few days before your puppy will be going into it on his own.

A wire crate is best as it will give your dog adequate ventilation and visibility. He can watch the family activities around him but feel protected from them. There are many good crates on the market that fold up and can be carried like a suitcase and easily moved from room to room. You will find the crate indispensable not only in your own home but when visiting friends and relatives. Confining an active puppy in someone else's home ensures a smiling welcome, especially as it will keep him from soiling the floors and carpets at will.

Make sure that your attitude toward using a crate is a positive one. Remember that you are doing your puppy a real favor,

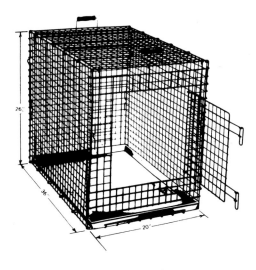

as his crate training will reduce his fear, insecurity, and stress. As he gets older, you will find your Vizsla going into an open crate by himself to nap. After time you will find yourself using the crate constantly for one reason or another. It can be placed in a car for safety during travel; it can be carried into a motel room to secure your dog if you are out of the room. Getting both yourself and your puppy used to his crate now will be a benefit throughout your dog's life.

Get a large enough crate size to be comfortable for your dog as an adult—approximately twenty-four by thirty-six inches. Place the crate in a corner of the family room or kitchen during the day. Keep a washable blanket or mat, never newspapers, on the floor of the crate along with several safe toys. Make sure the crate is not in a draft from air conditioning or heat ducts.

Wait until your puppy is tired, ready for a nap, and has been fed and exercised before attempting to crate him. If he cries, do not let him out. Because he is already tired, he will soon settle down. If you put your puppy in the crate at the same time each day to establish a pattern, he will quickly adjust to a schedule of rest. It will make your life easier if he is not constantly underfoot.

If your are away from home for short periods of time, confining the puppy to his crate means that you will not have to worry about what kind of mischief he is getting into while he is alone. Not only will you not have

chewed furniture or a mess on the floor, but you will also have a happier relationship with your puppy if he is not a problem.

Use the crate as a housebreaking tool since a dog generally will not mess in his sleeping area. He should not be confined for more than four hours at a time during the day, and he should be taken out to eliminate immediately upon release. Since he will not be able to soil at will, he will learn control of his bowels that much sooner and will come to associate his toilet duties as belonging outdoors.

Housebreaking

The hardest problem confronting the new puppy owner is housebreaking. When you bring your young Vizsla home, he may still be in the habit of using newspapers, both in the whelping box and on the floor. But if weather permits, there is no reason to delay outdoor training.

When your puppy opens his eyes in the morning, immediately scoop him up in your arms and run, do not walk, to the nearest exit. Go out with him and give plenty of praise as he does his business. Feed him breakfast and repeat the procedure. Take him to the same spot each time and he will associate the odor with the deed.

When inside, confine your puppy to an area of washable floors. Watch for signs and if he suddenly stops playing and looks for a place to squat, pick him up and run outside with him. Each time he wakes up from a nap and after each of his meals, take him outside. Take him out before bedtime and stay with him until you are sure he has had a bowel movement. He should be able to get through the night. Expect to go out with an eight- to ten-week-old puppy a minimum of ten times a day.

As he gets older, your puppy will have better control and you will be bragging that you have him "housebroken," but actually it is only that you have been trained to get him outside on time. One day, around fourteen weeks of age, something clicks in his brain and suddenly he has learned that it all belongs outside.

Never punish your puppy for an accidental puddle in the house by rubbing his nose in it. A Vizsla is smart and sensitive enough to know just from the tone of your voice that he has goofed. Clean up the puddle with a vinegar and water solution to kill the odor and do not make it a traumatic experience for either of you. Accidents will occasionally happen, and while he is learning he needs your encouragement and help.

Unless there is someone home most of the time with your young puppy, the training will be a long and frustrating job. It is unfair to expect him to go long periods without making a puddle. In fact, if he is not confined to a crate, it will seem as if he is making small puddles every few minutes.

If you have to leave him for long periods, make sure you have taken him outside to eliminate and then take him out again as soon as you return. While you are away, if he is not in a crate, confine him in a room with newspapers covering part of the floor. Do not punish him for anything he did while he was alone, especially if it was your fault for not being there to take him out when he needed it. And always remember to praise him when he eliminates outside where he should.

Suggested Housebreaking Schedule

Time	Activity
6:00 a.m.	Walk puppy. Return to crate. Place water in crate or pen for day.
7:00 a.m.	Feed puppy.
7:15 a.m.	Walk puppy and have brief play time. Return to crate or pen.
10:00 a.m.	Walk puppy and spend time with him afterward.
12:00 noon	Feed second meal. Walk 15 min. later Give pup a play time, then return to confined area.
3:00 p.m.	Exercise and potty the puppy. Return to confined area.
5:00 p.m.	Feed third meal.
5:15 p.m.	Walk pup. Bring pup into house with you.
7:00 p.m.	Walk pup, followed by brief play time.
9:00 p.m.	Feed fourth meal.
9:15 p.m.	Walk pup. Remove water from crate. Put puppy in crate near your bed for the night.

BASIC LESSONS

The first basic rule to understand is that you are not *asking* your Vizsla to follow a command, you are *telling* him to. Be firm. If you time your praises and reward the exact behavior you want, your puppy will learn easily, happily, and correctly after just a few times.

The first thing to do is give him a name and use it often. Every time you look at him, play with him, or feed him, use his name. Speak only in a happy tone, never an angry one. Let him get used to the sound of your voice.

Sit on the floor while he plays and call him to you. As soon as he comes to you, reward him with a piece of cheese or dog biscuit, and lots of praise. Repeat several times, saying his name and "come" every time he

Koppertone's Casey Baratom, owned by Marianne Megna, at five months of age, grew up to become an energetic agility competitor.

wanders off, rewarding him each time he comes back. Every call to you should be a pleasant experience.

As your puppy gets accustomed to his new surroundings, he will show more independence, especially if he is enjoying himself in some way, such as chasing a butterfly and you are calling him to leave his fun and come into the house. If he turns a deaf ear to your pleas, the time has arrived for the "come" command to be taught on leash.

Most new owners do not give their eight-week-old Vizsla enough credit for brains, but puppies love the training and attention that entails. The basics should include sit, stay, down, come, and waking on leash. Most pet owners ignore the training on leash since the only time their Vizsla might have to be on leash is for a trip to the veterinarian, but leash training is one of the basics of dog obedience and it is necessary to make your dog a true companion.

Coming when Called

Use a plain buckle collar for training puppy basics. Do not use a slip collar, or choke chain, on a puppy this young, as you can cause damage to the soft cartilage in the throat if you do a lot of pulling with the leash. Make sure the collar fits correctly and does not allow the puppy to get his chin under it. Never leave it on when he is unsupervised, as it could get caught on a fence or shrub and choke your dog.

Attach a leash or piece of rope to the collar; not surprisingly, it is easier to teach the come if your dog is within reach both mentally and physically. Call his name and "Come" and immediately give a slight tug on the leash and reel him in to you. Praise him as he comes. The word "come" is the most important word your dog will ever learn—it may even save his life one day.

Let him wander off on his own again without saying anything for several minutes. When he forgets that you are on the other end of the lead and focuses his attention elsewhere, call his name and "Come" again. Immediately give the leash a jerk to get his attention. As soon as he looks at you, praise him in an excited voice, and reel him in.

Spend only a few minutes each day with this exercise. Do not use it constantly while the puppy is on the leash. Let him have time to explore and then, when he is not expecting it, give the command. Once you are getting reliable instant responses, try it without any jerking of the lead and then, finally, completely off-lead.

If at first your puppy does not respond when you remove the leash, go back to working on lead and stress the fact that he *must* come when called. Make it more fun by running backwards as he is coming to you. Praise, praise, praise when he reaches you.

Walking on Leash (Heeling)

When your puppy has become sufficiently accustomed to the collar and leash, let him run and play while dragging the leash behind him. Soon he will become used to the weight of the attached leash, and then it is time to get him used to leash restraints. The timid owner who encounters frantic resistance to this early training is usually conned into stopping it, with the misconception that it will be easier to handle when the puppy gets older. But your puppy will only grow larger, stronger, and more determined, and will protest again, so it is always better to start leash training early.

Most Vizsla puppies adapt to the leash without protest, but the first few times your puppy will probably want to go the other way when you try to entice him to follow you. He might even stop and scratch persistently at his collar. After a few days of encouraging him to follow and stay with you on your left side, with praise and bits of food as a reward, however, he should be able to trot alongside without constant pulling on the leash. A quick jerk on the leash every time he surges ahead, should actually move his front feet back to the correct place at your side, even with your shoulders. Expect the heeling, or walking on leash correctly, to take several weeks of practice. Your puppy

A responsible child and a young Vizsla have a great connection.

must learn to stay near you when walking, no matter how interested he is in other things.

When he has accepted walking on leash, insist that he not wander in every direction on his own. Keep the leash shortened so that he doesn't trip you up, and coax and praise continuously with slight tugs on the leash. Do not make sudden jerks and pulls with the leash. Just hold it tightly enough that your puppy is comfortable when he is near your left side and uncomfortable when he tries to move from that position. Keep the leash in your right hand, leaving your left hand free to give him a pat every so often or to encourage him with a treat.

When your puppy starts walking easily beside you, begin making turns and changing directions. It will make it more interesting for your puppy and will help keep his attention on you. Make everything fun for him, and you will soon have a Vizsla puppy trotting along proudly at your side, unafraid, with tail wagging and head held high.

Teaching your puppy to eliminate while he is on leash is vitally important. If you do not have a fenced yard which enables him to go on his own, you will have to start the leash training early along with the housebreaking. The collar and leash may distract him at first, so keep repeating in a calm voice to "hurry up." As soon as he is finished, give a lot of praise. He will soon associate those words with his toilet. There will be many times in his life when eliminating on leash will be necessary. Get him used to it early.

Leash training and housebreaking should be done in the confines of your own yard if possible, until your Vizsla has had the time to build up his immunity to diseases with his full series of vaccines.

Sit

For teaching the sit, hold a piece of food in front of and just above your puppy's nose. Raise it slowly until he lifts his head. This position usually makes him sit in order to keep looking up. As soon as his bottom hits the floor give him the treat. As he progresses to an automatic sit in order to look up, tell him "Sit." When he does, praise him and reward him.

It is not important at this point how he sits. Training for straight sits is only important in obedience trials and that type of formal education can come later. All you want now is to teach him what the words mean, and to have a puppy that is happy and reliable.

Down

You can teach your puppy a down from either the sitting or a standing position. Using the food as an attraction in front of the puppy's nose, move that hand slowly straight down to the floor. As his head follows the food and his body drops, tell him to "Down." As soon as the elbows and rear are on the floor, reward him.

Stay

After your puppy is doing a reliable sit and down, you can begin to teach him the stay from either position. While he is still in

Young Vizslas can be taught to retrieve in the water. Swimming is also great exercise.

position, swing the flat of your hand, palm facing him, towards his face. Stop short of actually touching his face and tell him to "Stay." Back a short distance away from him, quietly repeating "Stay." If he does not remain in place, lead him back to the place where you told him "Stay" and repeat the procedure until he gets the idea and is able to stay in place for a few seconds. You may find it easier to teach the stay from the down position, but it is a good idea to teach and practice from both positions. If he is staying in place, do not praise him at this point since a Vizsla instantly responds to praise with a bounce and a wagging tail, and you do not want any movement from him.

Retrieving

Start your puppy retrieving soon after he settles into his new home. Since Vizslas have a natural retrieving instinct, he will already be carrying anything he can find. Give him a box of his own toys, especially stuffed animals. Encourage him to retrieve and carry different shapes and textures. You can have fun teaching him to bring his own toys in from the yard. He will also love retrieving a tennis ball, and at the same time will be getting exercise.

Staying Alone

In every puppy's life there will be times when he will be in an empty house. You need to help him accept and adjust to the fact that someone will not always be at his side.

Begin by leaving him in his crate, or bed, in a permanent place while you go about your chores in another part of the house. If you are sure he does not have to go out to eliminate, do not let him out if he cries. Stay in another room out of sight, but where he is still aware that you are nearby. Your puppy will soon learn that your activities do not constantly involve him. As he adjusts to not always having you at his beck and call, he will be able to adjust to being alone without stress.

It is wrong to expect an eight-week-old puppy to stay in his crate for more than four hours at a time. If that does not fit your schedule, make sure that you arrange for someone else to come in to let him out. This will lessen his time alone, give him his meals and exercise on time, and relieve his tension so that he will be able to nap. As he adjusts to confinement, the time periods he spends alone can gradually be lengthened.

Do not make a big deal out of the process of leaving home. Give your puppy time to exercise and play, then place him in his crate with plenty of safe toys for company, and leave a radio, tuned to a talk show, within hearing range. Leave the house without any fuss, and when you return, do it in the same quiet manner. Show him that you will always come back for him and that there is nothing to worry about. Communicating to him that you will be coming and going fairly constantly will help him learn to stay alone without stress.

BEHAVIOR PROBLEMS

A Vizsla never needs a heavy hand for any type of correction. All he needs is the sound of displeasure in your voice and firm gentleness in corrections or training. Vizslas are highly intelligent animals and training your puppy correctly will give him confidence in himself. The Vizsla's lovely temperament is probably the characteristic

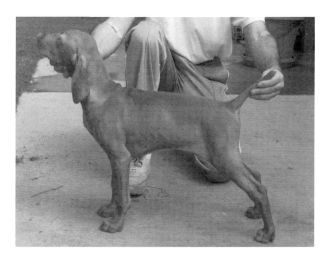

Training a young puppy early for the show ring. Owned by Mark Goodwein.

Four-month-old Covey finds the sofa an ideal place for his nap.

that most sets him apart from other breeds. How you handle and develop your dog's personality from the start will make all the difference in this wonderful dog. You cannot put him aside and ignore the affection and attention he will want to give and get.

Jumping on People

The Vizsla is a happy, outgoing, and sociable breed and if your puppy is being raised with love and affection, he will probably expect the same from everyone. However, if you allow him to jump up on you to give a greeting, he will also do it to visitors. Short of discouraging non-doggy friends from visiting, you will have to train your puppy not to jump up on people. And even if your friends like dogs and do not mind being greeted in this manner, muddy feet on clean clothes are not generally regarded happily.

One of the ways to prevent your Vizsla from jumping up to greet you is to get down to his level immediately as he tries to reach your face. He will be enthusiastic about getting all the hugs and petting he has been waiting for.

The alternative is to teach him not to jump up at all. As he starts to jump up, immediately press your hand against his nose and say "No" or "Off." Then turn your back and walk away. He will soon learn that jumping up and pawing is no way of greet-

ing you and that you are displeased with him. If pushing his nose down with your hand does not work, grasp both of his front paws firmly and thrust him backward. As a last resort, time a jab to his chest with a raised knee as he jumps up.

You must be consistent with the training. Do not expect your dog to understand that he is welcome to greet you when you are in old clothes but not when you are in new ones.

Climbing on Furniture

Maybe other breeds are content to lie on the floor, but a Vizsla seems to enjoy higher elevation. Although a sporting breed, the Vizsla is a very socially oriented dog that loves to be on your lap as you read or watch television. Of course, the easiest way to handle his desire to be on furniture is to allow it, or to allow it on one particular chair. It is very simple to throw a cover on a chair to protect it, and teach your Vizsla that it is the only furniture on which he is permitted. If you are never going to allow him on furniture, do not let him do this as a puppy and then try to change the rules later on in his life.

If you do not want your Vizsla in your lap every time you sit down, give him an alternative that will enable him to be close to you. Place a thick, folded blanket or a dog bed on the floor near your chair for him and be consistent with your commands. Do not allow him up with you. Do not reason to yourself "just this once won't hurt"—you will only confuse him.

Whether it is his crate or a blanket on the floor, get your Vizsla used to the command of "Go to bed" in the place he truly knows is his. Catch him before he wants his nap on the sofa or chair, give him a hug and a toy, and place him where he should be staying. A crate is the only guarantee, however, that he will never be on the furniture when you leave him on his own.

Better to chew on a rawhide bone than the chair leg.

Seven-month-old Lark thinking a bird in the hand is better than none in the bush.

Destructive Chewing

A Vizsla is born with the retriever instinct and, because of that, is very mouth-oriented and loves to be constantly carrying something. That sometimes rapidly graduates to chewing on sticks, toys, and even chair legs. If you wait for your Vizsla to outgrow this stage, you will have to replace shoes and furniture long before he decides to move on to another phase. Instead of trying to teach him not to chew, teach him what is permissible and safe to chew.

Keep a good variety of soft stuffed animals, nylon bones, and marrow bone for him to carry and chew. Give a sharp "No" if he starts to chew on anything that is not allowed. Puppies and adults have both been known to swallow items such as nails, bolts, needles, and tinfoil, all of which can cause intestinal problems.

Teach children to put away books, toys, shoes, and belongings, not giving your Vizsla the opportunity to get into trouble. Do not give your young dog an old sock or shoe to play with and then scold him when he damages a good one. He cannot be expected to know the difference and the inconsistencies of corrections will confuse him. You cannot change an inbred tendency, so channel it in the right direction with corrections and praise—and keep your closet doors closed.

Digging Holes

Vizslas love to dig, and freshly planted flower beds or gardens seem to hold a special attraction for them. If your puppy confined his digging to an area without any grass or flowers, the damage might not be of any consequence. But once started, he will be having too much fun to quit. Digging can become exceedingly persistent in a young Vizsla that is left alone in the yard without toys or another dog to play with. If the digging habit is allowed to continue, it will be difficult to break. Scolding does not seem to work. Apart from filling the holes with large rocks to discourage digging, the only alternative seems to be constant supervision and plenty of exercise.

CHAPTER SEVEN

The Young Adult Vizsla

Every Vizsla owner thinks that his dog is unique in his intelligence, but when owners get together and compare notes they find that each Vizsla is intelligent, friendly, sociable, happy, and interesting. There is never a dull moment with a Vizsla in the home. Watching him develop from puppyhood to adulthood will be satisfying and amusing. A Vizsla never loses his sense of humor and will find ways to entertain himself and his family well into old age.

An important aspect of your young dog's development is play and attention from you, his owner. Not only do humans benefit from contact with animals, animals benefit from the care and interaction with their owners. Companionship and care given mutually will help the owner and his pet live happier and healthier lives. No matter how busy or hectic things seem to be, be sure to spend time with your Vizsla. It is always best to set aside playtime as part of his regular exercise period, but also make time to cuddle, hold, and touch him.

GROWTH AND DEVELOPMENT

By fourteen months of age, both the male and female will have gained their full heights, but they will continue to mature during the next year as their rib cages spread and their chests widen and drop.

A male should look like a male. He should not be small or feminine-looking. You should be able to look at him and im-

mediately know that he is a male. He should have an attractive head, heavier and wider than the female's, good bone, substance and strength without any coarseness, and an ideal height of twenty-four inches. A female should be smaller, a little finer-boned, with a soft, feminine head, but she should still show strength of body. Her ideal height is about twenty-two inches, as a smaller bitch may lack substance.

As a full-grown adult, the weight of a bitch will usually average around forty-eight pounds, and that of the male around ten pounds more. Enough weight should be maintained to keep the ribs from showing, but a Vizsla should never be allowed to get fat or soft.

Your young male will start lifting his leg to urinate by the time he has reached one year of age. His hormones start working as he reaches the age of puberty. He will start marking his territory, covering areas where other dogs have been in particular. He starts to be very much aware of the fact that he is a *male*.

Most males have a moderate amount of discharge from their prepuce. If you are concerned about the appearance of this discharge, its color, or excessive licking and cleaning activity, it may be a sign of infection

Ch. CM Leitz, Camera, Action. Owned and photographed by Christina Freitag.

A very expressive head on this young boy. Ch. Caveat Tahoka CMF Rolleiflex, JH. Photo © Christina M. Freitag.

The Progress of the Average Heat Period in Bitches

Five to seven days for preliminary vaginal swelling, then:

First day: Discharge of bright red blood begins, marking the beginning of the true heat period.

Fifth to ninth day: Discharge changes gradually to light pink or becomes almost colorless. Bitch becomes playful and submissive to males.

Tenth day: Bitch will accept males for copulation. This is ordinarily the first day of possible conception.

Eleventh to fifteenth day: Bitch eager to accept males for copulation. Conception is very likely during this period.

Sixteenth day: Bitch may begin to reject males, but conception is still possible.

Seventeenth day onward: Bitch may be quite vicious and violent about rejection of males, although they are still interested in her. Conception still possible if the bitch has not yet ovulated.

Twentieth or twenty-first day: The heat is over, and conception is totally impossible.

and you should consult your veterinarian about a culture. As your male gets older, he should have annual physical examinations of his reproductive organs, since treatable disorders of the prepuce, testicles, and prostate gland are common.

The female will usually have her first season, or heat, between the ages of ten and fifteen months, but it is not uncommon for the first heat to be delayed well past that, even to almost two years. After the first heat, most bitches will regularly come into season every six or seven months.

The first signs of your bitch coming into season will be the swelling around the vulva. It may actually stay slightly enlarged for a few weeks before any bloody discharge appears. Your bitch may keep herself so clean that you miss the first few days, but when she starts to bleed in earnest and drips on the carpeting, keep her confined to her crate while indoors, or in pants with a protective pad.

The consistency, color, and odor of the discharge will change around the bitch's tenth day in season and will attract males. It is very important that she is not allowed outdoors without supervision at any time during her season since a determined male can and will climb a fence to get to her. If you live in the city or in a residential area, take her outside on a leash to eliminate and bring her back inside immediately. She can make up for the exercise she is missing after her season is over.

Because of the inevitable individual variation, the schedule indicated here may be off by two or three days in either direction, which is one good reason for guarding the bitch well from the moment she first comes into heat until she well out of it.

Quite often, after a young bitch has finished with her first season, her vulva will remain swollen for several weeks and her breasts will be enlarged and hard with blue discoloration around them. This could develop into a "false pregnancy," where she may eventually show signs of lactation, build a nest, and adopt articles and toys as surrogate puppies. If left untreated, the symptoms will slowly disappear by themselves, but if you are concerned about them and her personality changes, ask your veterinarian if hormone treatment is warranted.

The only reason not to have a bitch spayed (removing her ovaries and uterus) is if your future plans include the show ring and a breeding program. If that is not the case, then it is wise to have her spayed before she has her first season. By having her spayed, you prevent unplanned pregnancies, infections, false pregnancy behavior, and lessen the chances for the development of breast cancer. The bitch will not accumulate fat or be sluggish and lazy because of the spaying. These conditions arise from a decrease in exercise. Being spayed also means that any obedience or agility training will not be interrupted, since bitches in season are not allowed to participate in these events.

Neutering (removing the testicles) may make a male less inclined to mark his territory, especially indoors, and may make him less interested in roaming and looking for a bitch in season or picking a fight with another male. It may also lessen the chances of another male picking on him, since he will no longer smell of male hormones. Finally, neutering will help prevent infection or cancer as a male grows older, and may eliminate sexually linked behavior problems, such as the obnoxious habit of riding a person's leg.

TEMPERAMENT AND BEHAVIOR

As your Vizsla grows into young adulthood, all his energies and intelligence need to be channeled into correct behavior patterns in order for you to keep control over a dog that is a wonderful con artist. No matter how good-natured your Vizsla is, you should remember that behavior never stays the same. Your dog is constantly learning and developing. Interactions with people will

Donna, owned by Marcia Folley, shows the lovely feminine head characteristic of the Classic Vizslas.

Brooke Folley and Ch. Classic Barry Bakanal.

Vizslas gravitate to children and sometimes a kiss and a lick can cure anything.

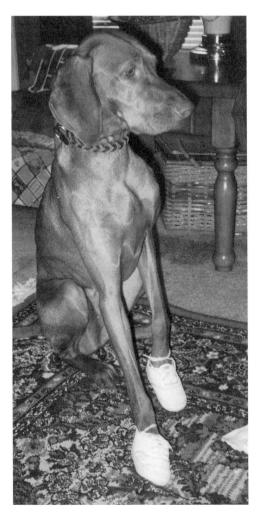

I've got my tennis shoes on—where's my racket and ball?

have a strong effect on any expression of affection. Vizslas love to show affection and usually respond to everyone they meet. Because of their happy, exuberant, loving nature, they are easy to love and spoil, and because of that it is possible to lose the essential control.

Dogs are pack animals by nature and every pack has a leader, known as the alpha, that dominates the other members of the pack. In your home, you and your family are the pack leaders, and it is your responsibility to establish yourself in the alpha position and make sure your dog understands. If you fail to do this, your dog will become the leader—it is his natural behavior. Dominance and alpha behavior are both important concepts that every dog owner should understand.

Every pack has its subordinates. The noisiest, boldest puppy will be dominant while the others will accept being lower down in the pack. Animals understand this rule, but for a human to become a pack leader, that person must have an attitude of superiority in order to get respect. There are several good books on the subject of dominance which may help you if you happen to have a dog that turns everything into a contest of wills.

Somewhere around the age of fourteen months, a male Vizsla will start testing your control; learning more about the alpha position will help you get through this stage. Your dog's hormones will have been working from the age of eleven months and his "testing" can be compared to that of a teenager who is starting to question authority. From your sweet, sensitive, soft male a stubborn and resistant streak can sometimes emerge. He may refuse to get out of your favorite chair and may even talk back when asked to obey. If he senses that you are uneasy and uptight about his behavior, he might become even more tense when you try to exercise control over him. You have to be the figure of authority to your Vizsla at every point. He has to learn that even with all the hugs and praises, you are still the boss and alpha figure. It is very important that you do not lose control at this time in his life or he will establish a pattern of behavior that will continue.

If you have been doing basic obedience training, a continued plan of advanced work has beneficial effects at this age. Obedience provides a subtle but enjoyable way to enforce your authority without any threatening position. Training is also a good way to dissipate a lot of your dog's surplus energy and give him an outlet for his exuberance. A contented and relaxed dog is less likely to chew, bark, or misbehave, and a confident dog learns to accept control from any family member once an effective pattern of behavior has been established.

Female Vizslas do not seem to go through any stubborn stages. Although dominance can be a problem with them also, mostly it is dominance over another bitch, which can turn nasty if you don't exercise control over it. A female will usually accept corrections or discipline as a matter of course, and then in a quiet, subtle way jump back up into your favorite chair as soon as you turn your back. They just sort of think that the rules are not for them.

Both dogs and bitches will be protective guardians, even though they are not an aggressive breed. The protective instinct develops strongly in their second year as they learn to discriminate. Although used for many years to guard the famous St. Stephen's Crown in their native Hungary, Vizslas are not usually thought of as guard dogs in the United States, but the underlying characteristic will become evident if it is ever needed. Certainly, Vizslas do not perform as well as most guard breeds because of their low aggression ranking, but they do give a good alarm and warning when a doorbell is sounded or when an owner is being threatened.

FEEDING PROGRAM

To the confirmed show ring exhibitor and the field trial follower, a dog's *condition* may mean two different things. To the show person, for a dog to be in condition signifies that state of appearance which enhances him to the judge's eye and enables him to go into the show ring and win. A show Vizsla must be adequately fed to maintain a shiny coat, clear eyes, and a happy, healthy attitude. He must be in good working shape, although not as lean as a field trial dog.

To the field enthusiast, his Vizsla must be lean and muscular, definitely not carrying any extra weight that may keep him from performing in the field for long hours. However, a Vizsla running in the field should not look gaunt, with hip bones sticking up. Since a field dog will utilize more food than a dog that stays quiet most of the day and only gets exercise on a weekend, he must be on a high-protein diet that can maintain the excitable and active hunting dog with adequate energy and weight in all kinds of weather.

Always feed a high quality food. Grocery store brands can put on fat, but may not provide all the nutrients required for optimum health. A dog correctly conditioned from the inside out will hold that condition against greater odds than the one whose outer appearance may simply be camouflage.

Food provides growth and energy, but the exact quantity your particular Vizsla requires for his maintenance, growth, and work will depend on his own individual rate of metabolism. It is a safe rule that, when determining how much food your dog should have, you judge more on the basis of his looks and actions rather than on trying to pinpoint a specific amount.

Growing puppies need a high-protein food since they are almost constantly active and burn up a lot of energy. If your young adult is still using up every bit of food he takes in, you may want to keep him on a good puppy meal containing a higher percentage of protein and fat than the adult meal. Some of these foods contain as high as a thirty-one percent protein. There is no set rule that says you have to take your dog off puppy food the day he turns one year old. Only you will be able to "eye-ball" him and make a decision.

Whichever food you do decide to feed for correct maintenance, stay with it. Do not keep skipping from one brand to another just because a friend tells you that her dog likes it. This will only result in a fussy eater. Dogs like and need consistency in their diet.

Every breed has its fussy eaters and the Vizsla is no exception. Apart from cooking special meals to constantly pique his interest in eating, force-feeding may be the only alternative if you have to put some weight on your dog. Mix the regular amount of meal and meat with a little bit of warm water. Add a full tablespoon of peanut butter and a tablespoon of honey and mix well. Holding your dog's mouth open with one hand, take a small ball of the mixed food and place it well to the back of his mouth with the other hand. Hold his mouth closed gently, allowing him to chew and swallow, but not spit it out. Feed him two meals a day, increasing the amounts as needed. This will take a little practice, but usually by feeding the same time each day, you establish a routine for the dog and he will eventually get hungry at that hour and decide to eat by himself.

For any dog, you can occasionally add vegetables and juice, cooked egg, cottage cheese, fish oils, broths, or soups to the meal for variety without creating a fussy eater. Dogs love asparagus, carrots, broccoli, green beans, and even melons and apples. The important thing to remember in feeding is to follow an established schedule and do not feed so many additives that you unbalance an otherwise balanced ration.

Exercise is critical in the development of muscle tone in a young show dog. Jnek's King Ralph shows good reach and extension. Photo © Greg Smith, Garden Studio, Inc.

Strenuous exercise should not be permitted for an hour before or after eating to ensure good digestion and eliminate the danger of bloat. Any evidence of vomiting or diarrhea is cause to withhold a meal until the problem is resolved.

COPROPHAGY AND PICA

The most unpleasant of all phases of raising a dog is when he takes to eating stools. This practice, referred to as *coprophagy*, is still an unsolved mystery in dog behavior. There is simply no clear explanation as to why some dogs do it.

At one time it was thought to be a problem affecting mostly bitches once they had a litter of puppies to clean up after. Another train of thought is that the dog is cleaning up after himself to avoid being punished as he was when he was a puppy and he made a mess on the floor. Others claim it is a sign of boredom, nutritional deficiencies, or the use of preservatives in dogs' food. It is argued that the preservatives give the food an appealing odor that survives the digestive process, but using meat tenderizers, garlic powder, or monosodium glutamate, all of which would give the stool a bad odor, does little to discourage a dog with this habit.

Unfortunately, the habit cannot be ignored if you are to enjoy your Vizsla to the fullest. If you are unable to correct the problem with a change in diet or the adding of enzymes, the only way to control it is with complete sanitation practices. Set up an established eating and exercising schedule for your dog, and follow him around the yard to remove all feces immediately.

Pica is a dog's craving for unnatural food such as ashes, dirt, grass, or paper. Whether he does this because he needs extra fiber in his diet, or because he has an upset stomach and is using the grass as an emetic to make himself vomit, it can become as much a habit as coprophagy. Unless the grass has been chemically treated, there is usually no problem if your Vizsla "grazes." However, a change in diet may be warranted, and a stool sample should be checked for parasites.

TRAVEL

As an important member of your family, your Vizsla naturally will be accompanying you on many adventures in many different places. With a little forethought and preparation, these trips can be just as enjoyable as the rest of the activities you share with your dog.

Car Travel

Most Vizslas love riding in a car, which makes traveling with them a pleasant experience. A young dog should be started out on quiet, short rides which can be gradually lengthened. Even if you had the problem

Have toys, will travel. Owned by Steven Shlyen.

A young Oakleaf's Everwhen Chances R in training in the field.

of a carsick puppy, he should be over it by the time he is old enough for longer trips to trials and shows. Carsickness is a byproduct of fear and nervous reactions. The usual remedy for a dog that vomits on rides is to leave him home, but that is precisely the wrong approach. If the only time he is ever in the car is for a painful trip to the veterinarian, he will never be cured. Instead, let your dog learn to associate car trips with fun times and his fears will soon be gone.

Rather than walking your dog to a park or field to run, drive him there. Take him for short trips to visit other doggy friends to help him understand there will be fun waiting for him at the end of a ride. Trips to obedience and agility class will be looked forward to with enthusiasm enough to overcome his nervousness and fear.

No matter how long or short the trip, your dog should be crated. If a crate has been a part of your puppy behavior modification program, he will already know the crate to be his sanctuary, and putting him in a crate in the car will help make him feel safe and secure. If your puppy continues to get carsick, try turning his crate so that he is facing towards the front of the car instead of sideways or backward.

Traveling in a crate while in the car or van means your dog will stay still. He will not jump from seat to seat, wrestle with children,

take up more than his share of room, or knock your elbow while you are driving. He will not get thrown through the windshield in case of a sudden stop, and he will not escape out of the car door when you open it.

Having a crate in a motel room means that your Vizsla will have his own place to nap while you are out sight-seeing or dining and that the maid will not accidentally let him out when she opens the door. The motels allowing dogs will welcome you as a responsible guest. Hopefully, you will have taught your dog not to bark while in the crate. Make sure to take along his favorite toys to keep him company, and a good chew toy to keep him busy.

If you are unable to place a crate inside your car, there are steel dividers that fit between the front and back to confine him to his own area and prevent him from jumping into the front seat with the driver. There are also dog seat-belt harnesses, available in pet supply stores, which will hold your dog in place and prevent him from moving around inside the car.

Get in the habit of putting a collar on your Vizsla every time he gets into the car, even if you are only going around the block. His buckled collar should be of flat nylon or leather with a brass identification plate displaying your name, address, and telephone number.

When traveling by car with your Vizsla, keep his leash handy for emergency stops. Keep it fastened to his crate and you will not waste time looking for it. Never allow your dog out of the car in a strange place without a leash. No matter how well trained he is, he may panic and bolt. Most rest stops on an interstate highway have areas set aside for dogs. Be a responsible dog owner and keep a small plastic bag or a pooper scooper handy to clean up after your dog. Do not allow your dog to sniff at other dog's feces.

Before any long trip, make sure your Vizsla's immunizations are current, as the risk of exposure to a virus is higher in rest stops and other public areas. Get boosters if needed, especially for parvovirus and coronavirus, both of which cause extreme diarrhea.

Take enough food and water for the entire trip so you will not have to make any dietary changes. If you will be gone for an extended time, fill a large container with water before you leave home and add to it each day of the trip so that the new water is diluted with the old; you can also purchase bottled water at most gas stops. Try to keep as close to your dog's normal feeding schedule as possible in order to avoid digestive upsets.

Pack a separate bag with medications and health supplies for your Vizsla. The most important thing will be an antidiarrheal drug—be ready to give your dog a dose at the first sign of trouble. Include a thermometer, ear and eye ointments, antihistamines, foot powder, Betadine, shampoo, triple antibiotic cream, antibiotics, and any medication your dog may be taking, especially for thyroid. And don't forget his heartworm preventative treatment.

Daily exercise will be a necessity if you want to travel with a happy dog. Exercise helps avoid stress, constipation, and boredom. It will be good for bored children too. With supervision, children can take their dog on walks in campgrounds, rest stops, and parks. A dog is a wonderful introduction and both your children and Vizsla can meet new friends that way. Your dog will be willing to nap in his crate if he has frequent walks.

While traveling during the day in hot weather, you may find yourself restricted to the use of a fast-food drive-through since you will be unable to leave your Vizsla in the car. Remember that the temperature inside a closed car in hot weather builds up at frightening speed and a dog can die within minutes from the effects of heatstroke. Heatstroke can cause a dog's temperature to reach as high as 106 degrees. Breathing becomes rapid, mucous membranes turn bright red, and the victim suffers severe muscle spasms. The dog steadily weakens, coma sets in, and death rapidly follows. It is a critical situation—never take the chance of it happening.

Starting your new puppy out with the correct training will make it easier later on.

Checklist for Traveling

- Crate
- Water from home
- Food and bowl
- Toys
- Collar with I.D. tag
- Leash
- Medications
- Health certificate if required or record of immunizations
- Dog's bedding

Plane Travel

Plane travel with your Vizsla is easy and fast, and can present less stress than a long trip by auto. Instead of a wire crate, you will be required to use a fiberglass shipping crate specially designed for safety in air travel. It must be large enough for your dog to stand and lie down comfortably. The correct size for the adult Vizsla is the #400. Place your dog's blanket in the bottom along with a toy; put proper identification on the top of the crate along with the flight designation. Paint arrows

on the crate indicating the crate's correct position, or use the words "This end up." This will also help you spot your own crate when it is being loaded.

Find out which airlines take the best care with animals. If you are traveling during hot weather, choose a flight that will leave and arrive during the coolest parts of the day. A nonstop flight is always best and will save you the worry about any transfer of your dog.

Tranquilizers are not recommended for air travel as they can cause adverse reactions. Do not feed your dog for several hours before a flight, although some airlines require that he have a container of water and food inside the crate. Make sure the crate is fastened correctly and securely. Before board-

ing the plane tell the gate steward that you are traveling with a dog and ask him to check if he has been loaded. Get positive confirmation each time you have to change planes on the flight.

By using sensible precautions, air travel with your Vizsla is safe and you will be able to enjoy the fun and competition of distant dog shows and field trials, or just relax on vacations with friends without leaving your companion at home or in a boarding kennel.

There will, of course, be times when it is better for your dog to remain at home. He should not travel if he is old, feeble, or recovering from any debilitating illness or surgery. It is also advisable to leave a pregnant bitch at home.

CHAPTER EIGHT

The Vizsla in Obedience

Of the many "career choices" for your Vizsla, none are more readily available to the average owner than obedience and agility. Even before you consider a field or show career for your dog, some basic obedience training will be helpful. Obedience training is the best way to get your Vizsla's attention and love. It will make him easier to live with and it will be a pleasurable hobby for you, leading to numerous opportunities to continue your dog's education. It can be enjoyed merely for the purpose of developing a more mannerly pet, or for performance at different levels of competition.

Vizslas love obedience work. They are extremely intelligent, fast, graceful, willing performers that love to please. Very sensitive, they do not do well under a heavy hand. Do not use any harsh, extreme corrections; the tone of your voice is enough. Lay a good foundation with the basics and let the fun start in advanced work with jumping and retrieving. The bonding that obedience people go through with their dogs is far more intense than that of most conformation owners and dogs.

Your Vizsla will always attract attention because of his beauty and enthusiasm while working. If you have over-trained or over-corrected to the point that you have an obviously unhappy dog working with his tail between his legs, you would be doing the breed a disservice to show him at an obedience trial where he would not make a respectable impression on exhibitors or spectators.

There are a lot of obedience books on the market, a lot of theories, and a lot of methods. You should decide whether a companion dog that you can train to be a pleasure to live with will be your main focus, or whether you are interested in competing for obedience titles. Most of the obedience classes will not accept a dog until he is at least six months old, at which time he should be able to pay attention and enjoy the training.

Pre-novice, novice, intermediate and advanced obedience classes are held in almost every community. They are sponsored by all-breed kennel clubs, humane societies, and training clubs specializing in obedience. Sometimes individual trainers also hold private classes. If you are interested in competing in obedience trials and gaining titles, check carefully for trainers in your area who not only are experienced and active exhibitors, but also who have competed in every class with several dogs, and who know all the rules and corrections that will help you compete.

You will need only two pieces of training equipment with which to start obedience training: a leash and a training collar. Cotton webbed or leather leashes will be the easiest on your hands. A training collar is called a *choke* and is a necessity in making corrections. Use a medium-weight nylon or chain

Ch. Jawnzeme N Dorratz In Sync, owned by Doris Ratzlaff, retrieving a dumbbell over the solid jump in Open exercise.

Ch. Dorratz Double Trouble, UD, MH, NA, owned by Doris Ratzlaff, shown winning first place in Utility A class. Photo © Chuck & Sandy Tatham, The Standard Image.

Anne Standen with her High in Trial Vizsla, Ch. OTCH Titan's Vintage Promise, UDX.

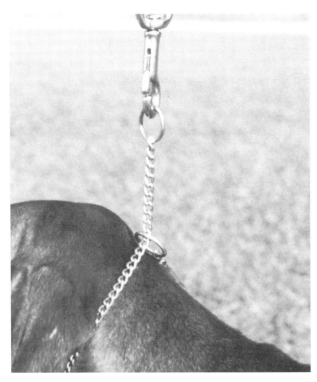

To make up the collar, lift one ring above the other and drop a loop of the chain down through the bottom ring.

The collar is put on over the dog's head so that it pulls in an upward direction. The lead gets fastened to the upper ring. There should be no more than three inches between the tightened collar and the ring for the leash.

Advice from a top obedience trainer, Anne Standen: "When all else fails, get your Vizsla to read the AKC obedience regulations."

Ch. Dorratz Double Trouble, UD, MH, NA, in the Heel Free exercise.

choke. The right size is important. Place a tape measure around your dog's neck and up over the occiput, pulling it snug. Add three inches to that measurement and you will have the correct size for your Vizsla. To make up the collar, simply hold one of the rings in each hand. Lifting one hand above the other, drop a loop of the collar slowly down through the ring in the lower hand until the two rings meet. Put the collar over the dog's head so that it pulls in an upward direction from right to left. Then fasten the leash to the ring which passes over the dog's neck. Never allow your dog to wear this type of collar when he is not actively being trained. It can catch onto things and strangle him.

AKC OBEDIENCE TRIALS

The American Kennel Club began its obedience program more than seventy years ago, promoting obedience as a sport and also as a way to improve the relationship of an owner and his dog. AKC regulations state, "The basic objective of obedience trials is to produce dogs that have been trained and conditioned always to behave in the home, public places and in the presence of other dogs."

Obedience trials test a dog's ability to perform a prescribed set of exercises on which he is scored. In each exercise your dog has to score more than fifty percent of the points possible for that exercise, and he must receive a total of at least 170 points out of a perfect score of 200. Each time a dog "qualifies" under that point system, he gets a "leg" towards the title he is working for. Three legs under three different judges are required for each title. There are three levels of obedience that your dog can compete in to earn a title. Each level is more difficult than the one before it.

Novice, Open and Utility classes are each split into A and B divisions. The Novice class yields the Companion Dog (CD) title. Novice A is for dogs that have not yet earned their title. It excludes handlers who have had a previous CD title, who must go into the Novice B class. After a dog has earned his CD, he can still compete in Novice B until he gets his first leg in the next class, the Open class, which leads to the Companion Dog Excellent

Veterans obedience class at the VCA Nationals. A three-minute down. Photo © Christina M. Freitag.

Edenvale PM Triple Play, at nine months, easily clears a solid jump. Owned by Anne Standen.

(CDX) title. In Open, the owner may enter either A or B, especially handy if he prefers one judge to another. The same methods and standards are used for judging and scoring the A and B classes. The final class, Utility, yields the Utility Dog (UD) title. Here also, the dog may be entered in either A or B. After the dog gets his CDX and his UD, he can still compete in Open B. A brief description of each class is given below, but in order to understand the exercises and requirements for competition, you should order a current copy of *Obedience Regulations* from the AKC.

Each judge must carry a mental picture of a perfect performance for each exercise and give a score based on how close the handler and dog come to it. Even though this perfect picture conforms to the *Obedience Regulations*, a dog is also judged on his willingness, precision, and enjoyment in performing. Standardized judging is a requirement; the judge is not allowed to inject any variation from exhibitor to exhibitor. The heeling patterns are the same for everyone, as is the positioning for each exercise. A qualifying score can never be given to any dog whose performance has not met the minimum point requirement as described above.

Unlike the breed ring, spayed bitches and neutered males are allowed in the obedience ring. Bitches in season are not permitted to compete, and a bitch that is so attractive to the males as to be a disturbing element may be excused. No dog is allowed to compete if he is bandaged or taped, even for medical reasons, and any dog that is lame can be excused from the ring. The judge is allowed to disqualify and excuse any dog that attempts to attack another dog or person, that appears to be dangerous to other dogs in the ring, or that is not under his handler's control.

Any loud command from the handler to his dog creates a poor impression in the obedience ring and should be avoided. Shouting is not necessary if your dog is properly trained to respond to a normal tone of voice. If a dog displays fear or nervousness or shies or runs away from his handler in the ring, it may indicate that too harsh a method was used in training. If your dog urinates in the ring because of fear and nervousness, he will be disqualified and excused.

Obedience trials can be held separately or in conjunction with either all breed or specialty (single breed) dog shows. Practice events, called *matches*, provide opportunities to prepare for "the real thing." Your local kennel club or training class can help you learn about dates, location, and entry procedures.

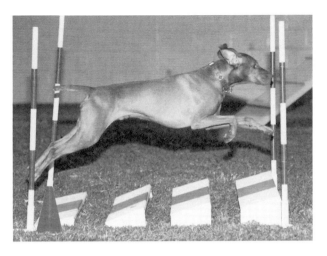

Dual Ch. Oakleaf's Everwhen Chances R, CDX, MH, NA, shows style on the jumps. Owned by Judy Richey. Photo © Critter Pictures.

Cariad's Vasaszfai Vadrosza, CDX, owned by Marion Coffman finishing a Retrieve on the flat.

Novice

The Novice class is basic obedience and provides the skills your Vizsla and you need to live together successfully. Your dog will have to heel both on and off leash at different speeds and turns, come when called (a "recall"), stand for a physical exam by the judge, and participate in a group sit, down, and stay.

In Novice it is permissible to guide your dog by his collar between exercises in order to place him in position for the next exercise. The easiest way to do this is simply put a finger through the ring on his collar to gently place him. No other physical control, like pushing with your knee or leg, is permitted. No food or bait is ever allowed in any class, so make sure your pockets are empty before walking into the ring.

In the Novice class, the first exercise is heeling on leash. Deductions in the scoring will be made for a handler who is constantly tugging on the leash to control his dog or adjusting his own pace to the dog's. The Vizsla is a fast-paced dog and looks better moving briskly. Not only will his attention hold better, but he will enjoy the faster movement. Vizslas can get very bored with the Novice class, so the sooner you can get through it, receive the CD title, and proceed to Open work, the better for both of you. Do all the exercises, especially the off-leash heeling,

Triple Ch. Cariad's Kutya Kai Costa, owned by Marianne Megna, going over the solid jump in Open B.

Ch. OTCH Titan's Vintage Promise, UDX (Tess), working with multiple scent articles for owner Anne Standen. Tess has had several High in Trials and three perfect scores of 200.

Ch. Surfstones Island Seachanter, bringing back the correct article to Doris Ratzlaff.

Ch. Dorratz Double Trouble, Toby, going over the bar jump in Utility.

very briskly. Encourage your dog to do a happy, fast recall to make a good impression.

Open

Your Vizsla's fun really begins with this class of jumping and retrieving. This second level puts your dog completely off-leash with exercises in heeling, dropping on a recall, retrieving a dumbbell both on the flat and over a solid high jump, and another jumping exercise over a broad jump. The group exercise of a sit and a down is done with the handler out of sight. Your dog receives his CDX title upon successfully completing his three legs in this class.

Points are going to be deducted in this class for a dog that does not move briskly in all exercises. He will be penalized for any slowness in picking up the dumbbell or in bringing it back, or for refusing to release it on command. He will be severely penalized for slow heeling, so it is important to start with good groundwork on the heeling training in Novice in order to carry it out in advanced classes. Vizslas always look good executing jumps, and combining this with their retrieving instincts and some natural flair for showing off to gain attention makes Open a fun class.

Utility

This third level of competition will be a further test of how smoothly you and your Vizsla work together. These are more difficult exercises and include silent hand signals, scent discrimination, directed retrieves, and directed jumping. This class demands close cooperation between handler and dog. After he qualifies in three shows, your Vizsla will be awarded his UD title.

Ch. Surfstones Island Seachanter retrieving the glove in the Directed Retrieve.

Tess clears a solid jump in Utility for owner Anne Standen.

Edenvale PM Triple Play (Logan), eight months old, clears a bar jump. Owned by Anne Standen.

Eight-year-old Tess clears a bar jump. Owned by Anne Standen.

The heeling exercise will be done the same as in Open, except that you may only use hand signals and must not speak to your dog during the exercise. The dog is left in a standing position and, after the handler has walked to the other side of the ring, must obey all hand signals to down, sit, and come on command. A dog that does not respond immediately and correctly to each signal will not qualify.

The principal part of the scent discrimination exercises is your dog's selection of articles you have handled—in this instance a leather and a metal dumbbell from among

Four OTCH Vizslas: Left: Ch. OTCH Titan's Vintage Promise, and Ch. OTCH Titan's PM Silhouette, both owned by Anne Standen. Right: Ch. OTCH Boelte's Kierra Classic, owned by John Morris; Ch. OTCH If'N I'Da Wendi of Witt's, owned by DeLois Witt. Photo © Alissa Behm.

the set of eight other articles—based on scent alone. He must promptly deliver the correct one to you. Minor or substantial deductions are made for a dog that is working slowly or that does not work continuously at finding the right article.

In the Directed Retrieve, three gloves are placed across the end of the ring with your dog being sent to retrieve one of them. Your dog must follow your hand signal to go to the glove specified, and retrieve it to your hand. In the Directed Jumping Exercise, the principle features are: The dog must leave you, go to the other end of the ring, turn and sit when commanded, and then obey a hand signal for both a solid jump and a bar jump in turn. Your dog will receive a non-qualifying score if he does not go out beyond the jumps, anticipates your commands, or returns over the wrong jump.

Because most dogs are taught and quickly learn the routine of exercises in the order of judging, the AKC changed the rules for Open B and Utility B class competition. The exercises in both those classes are scrambled and put in different order so that the dog can no longer anticipate the order as in the A class. The order of judging is posted before the start of the class for that day. When practicing or training your dog, it helps to keep him on his toes by never doing the exercises in the same order each time. That way he will not expect or be prepared for the next command.

Obedience titles can be compared to graduating from high school and college and then completing graduate work. The fun of training and competition become a way of life with many Vizsla exhibitors, who look forward to not only multiple titles on

Ch. Huntwyck's Woodland Cooper, VCD2, UD, TD, SH, MX, MXJ, NJP, VC, owned by Melissa Thomas, scored a perfect 200 in Novice B obedience.

Obedience brace owned by Doris Ratzlaff earned first place at the VCA Nationals. Left: Ch. Surfstones Island Seachanter, CDX, NAJ. Right: Ch. Dorratz Double Trouble, UD, MH, NA, VC, ROM.

the present dog, but future titles on the next dog.

Utility Dog Excellent

Many obedience-oriented owners want to continue their Vizsla's competition at trials after earning the Utility title. A dog that has earned his UD can go on to further competition and earn a UDX (Utility Dog Excellent) title. To earn the title, the dog must have qualifying scores in both Open B and Utility B classes on the same day. Qualifying at ten shows is needed to give him this advanced title.

Obedience Trial Champion

The best of the high scorers can compete for even more titles. An OTCH (Obedience Trial Champion) title is comparable to a doctoral degree for a college graduate.

Dogs with Utility titles can compete in Open B or Utility B to earn the required 100 points needed for their OTCH. Points are awarded according to how many dogs are competing in the class with you. You must have among your wins a first place in a Utility B class with at least three dogs in competition, a first place in an Open B class with at least six dogs in competition, and another first place in either class, with all three wins under different judges. To date, at least twelve Vizslas have earned the impressive OTCH title.

Tracking

Tracking tests allow a dog to demonstrate his natural ability to follow a human scent other than his owner's. Your Vizsla will need to qualify only one time in a tracking trial to earn his TD (Tracking Dog).

"Toby" in the Directed Retrieve exercise in Utility.

The dog must follow a track 440 to 500 yards long with three to five direction changes. The track is laid by a person unknown to him and must be allowed to "age" for thirty minutes to two hours before the dog starts. The goal is to use this track to locate an article dropped at the end of the trail by the tracklayer. You follow your dog on a lead twenty to forty feet long, facing an unknown track, totally at the mercy of your dog's nose. While training, you will have learned how to read wind currents that determine how your dog scents and his body language when he is on the track. And in the end, you will have learned to trust him.

The next level up from a TD is the TDX (Tracking Dog Excellent), in which the track is aged a minimum of three to five hours, is 800 to 1000 yards long, and has from five to seven direction changes. At present, five Vizslas have earned a TDX.

Advanced tracking titles are the VST (Variable Surface Tracking), which has a dog following a three- to five-hour-old track that may take him down streets, through a building, and across other bare areas; and the CT (Champion Tracker), awarded to a dog that has completed all three tracking titles (TD, TDX, VST). Owners who do tracking with their Vizslas enjoy the opportunity to see their dogs at work using their scenting skills.

Versatile Companion Dog

The Versatile Companion Dog 1 is an AKC title that honors the dog and handler who have continued successfully in multiple activities and earned the following titles: CD, TD in obedience and NA, NAJ in agility (see Chapter 11 for a discussion of agility titles).

The Versatile Companion Dog 2 title is awarded to dogs earning a CDX, TD in obedience and OA, OAJ in agility.

The Versatile Companion Dog 3 title is awarded to dogs earning a UD, TDX in obedience and AX, AXJ in agility.

The Versatile Companion Dog 4 title is awarded to dogs earning a UDX, VST in obedience, and MX, MXJ in agility.

The highest and most prestigious title that a dog and handler can earn is the Versatile Companion Champion (VCCH). This title is awarded after completion of an OTCH (Obedience Trial Champion), a MACH (Master Agility Champion), and a CT (Champion Tracker). A VCCH title is placed before the dog's name.

Any obedience title is intended to evoke admiration. To be worthy of this admiration, the title must be based on performances that fully meet the requirements of the regulations. Any handler who receives a deserved score of 190 points has reason to be proud of his dog. A score of 170 points should indicate a very creditable performance and fully justify the awarding of a title. While a score of 200 points is possible, it is extremely rare for a judge to have the privilege of scoring a dog and handler who perform perfectly all the exercises in a class.

CHAPTER NINE

The Vizsla in the Show Ring

The American Kennel Club was established in 1884 to promote the breeding, exhibiting, and advancement of purebred dogs. It approves and sanctions over 15,000 licensed events each year. Showing dogs is a great competitive sport, combining the fun and joy of completing a championship title on your Vizsla with being able to evaluate future breeding stock. Any dog that is individually registered with the AKC, is six months of age or older, and meets the eligibility requirements in the breed standard can participate in a conformation show.

The standard describes the characteristics that allow your Vizsla to perform the functions for which the breed was developed, and includes specifications for structure, temperament, size, and movement. A judge examines each dog and then may give him an award, based on how closely that dog compares to the judge's mental image of the perfect Vizsla described in the standard.

As you marvel over the beauty and smooth movement of your young Vizsla, the lure of the show ring may become more and more appealing. If you have already worked with a puppy for show ring in mind, you know how much training is in store. Basic training will start soon after you bring your puppy home, but only ring experience will provide the finer points of style and movement for both of you. You have to be enthusiastic, dedicated, and patient. If you have never gone to a show before, take the time to attend one and watch the procedures before you enter. A positive mental approach and a belief in your dog and yourself will go far in accepting losing as well as winning in the show ring.

Be truthful in evaluating your puppy, and do not waste time, money, and emotion on a mediocre dog. Make sure your Vizsla puppy is actually a good representative of the breed if you are going the dog show route.

Ch. Jnek's King Ralph, JH, owned by Kathy and Jeff Engelsman. Photo © Ashbey Photography.

Author Marion Coffman judging Sweepstakes at the 2001 Nationals. Photo © Christina M. Freitag.

Note how the lead sits just behind the head on this nicely stacked Vizsla. Ch. Classic Barry Bakanal, owned by Marcia Folley. Photo © A. E. Keil-Hopewell Ent.

Lightweight leads are used for the conformation ring. If a thin choke chain is used, it goes on the same as in obedience but is kept high on the neck, behind the ears. A thin lead is then attached.

EARLY TRAINING

If you plan to show your young Vizsla, it is very important that you start conditioning and training your puppy as soon as he has settled into his new home. Conditioning starts from the inside and is evident in a good coat, clear eyes, and a healthy appearance. Conditioning also requires proper exercise, since a show dog has to be in excellent physical shape. Your Vizsla puppy should be given the chance for active play in an area where he can really stretch out and run. He has to learn to extend, and running after another dog will help.

After your new puppy has had a chance to get used to the feel of his collar and the pull of the leash, gradually begin training with a show lead. You can choose from several different types, from a thin chain with a lightweight lead attached, to a one-piece thin leather or nylon lead. Whichever you prefer, it should be used for show training and the show ring only.

The lead goes on around your Vizsla's neck, snugly up behind the ears, and is kept in that position so that it does not slide down his neck. If you are using a thin choke chain, it goes on so that it tightens and releases across the back of his neck the same way an obedience training chain works (but do not use this thin a chain for any obedience work).

Remember to keep all training for the show ring light and happy. Once you have taken the enthusiasm out of a young Vizsla, nothing on earth can put it back. The show dog must enjoy what he is doing.

The lead will be held in your left hand only, with the end gathered in your palm. The correct place for your puppy to move while being trained is in line with your left leg and about one foot out from your body. Do not let him get in the habit of moving too close and crowding you. Practice at a walk until you have coordinated your movements, and then slowly increase your speed, being careful that your dog does not make any sudden moves in front of you, tripping you. Your lead should be an extension of your arm, with your dog thus becoming an extension of yourself.

The Vizsla moves beautifully with a long-reaching gait. As your puppy gets older, lengthen your stride and you will see him reaching and extending himself. Practice making figure eights, since your puppy will eventually have to learn inside as well as outside turns. When both of you have learned control, increase your pace to a smooth, slow run. Never use mincing steps with a Vizsla as this detracts tremendously from his movement. Along with mastering control, ring movement, and turns, your puppy should also be learning to stand and present himself.

When you come to the spot where you want your puppy to stop and stand, give the command "Stand" as you tighten up slightly on the lead. Simultaneously, extend your right hand in front of his face. If he attempts to sit every time you stop, slip your left toe under his belly and lift gently. He must learn not to sit while he is wearing a show lead.

When he has mastered stopping and standing, move in front of him and face him. Keep your body straight and do not lean over him. Do not worry at this point if he is not setting his body up correctly, since you are only teaching him control. As you proceed to improve with movement and control, gradually loosen the lead so that your puppy moves out freely. Make sure he is staying correctly on your left side. Be consistent. After he has learned each step and it feels comfortable and correct for both of you, practice the same way over and over, until it becomes second nature. But also remember that if you are working with a Vizsla puppy between the ages of twelve weeks and six or seven months, he will not have a long attention span, especially during the teething process. Keep training sessions short.

Stacking in the show ring is Am. Int'l Ch. CMF Leitz, Camera, Action. Breeder/owner/photographer C. Freitag. Handler, Pam Williams.

Stacking, or setting up your dog, simply means putting him into as natural and favorable a stance as is possible for the judge to view and examine him. The easiest way to teach a young puppy to stack is on a grooming table. This will take patience and a firm but gentle hand until your puppy understands what you want. Eventually you can graduate to the ground. Puppies learn quickly; only a few minutes each day on the grooming table and on the ground is necessary.

Your young puppy learns during stacking that his legs, feet, and head belong in a certain position. He will accept this if you move him with patience and praise. While stacking, always keep control of your puppy's head, either with a hand under his chin, a hold on his muzzle, or a hand under his collar. Practice doing the complete setup to the count of five, fast, smooth, and with a minimum of motion. Any fussing and you will lose his attention.

Practicing the stack in front of a mirror will show you where you are going wrong with the positioning. Start with your Vizsla's

When setting up the front correctly, the front legs will be the same distance apart on the ground as they are coming out of the shoulder.

With your right hand holding the muzzle, lift the left leg at the elbow and place it into position.

Holding the muzzle in the left hand, use your right hand to set the right front leg into position.

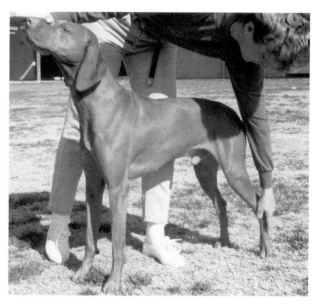

Holding the head facing straight ahead, run your left hand over the rear in preparation for placing the left rear leg.

Still holding the head straight, lift the left rear leg at the hock to place it in the correct position.

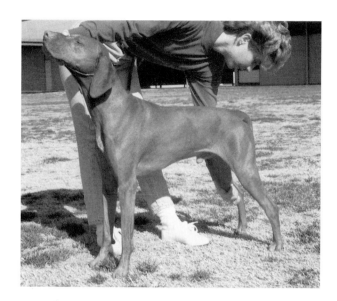

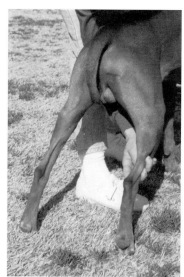

(far left) Set the right rear leg last. The rear feet should be the same distance apart as the hip bones.

(left) The rear can be set up by reaching over the dog's back or from underneath.

front. His forelegs should be exactly the same distance apart on the ground as they are coming out of his body. Holding his muzzle with your right hand to keep his head facing straight ahead, reach over his back with your left hand and, grasping the left leg at the elbow, lift it and position the leg with the foot pointing straight ahead. Change hands and do the same thing with the right front leg. If done correctly, both front feet will be under their respective shoulders. Do not try to change the position of the feet by handling them directly—always move them by lifting the leg at the elbows.

Now set the rear. Taking the muzzle in your right hand to keep the head straight, run your left hand down your dog's back so that he can feel you going to his rear. Your dog's rear legs should always appear perpendicular from the hock joints to the ground, and turn neither in nor out at the hocks. The rear feet should be the same distance apart as the hip bones.

Keeping an eye on the mirror, reach over your Vizsla's back and firmly taking hold of his left leg at the top of the hock joint, move the leg where you want it. Then do the same with the right leg, still keeping your right hand on his muzzle.

Do not let your dog lean on you. After you have stacked him, either kneel beside

Correct presentation of your Vizsla. The head and body are straight and the tail held perpendicular.

him or stand away from his body, with your right hand under his muzzle and your left hand holding the tail out.

Right from the beginning your Vizsla must get used to having his teeth examined since the judge will check his mouth in the ring to make sure he has the correct scissors bite. Handle your pup's mouth gently if he is still in his teething period; it may be sensitive. The correct way to show the judge your dog's bite is to place your right hand under the jaw and your left hand over the bridge of your dog's nose. With the left

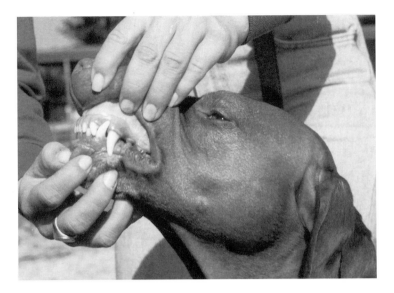

The correct way to show the bite to the judge. The mouth is closed and the teeth are together in a proper bite position.

index finger, lift the upper lip. Do not let the mouth sag open; the teeth must be shown in the correct bite position. Praise in a quiet voice as you work. If you have a male, also get him used to having his testicles handled in the same gentle way, praising him quietly. Touch the testicles lightly each time you groom or train him. A judge always checks a male to ascertain whether both testicles are down in the scrotum.

The more you practice, the more understanding your puppy will have of what you are trying to make him do. Remember to keep each session short so your Vizsla stays alert and enjoys what he is learning.

MATCH SHOWS

Before you consider entering an AKC point show with your young Vizsla, get some ring experience by going to match shows. A sanctioned match is an informal show at which purebred dogs compete, but not for championship points. These are excellent practice shows for both you and your puppy. You will learn many of the licensed point show procedures. Matches will give both of you exposure to slippery floors, congestion, noise, crowds, and strange dogs and people. They can be entered the day of the show and cost a lot less to enter than point shows. Match shows can help you solidify your work if you are unsure of your readiness for the point shows.

AKC CONFORMATION SHOWS

In order to enter an AKC licensed show, you must fill out an official entry form for that show. Entry forms must be in the hands of the show superintendent at least three weeks before the date of the show. Entries are also accepted online at the superintendent's web site. Ask friends who exhibit how to go about getting a premium list (a brochure giving details about the event) for upcoming shows. Most of the information you will need for the entry form is on your Vizsla's AKC registration certificate.

The Classes

The regular classes offered at an AKC show are Puppy, Twelve-to-Eighteen Month, Novice, Bred-by-Exhibitor, American Bred, and Open. All of these classes are divided by sex.

The Puppy class is for dogs that are six months of age and under one year. Your puppy is eligible for entering this class on the day he becomes six months old and can show in this class until the day before his first birthday.

The Twelve-to-Eighteen Month class is for dogs that are at least twelve months of age but under eighteen months, and that are not champions.

The Novice class is for dogs six months of age and over that have not, prior to the date of closing of entries, won three first places in the Novice class; a first in the Bred-by-Exhibitor, American Bred, or Open classes; or any championship points.

The Bred-by-Exhibitor Class is for dogs six months of age or older that are not champions of record and that are owned or co-owned by any of the breeders of record. The person handling the dog in this class must be the breeder of record and an owner of record of this dog.

The American Bred class is for dogs six months of age and over that were whelped in the United States from a breeding that took place in the United States.

The Open class is for any dog six months of age or over.

Non-regular classes offered at specialty shows include Veterans, Brace, Stud Dog and Brood Bitch classes.

Championship Points

To gain a championship title, your Vizsla must accrue a total of fifteen points in competition at licensed AKC shows. Included in those fifteen points must be two wins that are major points of three, four, or five, under two different judges. Points are determined by a scale for your area, and the number of points awarded depends on how many Vizslas you defeated that day. The highest number of points you can win in one show is five.

Brooke Folley winning the Veterans bitch class at the 1996 VCA Nationals with ten-year-old Ch. Cariad's Classic Mariah. Photo © Bernard W. and J. Kay Kernan.

THE SHOW RING

The judging program for each show you enter usually arrives in the mail about a week before the show date. It includes the time each breed will be judged, and the judges do adhere fairly close to that schedule. They will not wait for anyone, so you must always make plans to be at the showgrounds at least an hour before you are due to be in the ring. This will give you time to find your ring, get your dog settled down and accustomed to the noise and other breeds, and watch the pattern of judging which your judge prefers.

Get your armband from the ring steward and put it on your upper left arm so that the number is easily visible to the judge. Stay at ringside and be ready to go in when your number or class is called.

Brooke Folley in first place with her brace at the VCA Nationals in 1993. Photo © William L. Schobel.

Classes at an AKC Show

```
DOGS
  PUPPY  6-9 MOS.
         9-12 MOS.
  12 to 18 MONTH
  NOVICE
  BRED BY EXHIBITOR         WINNERS DOG
  AMERICAN-BRED             ONLY MALE TO RECEIVE
                            CHAMPIONSHIP POINTS
  OPEN
                            RESERVE WINNERS
                            DOG

BITCHES
  PUPPY  6-9 MOS.
         9-12 MOS.
  12 to 18 MONTH
  NOVICE
  BRED BY EXHIBITOR         WINNERS BITCH
  AMERICAN-BRED             ONLY BITCH TO RECEIVE
                            CHAMPIONSHIP POINTS
  OPEN
                            RESERVE WINNERS
                            BITCH

BEST OF BREED
COMPETITION

BEST OF WINNERS
BEST OF OPPOSITE SEX

SPORTING GROUP
HOUND GROUP
WORKING GROUP
TERRIER GROUP          BEST IN SHOW
TOY GROUP
NON-SPORTING GROUP
HERDING GROUP
```

Order of Judging

All male classes are judged first, one class at a time, starting with Puppy class. There are four awards, or placings, in each class.

After all the male classes are judged, the first-place winner in each class comes back into the ring to be judged again. From this group the judge awards one dog the title of Winners Dog, and it is to this dog that the points are given.

The Winners Dog leaves the ring and the second-place dog from the same class from which the winner was selected comes in to compete with the remaining first-place winners for the title of Reserve Winners Dog. No points are given for this win except that if for some disqualifying reason the Winners Dog is found to be ineligible for his win, he loses it and the Reserve Winners Dog gets those points.

When all the male classes have been judged, the bitches are judged in the same manner, with one of them being awarded Winners Bitch and the points.

The last class to be judged is the Best of Breed competition. This class consists of all the entered champions, the Winners Dog, and the Winners Bitch.

At some specialty shows, "non-regular" classes will be offered for Veteran Dogs and Veteran Bitches (over eight years of age), Stud Dogs and Brood Bitches, and Field Dogs and Field Bitches. The winners of these classes can also participate for Best of Breed.

The Best of Winners is chosen from the Winners Dog and the Winners Bitch. The winner may be able to gain additional points if the other sex had more entries and higher points. For example, if four points were awarded to the Winners Bitch and only two points were earned by the Winners Dog, but the male was chosen as the Best of Winners, he would gain the highest number of points available that day, which were four. The bitch would also retain her four points.

The judge will pick his Best of Breed winner and Best of Opposite Sex. The Best of Breed winner will go on to compete in the Sporting Group with other sporting dog breed winners. The winner of the Sporting Group then competes with the winners from the other groups for the coveted Best in Show award.

Gaiting and Ring Patterns

There are several patterns of movement that a judge can request, but only three of these are commonly used. They are the circle, triangle, and the straight line, or "down and back" as it is commonly called.

When you first enter the ring, whether it is alone or with others, the first movement is usually the command to "Take him around." Always circle counterclockwise with your Vizsla on your left. Start off easily and flow into a smooth faster run. Only you are going to know what speed is comfortable for both you and your dog. If you have practiced well, you will be able to feel when the timing is right. The judge does not want to see how fast your dog can move but, rather, if he can move correctly.

After the initial go-around your judge will examine and move each of the dogs individually. Keep your dog stacked and do not fuss with him as the judge starts to check the head, eyes, teeth, shoulders, testicles, and hocks. The best way to call attention to a fault is to fuss with it. Readjusting a slightly tuned hock while the judge is going over your dog is the first thing he will notice.

As the judge examines your Vizsla, get your hands out of the way. Steady your dog, but do not hamper the judge. As he moves to check the rear of your dog, hold your dog's head firmly and adjust any front leg or foot that may be out of line if you can do so without disturbing the judge.

Gaiting Patterns

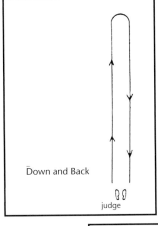

Down and Back

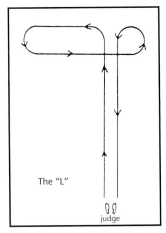

The "L"

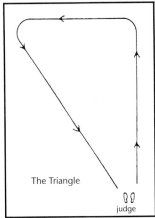

The Triangle

Do not let your Vizsla take command in the ring. One of the tricks he may try is holding a foot in the air and refusing to put it in place. Do not let him get away with this. Gently push him in the rib section to force his line of balance over to the side being held up. This will necessitate his replacing the foot or falling flat on his face. Do this anytime your dog's weight is not on a foot.

If your Vizsla protests about being stacked and tries to shy away by creating a bend with his body, immediately use your finger to poke him in the ribs on the side being bowed, forcing him to readjust to the proper position. If you find your dog leaning back, a hand just below an elbow can prod him back into an "up on the toes" look, or you can place a very sharp fingernail just below his last rib and push forward.

Checklist of Supplies to Take to a Show

Essential Items

For Me

Judging Schedule
Jacket with pocket, and comfortable shoes
Clothes brush and grooming smock or apron
Wet-wipes or washrag and paper towels
Trash bags
Pooper scooper
Rain gear

For My Vizsla

Drinking water and bowl
2 Show leads and collars (one to wear & spare)
Grooming tools
Crate with pad or rug in it
Several terrycloth towels
Liver or other bait
Rawhide chews and favorite toys
First Aid kit including diarrhea medication

Optional Items

Folding chair
Cooler with lunch or drinks
Dolly with wheels to roll crate & supplies
Change of clothes and/or shoes
Overnight bag including any needed medications

Grooming table
Shade cloth
Exercise pen
Obedience equipment (if also competing there)
Dog food (if overnight trip)

Keep corrections subtle and practice them in training before you use them in the ring.

The cowering dog is another problem, since a Vizsla does not present his best side when he is being shy. If your dog is tired, scared, or physically down on his pasterns, you need to distract him away from cowering by baiting with food or a small toy.

After the judge has examined and gaited the dogs individually, he will go down the line for another look, or have each dog move again. You will probably be asked to do a simple "down and back." Move your dog straight away from the judge to the farthest point in the ring, turn your dog around the outside of your body, and return to the judge in a straight line, stopping just a few feet in front of him. Your dog should be directly in front of the judge while you stand off to his side, allowing the judge a clear look. Make sure your dog stops with his feet and body pointing ahead.

The triangle pattern is also popular with judges as they can watch the dog moving from the back, from the side, and from the front. Just picture a triangle in your mind as you leave the judge in a straight line and travel to the end of the ring. Turn left and move across that section of the ring to the corner and then turn at a slight angle and return to the judge. If you are showing indoors with rubber mats on the floor, make sure that you dog moves on the mats to give him good footing.

No matter how many handling classes you attend, there is nothing like the experience of actually being in the ring. You will soon learn to simultaneously watch the judge, watch your dog, and make sure you do not fall over the ring barriers.

Insufficient training or improper and faulty handling can result in a lower placing than your Vizsla deserves, and could conceivably ruin an otherwise promising show career. In a wider sense and of even more importance to the breed as a whole is the impression your dog projects to the spectators. The Vizsla is a classy, showy breed that loves attention. School yourself to be at ease in the ring with your dog. If you are tense and nervous it will communicate to your dog and he will display the same emotional stress. And remember, if you don't win today there is always another show and another judge with another opinion tomorrow. You will see bad dogs and bad judges, and it may be hard to maintain your confidence. Handling well means a positive, enthusiastic attitude in spite of all the disappointments.

Your Responsibility as an Exhibitor

It is estimated that between twenty-five and thirty dogs can be judged in an hour and, based on this, each judge has his schedule set for the day. It is the sole responsibility of each exhibitor to be at ringside and ready when his breed is called, and not to delay the judging in any way. It is also the exhibitor's responsibility to be sure his Vizsla has been properly prepared and exercised and has eliminated before ring time. Not only is it an embarrassment to you if your dog fouls the ring, but it will irritate the judge if he is delayed while the floor is being cleaned.

There is nothing so exasperating to a judge as an exhibitor who is not paying attention. Watch the handler or class ahead of you so you will be prepared for the pattern of movement your judge will want you to do. Have your Vizsla under control in the ring and set him up smoothly and efficiently. The judge will not have the time to stand by and wait, nor is he expected to do so, while you try to set up an inexperienced and untrained dog.

It is your responsibility to present a clean Vizsla to the judge, not only a clean, shiny coat, but clean feet, mouth and ears. Tell the judge if you are showing a bitch in season that might still be attractive to the boys. Not only should your Vizsla be presented clean, but you should also make a good appearance. A female exhibitor should not try to attract the judge in the ring by wearing a low-cut blouse, bright jewelry, or a tight, short skirt. That type of dress has no

place in the show ring where it is the dog being judged, not the looks of the handler. A neat suit is always appropriate, as is a comfortable skirt, blouse and jacket. Low shoes with non-skid soles and tennis or running sneakers all make for comfort in the ring. You will probably notice that the majority of professional handlers wear suits or neat jackets. That is a good rule for all male handlers to follow if you want to have a tidy, clean look in the ring. Jeans and sloppy clothes are just not appropriate.

RECORDS IN THE SHOW RING

Top-winning Vizslas leave their impact on the breed and draw the breed to

Courtesy in the Show Ring

Do not crowd the dog in front of you.

Don't block the judge's view of another dog.

Be polite to the judge and other exhibitors.

Do not make excuses to the judge about your dog or yourself. He must judge your dog as he appears.

Keep bait and toys from distracting other entries.

Avoid making loud noises to attract your dog's attention.

If another handler blocks your dog from the judge's view, be courteous but firm in requesting him to move.

If another exhibitor deliberately interferes, you may ask the steward to move you, or you may file a complaint with her.

If you do not understand the judge, you may ask him to clarify. Paying careful attention to the dog ahead should avoid this problem.

Always take time to congratulate the winners.

Time to retire: Seventh Best in Show for Ch. Taunee's Loki Santana, CD, HOF, ROM.

Ch. Boelte's Brant of Penlee, winner of two Best in Shows, owner-handled by Pat Boelte.

the attention of show fanciers. The first Vizsla in the United States to earn a Best in Show was Ch. Napkelte Vadasz Dalos. Bred by Phil Wright in Canada and owned by Elsie and William Totten in California, "Danny" had his first top win on May 24, 1970. That win was followed by two more the same year. Danny also sired eighteen champions.

Ch. Debreceny Dezso was the second Vizsla to gain a Best in Show. Bred and owned by the Carpenters in California, Dezso gained his first top win on July 25, 1970. He was also the breed winner at two National Specialties. A lovely, dark dog, he made a lasting contribution to the Vizsla breed as the sire of forty-nine champions.

Ch. Taunee's Loki Santana, CD, owned by Marion Coffman and Linda Greenfield, made Vizsla history with his record of seven Best in Show wins and 120 group placements. He was fifth of all sporting dogs in 1974 and seventh in 1975. His record for a Vizsla male stood for twenty-five years. A beautiful, elegant, stylish dog in the show ring, he left a legacy as a top-

producing sire with fifty-two champions and was inducted into the VCA Hall of Fame for his outstanding contribution to the breed. His sire was Ch. Glen Cottage Loki Barat, CDX, also a member of the VCA Hall of Fame and sire of thirty-one champions. His dam was Ch. Cariad's Gaybine, CD, the dam of sixteen champions.

Ch. Boelte's Brant of Penlee, owned and handled by Pat Boelte, was the first Vizsla to be owner-handled to two Best in Show wins. Brant's sire was Ch. Taunee's Loki Santana, and his dam was the first Vizsla bitch to gain a Best in Show, Ch. Firebrand's Constant Comment.

The first bitch to gain multiple top wins was Ch. Harann's Tulipann, bred and owned by Anne Denehy. "Tuli" had four Best in Show wins. Following just a couple of years later was another top winning bitch, Ch. Cariad's Surfstone Szuka, owned by Paul Gornoski, with four Best in Show wins and 124 group placings

The next top winning bitch was Ch. Russet Leather Caveat Calla, owned by

Ch. Sandy Acres Russet Majesty, JH. Owned by Judy Barber, D. Clark, and M. Adams. Photo © Christina M. Freitag.

Junior Handler, Brooke Folley, with Ch. Classic Barry Bakanal. Photo © Bernard W. and J. Kay Kernan.

Diana Jones, Karen Hooks, and Kathy Rust. Calla had seven Best in Show wins. Ch. Piper Barben's Buttons'N Beaux, owned by Ben Zahn and Valerie Piper, had six top wins.

The top winning bitch of record is Ch. Sandy Acres Russet Majesty, owned by Judy Barber, with twelve Best in Show wins. Ch. Russet Leather Warrior's Mark, JH (Junior Hunter), owned by Seal Samuels and Bev Wanjon, is the top-winning male Vizsla with fourteen Best in Shows wins.

JUNIOR SHOWMANSHIP

Junior Showmanship classes are offered to encourage youth to get involved in showing. In Junior Showmanship competition, the abilities of the handler is judged, not the merits of the dog being handled. The purpose of Junior Handling is to teach good sportsmanship, poise, correct handling, grooming, responsibility, and care of dogs

to the breeders, exhibitors, and handlers of the future.

Each dog entered in a regular Junior Showmanship class must be owned by the Junior Handler or their father, mother, brother, sister, uncle, aunt, grandfather, or grandmother. Bitches in season are not eligible. A Junior is not allowed to handle dogs for pay nor to accept payment for handling dogs.

Novice

This class is for boys and girls who are at least ten years old and under eighteen years old on the day of the show, and who have not won three first place awards in a Novice class.

Open

This class is for boys and girls who are at least ten years old and under eighteen years old who have three first place awards in a Novice class. The winner of a Novice class shall automatically become eligible,

Multiple group placer and BISS winner, Ch. Koppertone-May Sweet Serenity. Owned by Vicki May. Photo © Meg, Callea Photo.

upon notice to the Open class steward, to enter and compete in the Open class at the same show, providing the win is the third first place award.

Either or both of these regular classes may be divided by age into Junior and Senior classes, provided the division is listed in the premium. A Junior class shall be for boys and girls who are least ten years old and under fourteen years; a Senior class shall be for boys and girls who are at least fourteen years old and under eighteen years old on the day of the show.

By learning to be at ease in the Junior Showmanship ring, a young handler will carry the attributes of courtesy, confidence, and experience over into all facets of his life. His entire future will benefit. Many handlers go on to be judges in the Junior Showmanship ring and from there to apprentices under professional handlers. If you are the parent of a Junior Handler, try not to do anything in the way of criticism that will take away his confidence in his handling. Do not stand outside the ring and glare at him if he is making a mistake or does not place in the class. Support his interest in handling with simple, quiet suggestions. With constant criticism he may get the erroneous idea that winning is more important than good sportsmanship.

Give your child a chance to develop friendships with other Juniors and help him have an open mind so he can learn from them. Remind him that his responsibility to his dog has to come first, and encourage a healthy, happy attitude toward competition, whether losing or winning.

Ch. Rosewood's Sweet Revenge, CD. Owned by Edwin Foster, Jr.

Ch. Rheingold Loge Anton Dvorak, SH. Owned by Steve Shlyen and Stan Miller.

Ch. Russet Leather Sacajawea, JH, AX, AXJ. Owned by J. Walton, C. Dostal, and B. Wanjon.

Ch. Eszaki Cinka Panna. Owned by Bill Wion. Photo © Ashbey.

Ch. Jnek's King Ralph, JH. Owned by Kathy and Jeff Engelsman. Photo © Booth Photography.

Ch. Stonepoint's Thunderheart, JH (Geronimo). Owned by Ute Plass and Suzanne Branch. Photo © Booth Photography.

Ch. Titan's Encore, CDX, NA, NAJ, ROM (Leia). Owned by Peggy Schmidt. Photo © Downey Dog Show Photography.

Ch. Cariad's Classic Mariah shown finishing her championship title at eight months, handled by breeder, Marion Coffman.

Ch. Russet Leather Red Cloud II, SH. Owned by Paul Palk-covic, M. Faulkner, and B. Wanjon. Photo © Photos Today.

Ch. Koppertone's Magyar Buszkea, CD. Owned by Bonnie and Mark Goodwein. Photo © Mitchell.

Ch. Koppertone's Redd Hott Jazz, CD. Owned by Cal Bern-stein. Photo © Ludwig.

BISS Am/BIS Int'l Ch. CMF Leitz, Camera, Action. Breeder-owner-photographer, Christina Freitag.

Ch. Koppertone's Cariad Baratom, CDX. Owned by Marion Coffman and Mark and Bonnie Goodwein. Photo © Meyer Photo.

CHAPTER TEN

The Vizsla in the Field

Vizslas are born with a natural instinct to stalk and point. Such desirable attributes as a good nose, style, and natural retrieving will be evident in a puppy from an early age and will make training him enjoyable and easy. It is obvious that the Vizsla needs to be taught by patient, kindly methods. He must regard most of his early work as a happy game so that he will mature into a bold and happy worker. However, he should not be allowed to do whatever he likes and then suddenly be corrected in an attempt to eradicate habits which had been permitted at the start.

EARLY TRAINING

While your puppy is still young, teach him to obey commands around the house, such as sit and come. You should have one major objective in mind—control. Control must be worked at gradually and steadily, so as not to take away your puppy's spirit and enthusiasm. Be consistent with each lesson and, at some point, your puppy will respond. Any response on his part to comply and perform correctly should be instantly rewarded with praise.

Voice tone is of major importance and you should give each command firmly and quietly. Make a conscious effort not to shout a command if your puppy is not obeying. Encouragement and kindness are necessary in training a Vizsla at any stage.

Early training to heel is a must—this should never be postponed since it is important later to off-leash control and acceptance of the check cord. As soon as you have

Retrieving in the field. Photo © Christina M. Freitag.

started the basics of come and sit, attach a lead to your dog's collar and teach the heel. He might not be too happy about it at first, but shortly should be moving with head high and tail wagging.

Start taking your puppy out to strange areas where the grass is of different heights. Encourage him to move through various types of grass and cover. As soon as he is able to walk on the leash without pulling, you can begin to think about off-leash work with him. To start him off-leash, simply drop the leash and let him trail along as you walk. This is also a good time to incorporate the use of the whistle.

As you call his name and "Come," use the whistle with the command. This will eventually be the signal you use while working in the field to call him to you from a distance. If he persists in not coming back to you, start using a longer lead or check line about twenty feet in length. Let him run loose, dragging the longer lead. Then give the command "Come" and either grab or step down on the cord, bringing your pup to a sudden halt. When he has become reliable on a recall, from either a voice or whistle command, discontinue the use of the check cord until your dog starts working in the bird field.

Heading for the starting line. Photo © Christina M. Freitag.

Dobrocat's CG Mire Belle at four months of age already showing promise in the field.

Natural First Points

Every owner of a Vizsla wants to know if his puppy will point. Most puppies do, instinctively. One of the easiest methods to find out what your puppy will do is to use a quail wing attached to a fishing line and pole (without the fish hook, of course). What you are looking for is intense excitement and interest in movement.

Hold the fishing pole at an angle so that the wing is just touching the ground. With your puppy playing loose, jiggle the wing slightly until he sees the movement. He will stop, look at it, and then suddenly make a lunge to grab it. Flip the line and wing up before he grabs it.

Repeat the procedure several times, moving the wing just slightly to keep his attention. After several attempts to grab the wing, he will realize that if he stalks and points it, the wing will stay still. If he tries to pounce on it, flip it up fast. Stop this game before your puppy gets bored. His attention span is very short when he is young. If you overdo, he may get discouraged when he is unable to get the wing. Also, since he is responding to movement and not smell, the game will not hold his interest all that long.

Introduction to Live Birds

Early successful training is dependent on the use of live birds. In order for your Vizsla to retain his intensity, he must be able to find birds. Since game birds are expensive and, at times, difficult to obtain, it is acceptable to use live pigeons. Until now your puppy has probably done nothing more than run around and play in the field, sniffing and picking up strange objects—pretty much normal puppy behavior. He has not yet truly discovered how to use his nose. Finding birds will rapidly teach him to search for game using his scenting abilities.

First dizzy your live bird and tuck its head under its wing to prevent it from flying off immediately. Place the bird in suitable grass cover and bring your puppy into the field on a long check cord. Come into the cover from a downwind direction to give him a chance to use his nose to locate the bird.

If your dog sees the bird and grass move, he will probably stop moving and stalk, or even flash point. Most puppies will flash, or sight, point and then rush in and try to catch the bird. Do not reprimand him too severely at this point. He will learn, after several failed attempts when the bird takes wing, to follow its flight and relocate it when it lands. Or he will come back to where he first found the bird and smell around the same area. He must learn to connect using his nose with locating something exciting—a bird.

Once the game is scented, your puppy's instinct to point will be triggered and he should freeze in his tracks. The bird will remain motionless to avoid being located. An uncertain nose and a wrong movement from your dog, because of a lack in the pointing instinct, will cause the bird to flush. However, both the use of his nose and the tendency to point are inherent in your Vizsla, and correct training will bring about the proper balance.

The desire to catch also is inherent in a hunting dog and is triggered once the bird moves, so you want the bird to stay still until you flush it. Continued training with a check cord will bring the control necessary to keep your dog from pouncing on and grabbing the bird. Remaining in a pointing position until the bird has been flushed, as the bird flies, and after the shot, is simply obedience to a learned command. The response to "Whoa" must be constantly reinforced.

Release cages for whatever bird you are using can be purchased from most training equipment suppliers. The cage has a spring-loaded lid which flies open when a metal arm is depressed. It can also be released from a distance by attaching a length of cord. When you use a cage during training an unsteady dog on point, the dog cannot dive in and catch the bird. By continued work with a check cord, he is encouraged to hold his point until you release the bird.

Since a noisy approach by you may break your dog's concentration, the check cord and a calm "Whoa" are required. The angle of approaching the dog when he is on

A young Vizsla eager to get to the field.

point is also an important consideration. Approaching from the front or side to flush the bird, instead of from the dog's rear, will keep him from interpreting your movements as a command to release his point. Always be careful never to walk between him and the bird if you can possibly help it, and never rush your approach. Excitement on your part is quickly transmitted to your dog, and will lead to an unsteady point.

When your Vizsla breaks his point, do not yell at him. Let the check cord out as he runs and then suddenly step on it and dump him head over tail, bringing him to an abrupt halt. Bring him back to where he had been on point, even though the bird is no longer there, and give a strong "Whoa" again. Keep him in that position for several seconds and then, after telling him the bird is "all gone," heel him off in different direction to hunt for another bird. This will help to get his mind off the departed bird.

Introduction to the Gun

Getting a Vizsla puppy accustomed to the sound of a gun is a most critical stage. If done incorrectly or thoughtlessly by an impatient owner, it can result in a problem which may be difficult or impossible to overcome. Correctly introduced, however,

Andre V. Schloss Loosdorf (Joey) is shown in these 1956 training photos by V. Halmrest.

Basics start with sight-pointing a bird wing attached to a pole and line.

Joey has found his bird and shows an an excellent style of pointing.

Joey has snapped to a point. The handler talks to him at all times, keeping him steady.

The handler encourages Joey to "steady."

The handler is pushing Joey's hindquarters and Joey is resisting, resulting in a stauncher point.

Again, with Joey on point, the handler is giving a slight forward push on his back. Joey resists by pushing forward, getting a tighter point.

Joey retrieves the downed bird and delivers it to his handler's hand.

gunfire should cause no fear and will soon be regarded as a normal occurrence.

Sounds of gunfire should be introduced gradually while your dog's mind is occupied with something he enjoys—finding a bird. With the dog running freely ahead of you, shoot off a blank pistol. In the excitement of finding and chasing his first birds, a young dog will not have much reaction to the noise. He may stop momentarily and look back at you, find there is nothing to be concerned about, and continue the chase. While he is still a distance from you and occupied with the chase, fire again. Provided he is still unconcerned, wait until he is closer to you before firing again.

When you are satisfied that your dog is not the least worried about the sound of the blank pistol, you can change to a .410 shotgun. The introduction to the shotgun should always be done from a distance at first. If you detect a nervous reaction from your Vizsla, you are pushing him too fast and you should revert to the blank pistol for a time before reintroducing the shotgun. Patience and a lot of praise will be extremely necessary.

DNFCH Csardas Lakeside Zephyr, SH. Owned by Nancy Staley.

Retrieving

Vizslas are natural retrievers and it would be unusual for a young dog not to have the tendency to chase a ball or stick when it is thrown. Retrieving is going to be required for a dog used in the field, so it is good to start encouraging a young dog, especially when the desire exists.

So far your Vizsla has probably seen retrieving as a fun game. Now you want him to do it for you, on command only, in order to ensure a steadiness to wing and shot.

The use of a canvas dummy in training will eliminate the necessity for strong correction that can arise if you use a real bird, even a dead one. Your young dog may find it hard to give up a bird.

Since the enforcement of a "Whoa" will be necessary, put your dog on his check cord and stand on the end of it. Give him the command to "Whoa" using a hand signal, and then toss the dummy. He may break when he sees the motion but will come to a sharp stop when he hits the end of the cord. Pull him back to you, and giving another command of "Whoa," pick up the dummy yourself. He has to learn that he can retrieve it only when you allow him.

Repeat the process of throwing the dummy while you continue to stand on the end of the cord. If he breaks again, correct him in the same way, but if he obeys the "Whoa" when you release him, give the command "Fetch" after taking your foot off the check cord. If there is any hesitation in bringing the dummy back to you, give the dog a lot of voice encouragement. Praise him when he comes back to you with his retrieve.

Vizslas learn fast and willingly. As a natural retriever, your dog will be in his true element. As soon as you are sure of your dog's steadiness in waiting for the command "Fetch," you can remove the check cord. Practice throwing the dummy in different directions, up close and far, and changing the length of time he has to stand and wait for the command. Never allow him to run in and retrieve as soon as the dummy hits the ground. He must wait for the command. It is not necessary that he sit when he brings the dummy back, but he should never be encouraged to drop it before you take it from him.

Add some fun to the exercise by tying bird wings around the dummy to keep his interest. He may become more possessive

An enthusiastic Vizsla has found his bird. Photo © Christina M. Freitag.

A happy Vizsla has retrieved his pheasant. Photo © Christina M. Freitag.

when it holds bird smell, so be quick to enforce any command, and use lots of praise when he performs correctly.

The "Whoa" is going to be the most important command your dog will learn. It will be necessary at every stage of his training and the dog that learns to obey it immediately is worth his weight in gold.

Steadiness to Shot

Steadiness to a thrown dummy is the first lesson in making your dog steady to wing. The next stage is teaching him to be steady to a gun being fired. You will need an assistant to throw the dummy and fire the pistol for this exercise; your concern will be watching that your Vizsla does not break.

As before, put your dog on his check cord, with your foot on the end of it in case he breaks in the excitement of a gunshot. Give him a sharp "Whoa" and signal your helper to throw the dummy and fire the pistol. Pause for a few seconds if your dog has stayed still, and then tell him to "Fetch."

Practice firing the pistol with your dog in a whoa, without throwing the dummy. After a pause, instead of sending your dog out, tell him "All gone" so he will not expect to retrieve every time a gun is fired.

Water Retrieves

Along with the early yard and field training, you must teach your young Vizsla to swim. Vizslas love to swim, especially if something is thrown into the water for them to retrieve.

When introducing your Vizsla to water for the first time, whether it is a lake or a swimming pool, walk out a short way into the water with him in your arms. When you are waist deep, lower him down into the water, letting him swim and follow you to the shore or steps. Never throw a young dog into the water—he can drown, mostly because he will panic, get tired from thrashing, and not be able to understand how to get out. While teaching him to swim easily without fear, make sure he can find the steps or shore.

Ch. Dorratz Double Trouble UD, MH, NA. Owned by Doris Ratzlaff.

As soon as your dog is comfortable in the water, start throwing the canvas dummy, a tennis ball, or a stick for him to retrieve. With a lot of praise and encouragement, he will soon do water retrieves with enthusiasm. Although not yet a requirement in Vizsla field trials, the water retrieve is always useful and fun.

CONTINUED TRAINING

Careless introduction to the gun, plus the lack of insisting on a staunch point, will lead to numerous problems as you advance in training with your Vizsla. In some cases, it will mean going back to the very beginning, this time slowly and patiently.

Blinking

Gun shyness can result in a young dog "blinking." Blinking is the tendency of a dog to ignore game while hunting, even though he has already scented it and is aware of it. Since the dog associates the gunshot with flushing the bird, he reasons that if the bird is not flushed, the gun will not go off. If he does find and point the bird, he may move away from it before his handler can come into position.

A dog that has been strongly handled in early training may also develop a tendency to blink. A threatening voice should never be used on the sensitive Vizsla and the "Whoa" command should always be given in a soothing, calm manner.

Quartering

The distance over which any individual dog will range while hunting can vary considerably, along with the owner's views on how far a Vizsla, supposedly a close-working dog, should range. A lot will depend on the type of ground cover and terrain where the individual is hunting. In Hungary, a dog works very close to his handler, since control is the first concern.

Every dog should show enough independence to leave his handler and quarter (cover ground) ahead and to each side so as to check the terrain thoroughly. He should leave the impression that, in all that ground he has covered, he has not missed anything. A dog that runs only far and straight without quartering is quite useless. It is the handler who should maintain a straight course while his dog hunts and quarters the terrain.

A Vizsla that consistently ranges too far can be controlled to a degree by experienced handling and the manner in which he is taught to quarter. Teach your dog to respond to whistle and arm signals if you find that he tends to work too far from you. If his range is too far to your right, give a couple of bleeps on your whistle to get his at-

tention. When he stops to look at you, signal with your left arm as you start walking in that direction. He should cross in front of you and start working his pattern on the left as you continue in a straight line again.

With experience, any dog should make use of wind direction while hunting. He will quarter into the wind, developing a fairly even pattern of covering the field ahead and to the left and right of you. If you have a young dog that is determined to hunt for himself and not obey directions, put him back on a long check cord until he learns instant responses to verbal and whistle commands, along with arm signals.

Backing (Honoring)

"Backing" means stopping during hunting and honoring the point of another dog. Ideally, when seeing another dog on point, your Vizsla should immediately stop without any command and honor the other dog by pointing also, whether or not he can actually smell or locate the bird. Many hunters will never need such a completely well-mannered dog unless they participate in field trials, but if you know someone with a good, well-trained dog, he will be able to help you with training sessions to teach your dog to back.

FIELD TRIALS

Field trials have been in existence for about the same length of time as dog shows, both having started only a few months apart in 1874. In that year the first field trial ever recorded was held in Memphis, Tennessee, by the members of the Tennessee State Sportsmen's Association. That initial trial, with an entry of only eight dogs, became the beginning of a healthy outdoor sport that has gained the enthusiasm of people all over the country.

When the Tennessee Club faded out of existence after a few years, other clubs began to spring up and in 1907, scores of clubs were in operation and a total of 410 trials had been recorded. By the late 1940s, more

Advanced training for field trials will include teaching your dog to honor another dog on point. Photo © William P. Gilbert Photography.

than 20,000 dogs were being run in trials each year.

Field trials were given their initial big push by The American Field, the oldest sportsman's magazine in America. In 1917 the Amateur Field Trial Club of America was organized and devoted attention to conducting amateur trials. This organization, along with the AKC, made a tremendous contribution to the development of pointing dogs by regulating and sanctioning field trials that comply with their rules and by recording wins and breeding records.

Since the first recorded field trial in 1874, the standards of performance for dogs have changed, particularly the element of range. At first, handlers were on foot as they directed their dogs around the course. Soon, however, wider-running dogs came into favor and handlers were permitted to complete the course on horseback. Although the Vizsla is naturally a close hunter, many handlers still make use of a horse in the backfield course in order to cover a larger area.

Field trials are one of the most exciting and highly competitive of all dog sports. Basically a field trial is a contest between dogs to establish the best dog in a particular classification for that day. A dog must live up to established criteria for performance while still competing against other entries. The sport is costly and not easily accessible, and the birds need to be constantly replaced. The Field Trial Championship title requires more work than many owners are willing to put into it. Training areas and trial grounds may be in out-of-the-way places and the distances you may have to travel to reach them may be too far. While your Vizsla is in training, he must be worked constantly, not just once in a while. He should be run on birds every single weekend, plus trained on basics during the week. It is a very time-consuming task.

However, from the first time you have seen your Vizsla in a rock-hard pointing position, so intense at the smell of a quail that he is actually drooling and quivering, you will probably become hooked on that way of life. If you feel that you truly want to develop the natural ability of your Vizsla, but do not have the time or training to progress past the stage of a companion gundog to a completely trained competitive field trial dog, a professional trainer can do it for you.

All in place for a successful hunt. Photo © Christina M. Freitag.

What's for dinner? Not much doubt with this big catch. Photo © Christina M. Freitag.

Choose one who is basically a Vizsla handler or who knows the breed well.

You will find that there is a constant influx of new Vizsla owners who are anxious to train and handle their own dogs. Locate someone who owns a really good, well-trained dog and ask if you can watch him work several times, especially to teach your dog backing. Make sure your own dog is already under control or you may get turned down. Like all competitive sports, training a field dog has protocol, general practices, and fine points.

Go to field trials as a spectator and listen and watch. There are no set rules for

There IS a bird in there. Photo © Christina M. Freitag.

training a field trial dog. There are as many training methods as there are trainers, but one method is sure to be the right one for you and your dog.

The best way to handle your dog under actual field trial conditions is to enter an AKC sanctioned Hunting Test. Since the dogs are not in competition with each other, it does not put any pressure on you or your dog, and is always a fun day with a group of other pointing breeds and their handlers.

Field Championship

A field trial is divided into several classifications, called stakes, with each of them being a separate test with placements in each of the stakes. The stakes offered are Puppy, Derby, Gundog, and All-Age. The dogs within a stake are run in braces, two dogs on the course at a time. A minimum of two judges score each dog based on the procedures and performances they give. The judges are not required to declare a winner if they feel that neither dog is worthy of it. To be recorded as a Field Champion (FC), a dog must have won ten points with at least three of them from a single win in an Open stake. No more than two points each can be earned in Puppy and Derby stakes, no more than four points won in Amateur stakes, and four points must be earned in a Retrieving stake at a club trial. Points are based on the number of starters in each class.

Amateur Field Championship

An Amateur is a person who has not accepted remuneration in any form for the training or handling of a dog in a field trial in the two years preceding the trial. An Amateur can run his own dogs but not more than two dogs that are owned by others. To be recorded as an Amateur Field Champion (AFC), a dog must have won ten points with at least two first placements, one of which must be a three point or better at a licensed field trial. No more than two points each can be earned in a Puppy or Derby stake. Championship points from first placements in Amateur stakes that are credited towards a Field

Championship will also be credited towards the Amateur Field Championship. Points are based on the number of starters in each class.

Puppy Stakes (Open and/or Amateur Walking)

Puppy stakes are open to any dog six months of age to fifteen months of age. They are run for at least fifteen minutes but not more than thirty minutes. A puppy must show desire to hunt, boldness, and initiative in covering ground and in searching the cover. He should indicate the presence of a bird but does not have to point firmly yet must show reasonable obedience to his handler's commands. He should be judged on his performance as an indication of his future as a Derby dog. If the premium states that blanks must be fired, a dog that makes contact with game shall be fired over.

Derby Stakes (Open and/or Amateur Walking)

Derby stakes are for any dog that is six months of age to twenty-four months of age. Derby stakes are run for at least twenty minutes but not more than thirty minutes. A Derby dog must show a keen desire to hunt, be bold and independent, have a fast, yet attractive style of running, and demonstrate intelligence in seeking objectives and the ability to find game. A Derby dog must establish point but does not need to be steady to wing and shot. He must show reasonable obedience to his handler's commands. If the handler is within reasonable range of a bird that has been flushed, a gun must be fired. A Derby dog must show promise as a high class bird dog for Gundog or All-Age stakes.

Gundog Stakes (Open and/or Amateur)

These stakes are for dogs six months or older. A Gundog must give a finished performance and must be under his handler's control at all times. A Gundog must show a keen desire to hunt, must have a bold and attractive style of running, and must

demonstrate not only intelligence in quartering and in seeking objectives but also the ability to find birds. A Gundog must hunt for his handler at a range suitable for the handler on foot and should check in front of his handler frequently. He must cover ground but never range out of sight for any length of time. He must locate game, point staunchly, and be steady to wing and shot. Intelligent use of the wind and terrain in locating game, an accurate nose, and style and intensity of point are essential. He must honor his brace-mate's point if the situation occurs. A reasonable move by him to mark a bird flushed after a point is acceptable but a break or delayed chase is not. At least thirty minutes shall be allowed for each heat.

All-Age Stakes (Open and/or Amateur)

These stakes are for dogs six months of age or older. An All-Age dog must give a finished performance and must be under reasonable control of his handler. He must show a keen desire to hunt with a bold and attractive style of running, and must show independence in hunting. He must range well out in a forward pattern seeking the most promising objectives, so as to locate any game on the course. Excessive line casting and avoiding cover must be penalized. He must respond to handling, but must

Dual/AFCh. Riverbend Deacon's Dandy, CD, owned by Kitty Pullen.

demonstrate his independent judgment in hunting the course and should not look to his handler for directions. He must find game, point staunchly, and be steady to wing and shot. Intelligent use of the wind and terrain in locating game, an accurate nose, and style and intensity on point are essential. A dog must honor his brace-mate's point if the situation occurs. At least thirty minutes shall be allowed for each heat.

Limited Gundog Stakes (Open and/or Amateur)

These stakes are for dogs six months of age or older that have won first, second, third, or fourth place in any Gundog stakes.

Limited All-Age Stakes (Open and/or Amateur)

These stakes are for dogs six months of age or older that have placed first, second, third, or fourth in any All-Age stake.

National and Amateur Championship Stakes

In 1978 the Vizsla Club of America approved the qualification requirements for a National and National Amateur Championship Stakes for Vizslas. Both are open to any Vizsla over six months of age. In the National Championship stakes, a dog must have placed in an Open All-Age stake, Amateur All-Age stake, Open Limited All-Age stake, or Amateur Limited Gundog stake to be eligible to enter.

In the National Amateur Championship stakes, a dog must have placed in an Amateur All-Age stake, Amateur Limited All-Age stake, Amateur Gundog stake, or Amateur Limited Gundog stake to be eligible to enter.

HUNTING TESTS

In 1985 the American Kennel Club designed their new noncompetitive hunting test after the basic test which the North American Versatile Hunting Dog Association (NAVHDA) had promoted, with the goal of testing a hunting dog's usefulness for the on-foot hunter in all phases of hunting except for water retrieves.

Since many owners of pointing breeds who do not compete in licensed field trials still want a type of related structured activity, the AKC wrote regulations for hunting tests to allow these owners to test their dogs against a practical standard. These hunting tests immediately became very popular as Vizsla breeders, in particular, were anxious to have some way of measuring their dog's natural abilities and ensure the continuance of these abilities in a breeding program—hence, the Dual Vizsla.

Dogs entered in these hunting tests are judged in one of three levels: Junior, Senior, and Master, based on the ability of the dog. Participating at any of these levels offers the owner both the fun of training and seeing his dog work, as well as the pride of accomplishment in earning an AKC hunting title.

Junior Hunter

The Junior Hunter is judged and scored on his bird-finding ability, plus his desire, boldness, and independence. He must show trainability, obedience to commands, gun response, and pointing. Only blank pistols are fired in the Junior class. A Junior Hunter must find and point birds to receive a qualifying score. Desire, speed, independence, and a useful pattern of running are the elements for the hunting category. A dog that is out for a run in the field and does not seem to be hunting, or a dog that does not leave his owner's side or that wanders around slowly should be scored low in hunting ability.

A dog that does a good job hunting should find birds. The number of birds a dog finds should not necessarily be considered as important as the quality of the finds.

The Junior Hunter is also graded on the basis of his willingness to be handled, his reasonable obedience to commands, and his gun response.

Gun-shyness cannot be tolerated in the makeup of any dog that is being evaluated as a hunting companion.

Senior Hunter

Judging for the Senior Hunter is more rigorous. Birds must be shot and the dog must retrieve willingly while being judged on handling, obedience, and gun response. The Senior Hunter must honor a brace-mate encountered on point in order to earn a qualifying score. Senior dogs must point and hold the point until the bird is flushed. A dog that breaks before the flush cannot receive a qualifying score. Gun response for the Senior is evaluated when the bird is shot.

Honoring is an additional element included under trainability. If a dog is given the opportunity to honor and refuses, he cannot receive a qualifying score. If he does not have the opportunity to honor, he is called back at the conclusion of the test to demonstrate his willingness to honor. A handler may give his dog a verbal command to honor, but if the dog steals his brace-mate's point he cannot receive a qualifying score.

Master Hunter

The Master Hunter category is graded very strictly, with no degree of tolerance or leniency. The dog must give a finished performance and show a keen desire to hunt with a bold manner of running, displaying not only intelligence in seeking the bird, but also a willingness to work with his handler and not range out of sight. After finding game, he must be steady to point and steady to wing and shot. He must honor not only during his brace-mate's point but through the entire flush and the bird being shot. A Master Hunter must retrieve to hand without any assistance from his handler in order to receive a qualifying score.

This level is the true test of a trained and finished gundog. All tests are done on foot with only judges and marshals on horseback.

Qualifying Scores

There are four categories of ability in

Ch. Dorratz Bebop at Birdland, CD, SH, ROM. Owned by Russell and Donna DeFelippis and Doris Ratzlaff.

Ch. Oakleaf's Dandy Dalton, SH. Owned by Jan Simer.

Junior Hunting tests and six categories in Senior and Master. All tests are graded on a scale of zero to ten. In order to receive a qualifying score, a dog must acquire a minimum score of not less than five on each of

Ch. Lakeside by Design, UD, MH. Owned by Nancy Staley.

DUAL CHAMPIONS

Numerous Vizsla owners have added the titles of Dual Champion and Amateur Field Champion to their dogs' list of accomplishments. An amateur is a person who, during the period of two years preceding a trial, has not accepted remuneration in any form for the training or handling of a dog. Amateur stakes have done a lot to encourage novice trainers and handlers to compete.

Many amateurs start out by way of the show ring or hunting tests. After gaining titles in other fields, they want to show the versatility of the breed. Interested in licensed field trial activities, they enter that arena. Some use professional help in training until their dogs have reached the stage where they are ready to compete and earn an Amateur Field Champion title.

A Dual Champion has earned both a show and a Field Champion title. In comparison to other pointing breeds, Vizsla have many Dual and Amateur Field titles due to the constant desire of owners to keep and promote the natural abilities for which the breed is known. By 2003 there were approximately fifty Dual Champion Vizslas and seventy with Dual and Amateur titles.

the categories, with an overall average score of not less than seven. A dog does not have to start at the Junior level if he is capable at competing and qualifying at a higher level.

A Vizsla qualifying in four tests at the Junior level will be awarded the Junior Hunter (JH) title. A dog qualifying in five tests at the Senior level will be awarded the Senior Hunter (SH) title; if he first has earned his JH, he will only need to qualify in four tests for his SH.

A dog qualifying in six tests at the Master Hunter level will be awarded a Master Hunter (MH) title; if he already holds an SH title, he will only need to qualify in five tests.

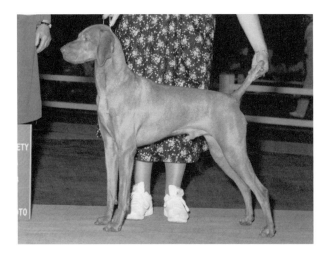

Dual Ch. Oakleaf's Everwhen Chances R, CDX, MH, NA. Owned by Judy and Gerald Richey. Photo © Pegini Animal Photos, Nugent.

NFC, CH, FCH, AFC, Hodag's Hunter, UDX, MH, NAJ and CH, FCH, AFCH, OTCII, MACH Legacy's DeChartay. Owned by Jack Sharkey. Photo © Christina M. Freitag.

CHAPTER ELEVEN

The Vizsla in Agility

In 1979, the Kennel Club of Great Britain designed tests for dogs as a form of competition where the animal's fitness and the handler's ability to train and direct his dog over and through obstacles are tested. It began as a spectator event, patterned after stadium horse jumping with modifications to accommodate dogs, at the International Horse Show in England. The sport caught on quickly and different obstacles were introduced until regulation was required.

Dog agility has changed a lot since those beginnings, with many organizations and governing bodies regulating and overseeing the sport in many countries. As enthusiasm and interest grew, the sport developed in the United States and was eventually accepted as

Cooper through the Tire Jump.

an AKC event. All AKC registered dogs twelve months of age or older are eligible to participate and earn titles. Several other agility organizations also offer trials and titles.

Some Vizsla owners simply want to play with their dogs and provide physical and mental stimulation, motivation, and confidence and have no desire to compete. Understand, however, that an unsound dog should never do agility. Your young dog must be healthy, fit, and friendly. The sport

Ch. MACH2 Russet Leather Anasazi, JH (Necka), doing weave poles at the VCA Nationals, where she earned first place. A top winner both in the show ring and in agility trials. Owned by Carol and Rick Dostal. Photo © Tien Tran Photography.

119

Ch. Poquito Chile RioVista Amigo, TDX, JH, MX, OAP, MXJ, OJP (Amigo). Owned by Melissa Thomas and Maria Zucconi. Photo © Sterling-Photography.

Coming out of the tunnel. Photo © Christina M. Freitag.

An enthusiastic Vizsla weaves the poles. Photo © Christina M. Freitag.

of agility encourages all breeds to compete, and since it is off-leash, your dog must never show aggression to other dogs.

Agility is an athletic sport so your Vizsla should be in top form physically. A few extra pounds will cause stress on the dog's body when jumping and running down the A-frame and will certainly make the timing slower. Conditioning is critical and should start with puppies, training with regular walks at four months of age. As the dog ages, walks should get longer and cover a couple of miles several times a week. Running freely after another dog in the yard is also excellent conditioning.

Puppies gain confidence in their abilities as they learn to climb or crawl through different obstacles. The learning process may be tough for any Vizsla afraid of heights or the darkness of a tunnel, but you can coax him with praise and a treat.

There should be no element of pressure in agility—the sport should simply be pure fun, but there are a lot of precautions. A young dog should not jump, since landing on immature legs and shoulders can cause injuries. He must be taught not to rush an obstacle such as the A-frame or dog walk. Never make him do an obstacle if he doesn't understand or is unable to do it. A dog's active life could be ruined and shortened if agility training is started too early or is rushed; waiting until he is over twelve months of age to start training will give your

The Pause Table. Koppertone's Casey Baratom is owned by Marianne Megna. Photo © Pam and Sherry, Pet Photographers.

Amigo over the A-frame.

dog time to grow and develop. It is recommended that an X-ray be taken to ensure that the growth plates are closed and that there are no underlying physical problems that could be made worse by this activity. While you are waiting for your Vizsla to grow up, do basic obedience classes from the time he is six or eight months old. He will have to learn how to be under control and follow commands when not on a leash. Remember not to concentrate so much on commands and corrections that you forget the praise and rewards.

The repetition of obedience training can become very boring to both your Vizsla and you, but you do need a good foundation in this before you can get into Agility classes. When you start agility training, you will find there is no place for training by compulsion—you have to build your dog's confidence by the use of encouragement and praise. Obedience needs the same teamwork as agility, and it helps the shy dog as well as the hyper and assertive ones.

Obedience skills will make agility easier since your dog will stay when told, come when called, and definitely will be easier to

train and show. To even think about competing in agility trials, you need to make sure that your dog stays with you and looks to you for directions and guidance in a very stimulating environment. Your Vizsla will need to know the obstacles by name, as well as the commands left turn, right turn, go back, come close, and stop. Having his attention is a real must.

Intelligence helps but isn't critical. Drive is the desire to move, and all Vizslas have it. A lot of drive is nice, but sometimes too much can cause frantic behavior—do not confuse drive with speed. Willingness to work is important, although a stubborn Vizsla, with the proper motivation, can be trained to do exceptionally well. The best dog is one that will work with lots of energy, is focused on the course, and is under control and working with you as part of a team. Even if you don't want to compete in trials, you will both enjoy agility training for the pure fun of it. Look for obedience clubs in your area that also offer agility training. They generally will have full sets of equipment to work on. You can also build your own at home.

AGILITY TRIALS

Agility trials are a fun, competitive way for an owner and his dog to work in a close, trusting relationship as a team. It offers an opportunity to refine a dog's skills and is an excellent outlet for a Vizsla's natural exuberance, enthusiasm, and intelligence. Agility has rapidly become the number one sport for Vizsla owners.

Essentially, an Agility trial is one in which the dog is required to progress off-lead through a timed, numbered series of various types of obstacles. There are open and closed tunnels, raised walkways, teeter-totters, A-frames, hoops, weaving poles, and a variety of hurdles. Each dog is scored on his performance and the time it takes to complete the course. The handler runs along with his dog, directing him in the correct sequence of jumps. It is a physically demanding, action-oriented sport for dog and handler and both should be in good running condition. Effective communication is essential—both verbal and body language.

Dogs can be faulted for knocking a bar off a jump, refusing to do an obstacle, or doing one in the wrong order, or for not completing the course within the allowed course time.

Running with your Vizsla in the series of obstacles is more than memorizing the sequence of the course and giving the commands to your dog. Body positioning, voice commands, and hand signals all play a tremendous role in course directions and speed. Dogs quickly learn the new vocabulary as the handler calls out the name for each obstacle. Each trial presents a different course, so the handler and dogs have to communicate quickly as they move through the series.

The jump heights are set according to the dog's height at the shoulder, and even Vizslas differ in size. Individual judging limits are 300 dogs maximum per day without regard to class level or type (Standard, Jumpers with Weaves, or non-regular classes). Almost every agility trial is immediately filled with entries because of the popularity of the sport.

AKC CLASSES AND TITLES

As in obedience competition, a dog must earn each title in turn before going on to the next level. A perfect score in agility competition is 100 points, with a qualifying score being not less than 85 points. Since agility is a timed event, the final score is based on a combination of time and mistakes, or faults. Three qualifying scores earned under two different judges are needed for each title. There are three levels for which a dog can earn a title and each is more difficult than the one before it.

Novice Class

In the Novice class the titles are Novice Agility (NA), and Novice Agility Jumpers (NAJ). As in obedience, the Novice A classes are for handlers who have never put an agility title on a dog and the B classes are for handlers who have previously earned a title. A dog may continue to be shown in the Novice B class until he has acquired a qualifying score towards his Open title.

At the Novice level, the dog must successfully complete a course of twelve to thirteen obstacles, including the A-frame, See-saw, Dog Walk, Open Tunnel, Closed

Amigo through the Closed Tunnel. Photo © Tien Tran Photography.

Tunnel, Pause Table, Tire/Circle or Window Jump, Broad Jump, Panel Jump, Double Bar Jump, and two or three additional jumps. The focus of the Novice Class is obstacle performance with minimal handling.

Open Class

In the Open class, the titles are Open Agility (OA) and Open Agility Jumpers With Weaves (OAJ). The Open class is for dogs that have completed a Novice agility title or Open agility title but have not acquired any qualifying score towards their Agility Excellent title. Open Jumpers With Weaves class is open to dogs that have acquired the Novice NAJ or the Open OAJ title but have not earned a qualifying score towards the Excellent AXJ title.

In this second level, the dog must do all the Novice obstacles, plus the addition of the weave poles and more jumps in a more complicated course with a total of fifteen to seventeen obstacles. The focus of the Open agility class is on enhanced obstacle performance with more handling required.

Excellent Class

In Agility Excellent class, the titles are Agility Excellent (AX) and Excellent Jumpers With Weaves (AXJ). Agility Excellent A class is open to dogs that have acquired the Open Agility (OA) title and to dogs that have acquired the Agility Excellent (AX) title but have not yet earned a qualifying score in the Master Excellent class.

The Excellent Jumpers With Weaves "A" class is open to dogs that have acquired the Open Jumpers With Weaves (OAJ) and to dogs that have already earned the Excellent Jumpers With Weaves (AXJ) but have not yet earned a qualifying score towards their Master Excellent Jumpers With Weaves (MXJ) title.

This final level is the cream of the crop, and in addition to much more difficult courses, even more jumps are added for a total of eighteen to twenty obstacles. Allowed times to complete the course also get tighter at this level.

Amigo clears the Triple Jump. Photo © Tien Tran Photography.

Ch. Russet Leather Sacajawea, JH, MX, AXJ, a top winning bitch, is also a top performer in the Agility trials. Owned by J. Walton, C. Dostal, and B. Wanjon.

Master Excellent

Only the best go on for another title. Agility Excellent dogs that continue to compete and earn legs in Excellent at ten shows become Master Agility Excellent (MX). Qualifying in ten shows in Excellent Jumpers With Weaves earns an MXJ.

MACH

Those who have earned the MX and the MXJ titles and want to keep going have the challenge of going for the Master Agility Champion (MACH) title. This is very difficult to earn. Twenty times the dog and handler must run cleanly in both the Excellent Standard and Jumpers With Weaves classes on the same day. In addition, they must earn 750 "speed points." These are gained for every second that the dog is under the standard course time in each class. If the dog places first in their division, the "speed points" for that run are doubled. If they place second, the "speed points" are multiplied by a factor of 1.5.

The MACH title can be earned multiple times, with the title being designated as MACH2, MACH3, etc. Several Vizslas and their handlers that have completed multiple MACH competitions. It is an exciting and challenging goal.

Ch. Poquito's Chile Sandia Verde, VCD2, CDX, TD, AX, MXJ, owned by Melissa Thomas and Maria Zucconi, was the first Vizsla to earn the VCD2 title. Photo © Tien Tran Photography.

UNITED KENNEL CLUB AGILITY

For the many owners who want more than the available agility trials sponsored by the AKC, the United Kennel Club offers another source of active competition in every field. The United Kennel Club is the second oldest and second largest all-breed registry in the United States. It was founded in 1898, and supports the idea of the total dog, with performance programs that include conformation, obedience, agility, field trials, and hunting tests, always encouraging the owner-handler to participate in events without the use of professional handlers. The UKC was the first to offer DNA profiling as a foolproof method of identification and proof of parentage. It was also the first to take an aggressive stand against puppy mills and was the first to publish and enforce the Breeder's Code of Ethics, reserving the right to inspect kennels and registrations and to bar anyone from the club if violations were found.

UKC events are encouraged for those who want to avoid the stress that is evident when participating in high-activity AKC events. Dogs have to be registered with the UKC in order to receive titles.

Agility Trials

Some of the rules for AKC agility participation are the same in the UKC, with all activities conveying the image of fun and enthusiasm, companionship, and a working relationship between dog and handler. There are three levels, or classes, with corresponding titles, once again with Agility Champion as the ultimate aim.

Standards for Performance

Willingness and enjoyment on the part of the dog is important, and dogs showing fear or extreme hesitancy in following a direction may be given a non-qualifying score. Excessively loud commands are penalized, and any dog relieving himself at any time, whether while entering, performing in, or

Prairie C'Cruiser Pistolpete, NA, NAJ, a SAR dog owned by Sharon Malnar, takes time off from work for his Agility training.

Weaving the poles. Photo © Christina M. Freitag.

leaving the ring will be disqualified. No food is allowed in the ring.

Performance faults are those that are committed by a dog or handler during the actual running of the course, or committed while moving from one obstacle to the next or returning to re-enter an obstacle.

Time faults are assessed for the amount in excess of the assigned course time requirements for the dog to run the course. There is a maximum time allowed to negotiate a single obstacle. If a dog refuses an obstacle and there is a substantial amount of time lost, the handler may be directed to skip that obstacle and continue the course, and will not qualify.

Faults quite often are assessed as being handler's errors. Although regulations have been written to provide rather extensive guidelines for scoring faults, each judge establishes his own guidelines for judging each aspect of the performance. There are no restrictions on the types of signals, verbal commands, or praise given by the handler as long as they are not harsh.

A dog and handler team is judged on the basis of the time required to complete each course and the precision with which the course and the obstacles are negotiated. Deductions for faults are assessed against a total of 200 points. Qualifying scores require the completion of all the obstacles and a score of 170 or more.

Within the three classes, the length of the course can vary from 120 to 200 yards. A minimum of 3,000 square feet is necessary for an Agility I course and 4,000 square feet for Agility II and Agility III. Although no specific outline of the course or sequence of the obstacles is prescribed, the safety of the dog is considered. Certain arrangements of obstacles on each course must to be set for the dog to safely negotiate, while at the same time the number of obstacles, relative difficulty of the obstacles, and the type of maneuvers required to get around the course present an increasing level of difficulty between the Agility I and Agility II classes.

Agility I Class (UAGI) A and B

Agility I is the entry level class with thirteen obstacles included in the course: six non-hurdles, six hurdles, and the Pause Table. The class is divided into A and B. Agility I-A class is open to dogs that have

Koppertone's Casey Baratom comes out of the tunnel still running. Owned by Marianne Megna.

not earned any UKC Agility title. Agility I-B is open to all dogs.

Agility II Class (UAGII) A and B

Agility II class has sixteen obstacles in the course: seven non-hurdles (all which have to be different than in Agility I class), eight hurdles, and the Pause Box. More difficult challenges are used in designing the course. Entry in this class does not require an UAGI title and an owner and dog can compete in both Agility I and Agility II on the same day. Agility II-A class is open to dogs that have never earned a UKC title. Agility II-B class is open to all dogs. All points towards the United Agility Champion title (UACH) must be earned from the Agility I-B and Agility II-B classes.

Agility Champion (UACH)

All the points toward the United Agility Champion (UACH) title must be accumulated from the Agility I-B and Agility II-B classes. One hundred points are needed to gain the title. Points are awarded based on scores of 196 to 200.

Agility III Class (UACHX)

Entry to this class requires the completion of the Agility Champion (UACH) title. The level of difficulty is significantly greater than in the earlier levels; certain challenges and maneuvers are required. Sixteen obstacles are included in the course: eight non-hurdles, one of which must be either the Pause Table or the Pause Box, and eight hurdle obstacles.

CHAPTER TWELVE

The Versatile Vizsla

One of the reasons that the Vizsla is so appealing to the one-dog family is the versatility of the breed. There are many options with this truly wonderful dog that the word "versatile" can have different meaning with each owner.

To the Vizsla owner with no other desire than a loving dog to live with, a versatile dog can mean fun and enjoyment, protection, and guardianship. To some owners, a versatile dog is one that can compete in obedience, agility, and the show ring, gaining titles in all areas. To Vizsla owners who truly love and believe in the versatility of the breed, the term also includes the breed's natural ability and intelligence in the bird field.

For the many owners who want the companionship of a hiking companion, backpacking will be a favorite sport. Biking, jogging, boating—the list of fun things to do with your Vizsla is endless.

Because of the need for more security at airports, Explosives Detection Canine (EDC) dogs are used extensively for sniffing out bombs. Several Vizslas have been trained for this work, mostly at the Transportation Security Administration's training center in San Antonio, Texas. These dogs are trained to identify a multitude of explosives. Dogs have twenty to forty times more receptor cells in their nasal cavities than humans and can detect explosives far better than the luggage scanning machines at airports. The newest Vizsla to be trained for this job is Roy, patrolling and working security at Reagan National Airport near Washington, D.C.

The same training that goes into finding explosives goes into drugs detection work. Vizslas are on duty doing this job at several airports, including Houston.

At least one Vizsla in the country has already been trained and is working as an arson detection dog for a fire inspector and can identify over twenty inflammable substances, such as kerosene and gasoline, at suspicious fires.

Vizslas trained to find victims at crime scenes are making an excellent showing for themselves, detecting not only buried bodies, but also drowned ones.

For several years Vizslas have been used as therapy and service dogs. Because of their gentle and sensitive nature, Vizslas are able to communicate with institutionalized people without speaking, simply by showing love and trust.

With the advent of the Obedience Champion title, the Hunting test title, and the Agility titles, along with Field Championships, the possibility of multiple titles is a never-ending challenge to action-loving owners and their dogs. Vizlas have earned a place in canine history by being the first breed to earn the Triple Champion title and the Quintuple Champion Title.

Cooper through the Weave Poles. Photo © Tien Tran Photography.

Triple Ch. Cariad's Kutya Kai Costa on the day he earned his final OTCH point to become the first Triple Champion in AKC history. Owned by Marianne Megna.

TRIPLE CHAMPION
Cariad's Kutya Kai Costa

Cariad's Kutya Kai Costa made history not only for the Vizslas but also for the AKC by becoming the first dog of any breed to finish titles in three categories. Until then, no other dog had done so much to exemplify the versatility of a breed.

Kutya was owned and trained by Marianne and Robert Costa of Staten Island. He completed the requirements for his Breed Championship in 1976 and in that same year earned his CD in obedience and had started on his Field Championship. On October 16 in the following year he completed the Field Championship, making him a Dual Champion.

During the next two years, Kutya earned his CDX and UD obedience titles while working towards his Amateur Field Championship. He was the top obedience Vizsla in 1978, 1979, and 1980, as well as the fifth best Sporting Dog in Obedience, the first Vizsla to place in that elite category.

With the advent of the Obedience Trial Championship by the AKC, Kutya was in constant competition in the obedience ring to gain the required points for an OTCH. He gained his final points on October 25, 1980, becoming the first dog in history to gain the three titles: Breed Champion, Field Champion, and Obedience Trial Champion.

QUINTUPLE CHAMPION
Legacy's DeChartay

Another milepost in our breed's accomplishments took place in June 2000 when Chartay, at nine years of age, became the first dog to earn five championship titles in the 116-year history of the AKC. Owned and trained by Jack Sharkey of Virginia, Chartay earned her Breed Championship in 1993, her Field and Amateur Field titles in 1995, her OTCH in 1997, and her MACH title in June 2000.

"Chartay has earned a permanent place in the record books of AKC and is a very special dog that has used her breed's natural instincts and her love of competition to work with her owner in achieving this remarkable feat," said the AKC president.

SEARCH AND RESCUE

In the aftermath of the destruction of the World Trade Center in New York City, hundreds of Federal Emergency Management Agency (FEMA) certified search and rescue dogs of different breeds from all over the country came to the site to do the job they had been trained to do. Among the twisted steel and clouds of dust, a Vizsla, Prarie C'Cruiser Pistolpete, and his owner and handler Sharon Malnar helped search for survivors and victims. Search and rescue (SAR) dogs are accustomed to locating bodies under many conditions including in the aftermath of tornados and earthquakes, but the horrifying situation at this bombing site truly tested the stamina and courage of all the dogs involved.

Pete started his training on human scent at nine weeks and learned quickly. SAR uses hair, teeth, fingernails, skin, and other items in training. These items are hidden high in trees, in buildings behind light switches, in cars, under rocks, underground, and in lakes and streams. Pete and Sharon also learned how to work in areas where there was nothing to be found, since Pete had to be able to let Sharon search when a site was empty. When Pete found something, he touched it or went to Sharon and spoke to her and then rushed back to touch it again.

Sharon explains that you have to trust your dog in every situation, since he is the one that can tell you if anything is present or not. You have to trust that your dog does not lie—he will not say something is there if it isn't. Sharon feels that Pete made a name for the Vizsla within SAR because of his cadaver ability.

Besides being certified as an HRD (Human Remains Detection) dog with Canine Solutions International (CSI), Pete also had a Novice Agility title. Sharon and Pete have worked with local and national law enforcement agencies as well as Park Services and Game and Fish. They covered a lot of drownings, missing persons, possible murders, buried bodies, tornados and disasters, as well as being deployed to New York City on September 11, 2001. Internationally certified in forensic work and cold cases, Pete has also worked historical sites of civil war battlefields and very old graveyards.

Ch., FCh., AFCh., OTCH, MACH Legacy's DeChartay, UDX, MH, owned by Jack Sharkey, was the first dog in AKC history to earn five championship titles. Photo © Christina M. Freitag.

Prairie C'Cruiser Pistolpete (Pete), SAR dog owned by Sharon Malnar, has found blood and hair in this tree. Pete took part in the search and rescue efforts after the terrorist attack of the World Trade Center.

Kallmee Vizcaya's Sassy Dax is trained to find corpses and also old burial sites.

in October 1998. She also has worked with the FBI on several successful searches for murder victims

CANINE GOOD CITIZEN

The Canine Good Citizen program is a certification program that tests dogs in simulated everyday situations in a relaxed atmosphere. The purpose is to ensure that a dog can be a respected member of the community because he is trained and conditioned to act mannerly in the home, in public places, and with other dogs.

Most Vizslas are taught house manners to make them welcome family members, and now they are encouraged to function acceptably in public. Each dog must know how to respond to four basic commands: heel, sit, down, and stay. Response to these commands gives your dog the social skills that foster good citizenship. Passing a test gives your dog an AKC certificate proclaiming him to be a Canine Good Citizen (CGC). This is an award, not a title, but the training provides a firm foundation for participation in future activities.

Training results in a controlled dog, stimulated intelligence, and good manners. Training for the CGC test is fun and the activities are useful in everyday life. There are several steps in the test, which involve the dog accepting a stranger, sitting politely for petting, accepting grooming, walking correctly on a leash in a crowd, coming when called, responding calmly to the approach of another dog, jogger or bicycle, obeying a sit or down on command, and remaining calm with the owner out of sight.

Tests for this award are held at some of the larger dog shows with the information being printed in the show premium. Any dog participating must be over six months old and have proof of inoculations. Tests are also sponsored by dog clubs and service organizations, since CGC certification is basic for any therapy dog visiting institutionalized people.

Pete loved his work, but it may have been the cause of his early death at eight years of age. Exposed to many chemicals while working, any of which may have caused cancer of the liver, he died in August 2003—a tremendous loss to the Vizsla breed and to SAR.

Kallmee Vizcaya's Sassy Dax, owned and handled by Rita Martinez in California, is another Vizsla trained to find victims at crime scenes, but she was also involved with helping uncover an ancient Ohlone Indian burial site. One-thousand-year-old remains have been found in downtown Fremont. This was the first time that forensic dogs were used in the field of archeology to map a site for ancient bones. Dax is one of only four dogs chosen for the search. This work could lead to a new specialty for trained dogs. Artifacts as old as 3,200 years have been found in the area, which was once a prehistoric Indian village.

Dax was the first Scent Specific Specialist in Human Remains Detection in the state of California and the first Vizsla in the country to be certified for that work

THERAPY DOGS

Virtually every major newspaper and human interest magazine has featured stories about the therapeutic benefits of animals. Dog clubs all over the country have enlisted members with friendly and obedient dogs to visit nursing homes and other institutionalized residents. Associating with an animal provides physical and emotional benefits not only to healthy individuals, but also to those who are sick or emotionally ill. *Pet-facilitated therapy* refers to any treatment in which interaction with an animal is used as part of the healing process.

Although pet owners had been visiting nursing care centers with their dogs for years, it was not until 1980, when the organization Therapy Dogs International (TDI) was formed to unite and increase the number of therapy dogs available, that they gained recognition and hospitals and other institutions were alerted to the importance of animals as therapy. Therapy animals are not legally defined by federal law, although some states do have such laws. The dogs usually are personal pets

The balance in a therapy dog between calmness and friendliness is a difficult one. Even an excellent obedience-trained dog may not be a good therapy dog if he shows little interest in meeting people. An aloof dog may be calm, but may cause patients to feel rejected. A good therapy dog is calm, tolerant, and friendly. The visits must be pleasurable for all involved. You cannot force therapy work on a dog.

The successful therapy dog has been trained to maintain focus and respond to cues from his owner despite distractions. In a health care facility, the therapy dog can experience many environmental distractions: people bustling, food carts clanging, the clattering and beeping of equipment. The dog has to know to approach others only when permitted, perform specific behaviors on cue, ignore distractions, and have impeccable social manners. He also must possess excellent resiliency and adapt-

Int'l Ch. Eli's Akela Dragam, CD, SH, OA, NAJ, is a registered Pet Partner with the Delta Society, listens to a story. Owned by Kit Richards.

ability. The owner depends on his dog's ability to remain unstressed by unexpected emotional or physical outbursts or erratic behaviors from people who have Alzheimer's, dementia, and autism. One moment a dog might be hugged tightly while a patient weeps uncontrollably and the next he can be pushed away when the person no longer wants to interact with the dog. This requires enormous flexibility in a dog's attitude.

A good therapy dog pays little attention to age or physical ability, but accepts people as they are. Autistic children, unable to respond to anything else, have bonded immediately with friendly visiting therapy dogs. Unresponsive, older patients have

Ch. Acadian's Copper Cajon, CD, owned by Bev Edwards, spends time giving demonstrations on service and therapy dogs.

taken a renewed lease on life after a visit from a dog that they can relate to. Many in hospitals and nursing homes have had to give up pet ownership and miss the interaction. An animal visit can be a welcome distraction from pain and infirmity. People often talk to dogs and share with them their thoughts, feelings, and memories. Petting the dog encourages stretching, turning. and use of hands and arms. Stroking a dog has been proven to reduce blood pressure.

Many Vizsla owners across the country have become interested in this program. While most therapy dogs are also involved with obedience or agility, many are also show and field dogs. Used to different people and different situations, these dogs visit all kinds of day care centers, VA hospitals, nursing homes and children's hospitals, bringing joy to sometimes depressing situations.

SERVICE DOGS

The use of a trained service dog can reduce a disabled person's need for a human attendant. For example, a dog trained to help a person walk might be referred to by different sources as a "mobility dog," or a "support dog." In addition to the wide variety of terms used, many service dogs are cross-trained to perform more than one category of work, such as guide and mobility for a person who is blind and has severe arthritis. Most individuals choose to identify their dogs generically as "service dogs" because it stresses the dog's role for them without disclosing the specific nature of their particular disability.

Service animals are legally defined and are trained to meet the disability-related needs of handlers. Federal laws protect the rights of those individuals by allowing them to be accompanied by their dogs in public places. Service animals are not considered pets.

According to the Americans with Disabilities Act (ADA, 1990), a dog is considered a service dog if he has been individually trained to do work or perform tasks for the benefit of a person with a disability. A disability is a mental or physical condition which substantially limits a major life activity such as caring for one's self, performing manual tasks, walking, seeing, hearing, speaking, breathing, learning, and working. Some disabilities many not be visible, such as deafness, epilepsy, and psychiatric conditions.

Service dogs are trained to do specific tasks for their handlers, but not for others. Their work demands that they focus exclusively on the handler, ignore other people, and work reliably amidst many distractions. Service dogs generally interact with others only when directed to do so by their handlers. They must remain neutral to all types of environmental stimuli—such as car horns honking, buses backfiring, people whistling, shopping carts, and even children who grab or hug the dog without warning—so that they can be considered reliable when responding to a handler cue. These dogs provide a source of enthusiastic help, unconditional love, and a sense of freedom and independence.

Most service organizations depend on donations of puppies or dogs. These dogs must exhibit intelligence, sound temperament, physical soundness, and adaptability. Many training schools select dogs to assist blind, hearing-impaired and physically challenged persons, and give extensive obedience training. Other schools train support dogs to help with balanced walking and wheelchair movement. Often these schools not only teach dogs to bring independence to disabled people, but also teach individuals the leadership skills necessary to master their dogs and gain the most from their use. They also provide dignity and purpose for dogs that are eager, anxious, and capable of working.

The training of a hearing dog takes three to four months and training a service dog requires six months to a year. During this time the dog is taught house manners, basic obedience commands using both hand and voice signals, as well as sound response, retrieval, and other specialized work. Both guide dogs for the blind and the hearing and service dogs are socialized and trained to work and behave in public situations like restaurants, malls, and public transportation, as well as around other dogs and animals.

The Vizsla meets every criteria for a service dog, and after years of focus on the Golden and Labrador Retrievers, the service dog associations are now taking a longer look at this breed. Concerned over the inability of the young, old, blind or handicapped person to groom and handle the larger, stronger Retriever, schools now see that the Vizsla fills the need for a small but robust, intelligent, easy-care companion.

When approaching a service dog and handler, it is correct procedure to speak first to the person. Do not touch either the ser-

Skidaddle's Sassy Sage Vennka, RPP, is an Advanced Registered Pet Partner (Delta Society), and at fifteen years old, is still used for demonstrations. Owned by Kit Richards.

vice dog or his person without first asking permission. Touching the service dog might distract him from his work. Touching the person might be interpreted as assault. Resist the temptation to offer treats to a service dog.

RALLY

Rally is called the bridge between the Canine Good Citizen and formal training for competition in the obedience ring. It requires strong teamwork in its combination of obedience and agility. It is a good confidence-builder for dogs and their owners since it is informal and handlers are encouraged to talk to their dogs as they perform the exercises. The course is set up with numbered stations, with instructions for a particular exercise posted at each station. The dog heals on leash, with no commands from the judge after the start. The judge will make deductions for errors, but will be less exacting than in the obedience ring.

Your Vizsla benefits from Rally because he loves working closely with you, and you will benefit from teaching him to focus in the ring as he does in practice. Both of you will be better prepared for showing in regular obedience classes when the time comes. The Rally A class provides fun competition while preparing beginning teams for the Novice and agility classes. Rally B class is for the advanced exhibitors.

FLYBALL

Flyball is a game played by highly energized dogs that are ball-crazy. It is a very noisy sport with a lot of excitement, barking, and cheering dog owners and spectators. It is actually a relay race, with a team consisting of four main dogs and handlers and two alternate dogs with handlers. In competition, two teams compete against each other in two side-by-side racing lanes, each lane containing four jumps (called hurdles) set ten feet apart. The racing lane is 102 feet overall—51 feet down and 51 feet back, with the last hurdle placed 15 feet from the flyball box. A flyball box is a wedge-shaped box with a spring-loaded front that releases a tennis ball when the dog steps on it.

At a flyball tournament, a green electric timing light records the total time each team takes to finish their race. The first dog can get a running start but cannot break the laser beam at the start/finish line before the green light. The three remaining dogs on the team cannot pass the start/finish line before the previous dog returns. All the returning dogs must jump all of the hurdles and must have the tennis ball in their mouths as they cross the start/finish line.

The first dog running should be at the start/finish line as it turns green, and he must be completely focused. He jumps over the four hurdles, pushes the ball box, a ball flies out that he catches, and he returns over the four hurdles. The second dog and first

dog should pass nose to nose at the start/finish line. The relay continues until all four dogs have run.

Several years ago at the big Houston show in the Astrodome, a team of rescued Vizslas competed in the flyball competition and won. Dogs of every breed and from all over the country have fun in this highly competitive sport. Vizslas are fast, active, and enthusiastic, so this is a wonderful sport for them, although not AKC sanctioned.

NAVHDA

On the continent, and among a group of people in North America who founded the North American Versatile Hunting Dog Association (NAVHDA) in 1969, the term "versatile" is interpreted to mean a dog that can point game, retrieve from land and water, and track wounded game.

NAVHDA is a non-profit organization whose purpose is to foster, promote, and protect the versatile hunting dog breeds. It does this through sponsoring field tests that provide standards for evaluating the dogs with the ultimate objective being the conservation of game by encouraging hunters to have dogs well trained to work both before and after the shot.

There are two types of versatility tests: Natural Ability tests and Utility Field tests. In the Natural Ability test the dog is judged only on his hereditary characteristics, and he is only eligible for this test up to sixteen months of age. The test covers seven different hereditary characteristics that should disclose the latent natural abilities that are required to develop a dog into a versatile hunter.

Natural abilities manifest themselves at an early age and any hereditary flaws will show up in a young dog. It is the Natural Abilities test that a breeder looks to in order to assess his present breeding program or plan a future one. No other test is so important for the breeder who is honestly interested in improving his breeding program.

Each dog is tested for the following: use of nose, search, love for water, pointing, tracking, desire to work, and cooperation.

The Utility Field test measures not only the natural ability but responsiveness and obedience. In critiquing the dogs in terms of hunting instinct and trainability, the NAVHDA judges also evaluate each dog for basic conformation and temperament. This test is designed to test a dog's usefulness for the on-foot hunter in all phases of hunting—before and after the shot, in field and marsh, and on different species of game. A Utility Field dog should display self-confidence in the presence of game as well as when the gun is fired. He should be steady without a command until ordered to retrieve. On command, he should go to the bird, pick it up, and return happily to his handler.

Another function of NAVHDA is to help owners of versatile hunting dogs enjoy their dogs through proper training. Before NAVHDA, many hunters never had the opportunity to learn firsthand the various steps involved in training.

VCA VERSATILITY TESTS

Versatility tests were designed by the Vizsla Club of America to help in the overall improvement of the breed by promoting the Vizsla as a versatile, attractive, obedient hunting dog, and to encourage breeders to breed for the all-around dog. All licensed Vizsla clubs are eligible to hold versatility tests as long as the club follows the guidelines set up by the VCA. Since the program is a VCA event, the results of each test are sent to the versatility chairman appointed by the VCA. The chairman is responsible for all the ratings on each dog and grades them as "pass" or "fail."

The Versatility Test consists of three categories: Field, Obedience, and Conformation. In order to receive a Versatility Certificate, an eligible Vizsla must pass all three category tests three times under three different judges.

Searching out the bird in a field of straw. Photo © Christina M. Freitag.

Any registered Vizsla over six months of age may be entered in the Field or Obedience category, but he must be twelve months old to be entered in the Conformation test. Your dog may be entered in as many Field and Obedience tests as it takes to earn a "pass," but there is a limit of three failures in the Conformation class, after which a dog is no longer eligible for entry.

Field Test Requirements

This test consists of at least ten minutes, but not more than fifteen, in the backcourse, and at least five minutes, but not more than eight, in the birdfield in which two game birds have been planted.

The Vizsla must show a natural desire to hunt and must locate, point, and retrieve. He must show a keen willingness and desire to find game, hunt with intelligence, and show an aggressive style of running. He also must be obedient and respond to commands.

In the birdfield he must locate the bird and then point with style. After the bird is shot, he must be willing to retrieve it without mauling or mouthing it.

Ch. Huntwyck's Woodland Cooper, VCD2, UD, TD, SH, MX, MXJ, NJP, VC. Owned by Melissa Thomas.

Any Vizsla that is a Field Champion, an Amateur Field Champion, the holder of Senior or Master Hunter titles, or has had a placement in three field trial retrieving tests may receive his Field Certificate without testing, upon providing proof of performance.

Conformation Requirements

Any Vizsla that is already a Breed Champion and is over eighteen months of age need only be measured to apply for a Conformation Certificate.

If he is not already a Breed Champion, three major wins under three different judges in any class but Puppy will suffice in applying for the certificate, along with the age and measurement requirements. All measurements must be conducted by a Versatility Test committee or test judge at a test site.

Obedience Test Requirements

Any Vizsla that has already earned any obedience title is eligible for his Obedience Certificate simply by applying to the Versatility chairman. A Vizsla taking the Obedience Test must score at least fifty percent of the points required for each exercise.

Heel on Lead	(20 points)
Heel Free	(20 points)
Stand for Examination	(30 points)
Recall	(30 points)
Stay	(30 points)

Qualifying dogs receive a Certificate of Versatility from the VCA and the letters VD may be used after their registered names in VCA events.

CHAPTER THIRTEEN

Preventative Health Care

Preventative health care is a wise investment since the prevention of viruses and diet problems cost substantially less than any treatment. Good health is the result of a simple program of exercise, training, vaccinations, dietary management, and regular veterinarian checkups.

Close association with your veterinarian is important. Select one who is willing to give the time to answer any questions regarding your Vizsla's general well-being, but do not wait until the annual checkup to present him with a list of problems. Learn which part of a preventative health program you can handle at home, and which needs a skilled professional.

NORMAL VITAL SIGNS

Unless you know what is normal for your dog, you will not be able to recognize a problem when it arises. The normal temperature for an adult dog is 100 to 102°F. Using a digital thermometer, coat the tip lightly with Vaseline and insert half of it into the anus. Hold it there until it beeps, and do not let your dog sit.

A well dog breathes ten to thirty times per minute, but after any exercise or stress this rate will increase. Watch your Vizsla as he breathes through his nose while lying quietly and count the chest movements.

The average heart rate of an adult dog is 70 to 130 beats per minute; puppies have a faster rate. The beat, or pulse, should be firm and steady. With your dog lying down, take your index and middle finger and press on the inside of his thigh near the point where his leg joins the body. You will be touching his femoral artery which reflects the heartbeat. Count the beats for one minute, or count for 6 seconds and multiply by 10.

Your dog's urine should be a clear yellow color. Bloody or cloudy urine is indicative of a problem. The intensity of the color will increase if the quantity that he excretes decreases. A sudden increase in water intake along with the volume of urine produced may be an indication of disease.

Small blood vessels, or capillaries, carry the blood supply to the skin. Pressing a finger against your Vizsla's gums will cause the gums to grow pale. When you remove your finger, that area should refill with blood and regain the normal pink color rapidly (within 1 second). A slow return to color (more than 3 seconds) could indicate shock or anemia.

A healthy dog has clear, bright eyes, a wet nose, and shiny coat. He carries moderate weight, evidenced by the ability to feel, but not see, the ribs when he is standing. A healthy dog is alert, interested and responsive. A dog that is ill may act depressed, uninterested, or may uncharacteristically seek out a

How to Recognize a Healthy Versus a Sick Dog

Signs of a Healthy Dog

Normal temperature 101 to 101.5°F
Normal pulse rate 70 to 130 beats per minute
Normal respiration 10 to 30 per minute
Eyes clear
Nose moist
Gums pink
Appetite good
Glossy coat
Active and alert

Signs of Illness

Temperature 102°F or above, or under 100°F
Rapid or slow pulse when dog is resting
Labored breathing
Eyes dull, cloudy, red, watery, or filled with pus
Pale gums
Change in appetite
Dull coat
Drinking increased amounts of water
Change in behavior; hyperactivity, listlessness
Blood in stool, urine, or vomit
Constipation or diarrhea
Convulsions
Dehydration
Lameness
Pain in abdomen, limbs, ears, etc.
Pawing or scratching excessively at an area
Strong odor from mouth or anus
Stomach distended
Straining to urinate
Vomiting
Weakness

quiet corner to be alone. His eyes or coat may look dull. You may notice a change from his normal behavior. He may have runny eyes or nose, cough, have loose stools, lose his appetite, or drink excessive amounts of water.

By making a point of examining your puppy or adult dog every day, you can easily monitor his overall health at home and become aware of any signs of a low level of health or of impending problems.

EAR PROBLEMS

Vizslas can be prone to ear problems since their ears hang down and prevent good air circulation. The inside forms a warm incubation area for ear mites and infections. A dog with ear infection will hold his head low and shake or scratch at it. The external ear will be inflamed and sore and will have a smelly discharge.

Routine cleaning of the ear canal is not usually necessary and may be contraindicated in the healthy dog, Mild to moderate amounts of wax, or cerumen, is normal. Cerumen has antibacterial properties which help to reduce the overpopulation of bacteria and yeast. Cleaning, when necessary, should be complete and non-irritating. A mixture of vinegar/water (1:10) is a good degreasing solution to remove wax and dry excessive moisture in the ear canal. The liquid should be gently applied in the canal, the ear massaged to allow breakup of the cerumen, and cotton balls used to wipe out the excess liquid. Never put anything farther down into the ear canal than you can see. To do so only pushes the material farther into the canal and could potentially rupture the eardrum. Never use ear powder, as it builds up, predisposing the ear to the development of secondary infections.

Accumulation of cellular debris and exudates indicate the presence of ear disease. Swabs of this material should be cleaned out and the ear canal rinsed. The color, texture and odor of the exudate can provide clues regarding the underlying primary cause of the inflammation. Dark brown, granular, dry discharge (coffee grounds) characterizes infestation of ear mites. The ear mites live on the surface of the ear canal and feed on it by piercing the skin and causing irritation, infection, and discharge. Ear mites can possibly be controlled by constant supervision and treatment and the administration of antibiotic ointment for the bacterial infection.

A moist brown discharge tends to be associated with bacteria and yeast infections. An overgrowth of yeast may occur following antibiotic therapy. The discharge is thick, dark, and sweet-smelling. Purulent creamy to yellow discharge is most often seen with bacteria such as Pseudomonas. Thorough cleaning of the ear canal is vitally important for successful management of otitis for several reasons. Wax and oily cellular debris may be irritating, prevent medication from contacting the canal epithelium, and produce a favorable environment for microorganisms to proliferate. They can also inactivate certain antibiotics.

Cerumene is an agent that will emulsify the waxes and flush them more readily from the ear canal. A drying agent such as Epi-Otic can be applied after the ear has been cleaned and is relatively dry. Cleaning cannot be done on very swollen, partially closed, ulcerated or painful ears. Such cases need to be treated symptomatically to start with and then cleaned later when the inflammation has been reduced.

Reasons for ear irritation include climatic variations, since humidity, rainfall, and temperature correlate positively with increases in otitis. Dogs used for activities in the field are at increased risk for ear disease since foreign bodies, especially plant material such as foxtails, sand, loose hair, and impacted wax often become trapped in the canal.

Any increase in the moisture of the ear canal can lead to softening and/or wasting of the tissue. Moisture in the canal introduced by swimming, bathing, or poor cleaning methods, may cause inflammation of the external part of the ear canal. A combination of water retention and increased gland activity and secondary infections may be responsible for disease. Vizslas that are swimming a lot may benefit from prophylactic treatment with a drying agent.

Inhalant allergy is common in Vizslas. Allergic dogs tend to have itchy feet and itchy ears. They are predisposed to secondary skin and ear infections that tend to recur after treatment unless the underlying allergy is well controlled. The clinical signs are seasonal. Diagnosis is based on history, clinical signs, exclusion of other diseases, and skin tests. Food allergies should be considered in any young dog. Contact allergy can result from medications used to treat the otitis (ear inflammation) and will only make it worse.

Endocrine disorders such as hypothyroidism and Cushing's disease are the most common endocrine diseases that can cause otitis. If a middle-aged dog keeps relapsing with otitis and is not itchy, then endocrine diseases should be considered as possible underlying causes, along with autoimmune disorders such as lupus.

Ch. Acadian's Copper Cajon, CD. Owned by Bev Edwards.

EYE PROBLEMS

An inflamed eye may be caused by almost any kind of foreign object such as dirt, sand, pieces of bark, pollen, chemicals, and other infecting material. If you see your Vizsla squinting, look under the eyelids. If you find any foreign material in his eye, remove it by flushing it with warm water or eye drops, or even by using the tip of a handkerchief. If the eye is red and irritated, your veterinarian can prescribe an eye ointment for treatment.

Due to a slack, inverted lower eye margin in many Vizslas, a pale mucous discharge will often collect. A daily check and cleaning of your dog's eyes may be necessary. If the discharge is yellow, it may indicate an infection and the use of antibiotic ointment may be indicated.

Letting your dog hang his head out of a moving automobile can result in eye injuries from flying stones and debris. An injury to the eye can ulcerate the cornea, causing excessive pain and, ultimately, loss of sight.

TOOTH CARE AND GUM DISEASE

Gingivitis, or inflammation of the gums, is characterized by tender gums that bleed when probed. Pockets alongside the teeth retain food which causes bacterial infections that spread to the roots, destroying the support of the tooth within the jaw. Without treatment, extraction of the tooth may become necessary if the root becomes abscessed.

Examine your Vizsla's teeth periodically for any buildup of dental plaque, or tartar, which is an incrustation on the teeth consisting of salivary secretions, food residue, and various salts. Left uncleaned, it can cause severe gum inflammation. Blood on the gum line and a bad odor are the best indication of trouble, since dogs often do not show any signs of pain or tenderness as they chew.

Weekly brushing of your dog's teeth with a soft toothbrush and paste or cleaner will remove food particles and buildup of tartar. Do not use your own toothpaste on your dog's teeth. There are pastes specially made for a dog's system. If your dog already has a layer of tartar, it will be necessary to use a dental scaling tool to remove it. Since Vizslas like to chew on sticks and stones, check also for broken or damaged teeth. Your veterinarian can also do a twice-yearly cleaning with a light anesthetic and a fast laser tool.

ANAL GLANDS

The two anal glands are located on each side of the anus. They are about the size of small cherries and can enlarge if they get overfilled with secretions. Normal bowel movements help to express the glands and keep them from becoming irritated, but soft stools caused by incorrect diet or parasites will lead to retention, impaction, and eventual infection of the glands.

Scooting on the rear may not always be a sign of irritation by worms. If your dog shows discomfort in sitting, pain, or constant licking at the anus, it could be from impacted anal glands. Continued impaction can cause abscesses.

Learn to express the anal glands yourself since chronic problems can cause frequent trips to the veterinarian. These smelly secretions can be expressed with a little practice. Apply gentle pressure with a thumb and forefinger on each side, just below the anus. Milk each gland toward the anal opening. Be sure to cover the area with a paper towel, and stand to one side, as the secretions may come shooting out under pressure.

FOOT PROBLEMS

Occasionally too much running over wet ground, or even an eczema condition, will bring about an angry, sweating, redness between your Vizsla's toes. Foot trouble of this kind is aggravating. The first sign you may have of anything wrong is when your dog starts limping or licking at a foot. For temporary relief, sprinkle human foot powder, or even cornstarch, between the toes to relieve the pain and redness. There are several good fungal foot powders on the market which will dry up the moisture which is causing the irritation. If the condition persists, your veterinarian may have to take a culture to determine the exact cause in order to prescribe treatment. If the irritation is caused by a contact allergy, it may be from the secretions of several night-crawling worms. Early morning dew promotes the exposure to your dog's feet. Keeping your Vizsla inside until the grass dries is impossible, so boots may be necessary. Boots can be bought in most pet supply catalogs or stores. Keeping the area between the toes dry can go far in relieving the irritation and licking.

If the irritation is caused by a food allergy and is also apparent on other parts of the body, such as the eyes and ears, a change of diet may be warranted.

GASTRIC TORSION (BLOAT)

Bloat is an emergency situation. It has been linked to the feeding of dry food, large consumption of water, gas or swallowed air, and exercise too soon after eating.

Bloat is associated with all deep-chested breeds and can occur at any age. Signs are prostration, severe abdominal distention, unsuccessful attempts at vomiting, and difficulty in breathing. The distention of the stomach may cause it to rotate at the opening into the intestines. This torsion cuts off the blood flow, sending your dog into shock. Emergency treatment will be required to release the gasses trapped by the rotation and to counter the shock. Surgery may be necessary to reposition the stomach. Without immediate professional help, your dog can die from gastric hemorrhage and ulceration, severe electrolyte disturbances, and shock.

Feeding two smaller meals a day, instead of one large one, may help to prevent bloat. Moisten dry meal before feeding in order to prevent a large consumption of water after eating, and restrain your dog from excessive exercise both before and after eating.

CANINE HIP DYSPLASIA

Hip dysplasia occurs in almost every breed that matures at over twenty-five pounds. *Dysplasia* is a term applied to any abnormality of a joint, and hip dysplasia is a condition where the hip joint is malformed. Instead of fitting neatly between the top of the thigh bone and the pelvis, the edges are rough and uneven, losing close contact and resulting in a looseness in the joint. The shallow acetabulum, which is a cup-shaped socket of the hip joint that receives the head of the femur, can be too flat to hold the femur in place.

Generally, hip dysplasia can be controlled and prevented by breeding only Vizslas that have been X-rayed and verified as sound. While it has been proven that the problem is usually inherited, evidence exists to suggest that environment also plays a big role in the development of bad hips.

The condition can start in the whelping box with a smooth surface, which presents a problem to the small puppy trying to get on his feet. Raising a litter on a blanket will offer firm footing. Smooth, slippery tiles or linoleum floors would compound the problem as the young puppy learns to run and play. Hip dysplasia can also be the result of poor nutrition—a lack of vitamin C causes weak muscles and ligaments around the joints. It can also be a disease affecting the elasticity of the pectineus muscle. The pectineus is a small, strong, spindle-shaped muscle on the inner surface of the thigh. It originates on the lower surface of the pelvis and has a broad body that tapers into a long tendon attached along the femur. The hip joint changes are not primary; they are seen as secondary changes.

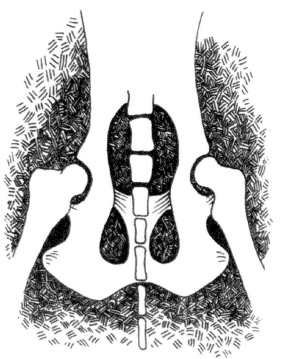 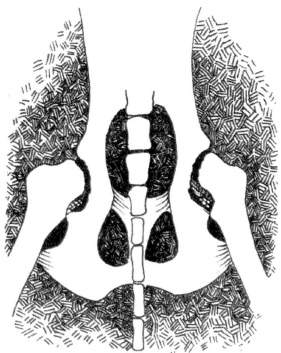

Normal hips with well-rounded ball and socket.   *Severe hip dysplasia, with flattening of ball and socket.*

It has been shown that a degenerative lesion occurs in the spinal cord at the level of the fourth and fifth lumbar vertebrae and nerve, which is the loin area. This lesion in the spinal cord is in the neuropathway of the pectineus muscle. Once the nerve is destroyed at the spinal cord, changes occur in the pectineus muscle. This degeneration begins to appear in the muscle between the 10th and 121st day of age. Once the pectineus muscle becomes diseased as a result of the alteration of its blood supply, its growth stops. The muscle does not grow, but the shaft of the femur continues to grow and lengthen. Because of this, an upward pressure develops, with the femoral head resting against the rim of the acetabulum. As the pectineus muscle stops its growth, and the shaft of the femur continues to grow, the rim of the acetabulum begins to deflect upwards due to the constant pressure applied to the femoral head. This produces the shallow socket that is seen in radiographically evident hip dysplasia. In extremely painful cases, surgery to sever the pectineus muscle can relieve both lameness and pain.

Whatever the cause, it is heartbreaking for the owner when his young Vizsla is suddenly unable to get up on his hind legs or is reluctant to run, play, or climb stairs. Decreased activity may be the first indication of the problem, along with an uneven gait with the rear legs moving together under the dog because of the inability to extend them back. The rear legs will slant in a "cow-hocked" position from the weak muscles.

Another hip dysplasia suspect is the young adult that noticeably lacks rear angulation and appears to have an extremely well developed front; he must carry the weight of his body forward. He will stand with his hind legs close together and tucked under his body, thus shifting his weight forward.

The disease is a progressive one and, at times, even crippling, but many dogs build a muscle mass around the affected joint, holding it in place, and show no signs at all of the abnormality. However, as an affected dog ages, arthritis may present a problem, depending on the severity of the dysplasia.

Providing your Vizsla with a warm, soft bed away from drafts, keeping his weight down, giving anti-inflammatory medication, and providing moderate exercise will ensure a comfortable life most of the time. Spaying or neutering is a necessity, since no Vizsla diagnosed with any degree of hip dysplasia should ever be used for breeding.

Vizslas have a low incidence of dysplasia compared to many other breeds of the same size. The use of diagnostic X-rays and responsible breeding practices have kept the problem to a minimum. The hip X-ray has to be performed by a veterinarian while your Vizsla is under a light anesthesia in order to keep him absolutely still and get the best picture. The X-ray should be sent to the Orthopedic Foundation for Animals for diagnosis and certification. Your dog has to be at least two years of age to be issued a number and certification of fair, good, or excellent.

Fences keep your dogs safely in the yard and stray dogs out.

VIRUSES AND VACCINATIONS

The goal of vaccination is to stimulate your dog's own immune system by giving a killed or weakened form of an organism. The animal will then be protected from becoming ill when exposed to the real disease. For the most part, veterinary vaccines are safe and efficacious and have saved many animals' lives. An important point to remember is that vaccination is a medical procedure that should include the same considerations and reasoning required when deciding to use any medical treatment or surgical procedure. The goal should be to vaccinate individual animals less frequently and only for disease for which there is a risk of exposure. The potential risk of exposure to various diseases must be determined for each individual dog.

Newborns can respond immunologically at birth, but the response is slow and inferior compared to older dogs. Protection for newborns is provided by antibodies that are passed in the colostrum from the dam to the puppies during their first twenty-four to seventy-two hours after birth. Almost ninety percent of the maternal antibodies come from the colostrum, while only two to eighteen percent of antibodies are transferred in utero. The amount of antibody each puppy receives depends on the antibody titer of the dam and how much colostrum each puppy receives. Maternal antibodies can interfere with the ability of puppies to respond to vaccination by inactivating the vaccine just as if it was the real disease. Vaccination, therefore, starts at six to eight weeks of age when the levels of maternal antibodies are waning. This is a critical period of susceptibility to disease for puppies when there are not enough maternal antibodies to protect the puppy from disease, but too many antibodies to allow for active immunization. Exposure to disease, especially parvovirus, at this time may result in sick puppies even though they have received one or more vaccinations.

If humans generally receive only childhood vaccinations, then why do dogs have annual revaccinations through their entire lives? This has been an area of intense research and controversy in veterinary medicine for the past few years. Most vaccines produced before 1995 were only evaluated for efficacy for several weeks after the last vaccination was given and the recommendations for annual revaccination were arbitrary, even then. Most veterinarians are now evaluating the use of titers to determine how often vaccine is needed in individual dogs. The exception, of course, is rabies vaccine that must provide a one- or three-year duration of immunity in order to comply with laws for a state or county.

Core vaccines are those which should be given to every dog to provide protection against diseases that are serious, common, or a risk to humans. These include parvovirus, distemper, adenovirus (infectious hepatitis), and rabies. Non-core vaccines are those given on the basis of risk assessment. These vaccines include coronavirus, parainfluenza, leptospirosis, bordetella, Lyme disease, and giardia.

The two most common types of vaccine are modified live and killed. The infectious agent in modified live (MLV) vaccine has been modified so that it will produce an immune response but will not cause disease as it replicates in the body. The advantages of MLV vaccines are that they provide rapid protection of a long duration, are less allergenic, overcome maternal antibodies more quickly, and can protect with one dose. Killed vaccines have the advantage of being safer in immunocompromised animals, and more stable in storage. The disadvantages of using killed vaccines, however, are that they are likely to cause allergic reactions because they contain more foreign proteins, and they require that two doses be given initially, along with more frequent revaccinations.

Not all vaccines will effectively immunize due to host factors, vaccine factors or human factors. Host factors include whether the dog is incubating a disease or is debilitated or malnourished, has a high temperature, or has existing maternal antibodies. Vaccine factors that may cause failure to immunize include improper storage or handling. Human factors that cause vaccine failure are improper vaccination protocol, improper mixing, improper route of administration, and vaccine interference.

Distemper

Distemper is an airborne virus, and droplet infection from secretions passed by an infected animal is the main source. The illness usually begins with an elevated temperature lasting one to three days, slowly subsiding, and recurring again in a few days, along with purulent material in the eyes, diarrhea, listlessness, vomiting, cold-like symptoms of a runny nose and coughing, and, in a severe case, convulsions and paralysis. Any chance of recovery is poor and intensive care is necessary over a long period of time.

Vaccinations against distemper usually produce solid, long-lasting immunity. If distemper in puppies is a problem, a measles vaccine can be used for the first vaccination between eight to twelve weeks of age. It will protect puppies from distemper if they still have maternal antibodies. Puppies receiving the measles vaccine require two more distemper vaccinations to provide full immunity.

Infectious Hepatitis

Hepatitis is a highly contagious disease with signs varying from a slight fever and congestion of the mucous membranes to severe depression, vomiting, lack of appetite, intense thirst, and a blue cloudiness over the cornea of the eye. There is a direct correlation between the severity of the disease and blood clotting time. Controlling a hemorrhage is difficult for that reason, and a long recovery period with antibiotics, vitamins, and close nursing care is required. The main route of infection is from urine, feces, and saliva from an infected animal, and the mortality rate is highest in young dogs that may have a low level of passive antibodies when exposed.

Leptospirosis

Leptospirosis is spread by a bacterial infection in the urine of a diseased animal, usually a rat. It can enter your Vizsla's system through a break in the skin, or if he drinks urine-contaminated water. The disease can

Your Dog's Medicine Chest

Include the following items:

A rectal thermometer
Liquid antiseptic soap such as *Betadine®*
Cotton swabs and cotton balls
Hydrogen peroxide
Gauze pads and bandage wrap
Clean towels
Blunt-nosed scissors
Styptic powder to control bleeding
Kaopectate® concentrate
Biosol M® or *Amforal®* for diarrhea
Rectal suppositories
Artificial tears or boric acid eyewash
Gauze or nylon stocking for muzzle
Dramamine® for motion sickness
Otocide® for ear mites
Antacid tablets
Panalog® neomycin sulfate wound ointment
Antibiotic or sulfa tablets
Variton® cream for moist eczema
Bitter Apple® to prevent chewing
Activated charcoal as universal poison antidote

Conversion table for medications:

16 drops = 1 cc or 1/4 tsp.
5cc = 1 tsp.
15 cc = 1 tablespoon
1oz = 30 cc or 2 tablespoons
1 qt = 1 liter; 4 cups

Dosage by weight of dog:

Aspirin—one 5-grain tablet per 30 lbs. every six hours
Charcoal—one tablespoon in four ounces of water per 30 lbs.
Dramamine—25 to 50 mg one-half hour before traveling
Kaopectate—one teaspoon regular strength per 5 lbs. every four hours
Milk of Magnesia—one teaspoon per 10 lbs. every six hours

---

have a sudden onset with weakness, vomiting, high fever, lack of appetite, jaundice, ulcers in the mouth, extreme weight loss, and mild conjunctivitis. In a few days the body temperature may drop as low as 97°F with breathing and swallowing becoming difficult. Symptoms include increased urination, thirst, bloody diarrhea, and vomiting.

Because of the serious damage to the kidneys and liver, intensive care is necessary, along with antibiotics and control of vomiting and diarrhea. Rodent control is important to reduce the chance of exposure to any rodents carrying the disease. Leptospira bacterin is the most allergic component of the majority of the vaccines and can result in anaphylaxis. Vaccination reduces the severity of the disease but does not eliminate the possibility of a dog becoming a carrier. Any immunity that is developed is of short duration (six to eight months.) Puppies should not be given the lepto vaccine until they are nine weeks of age, because the bacterin can be immunosuppressive in young pups.

Kennel Cough

Infectious tracheobronchitis can be caused by multiple agents that include parainfluenza, bordetella, and adenovirus. It is especially contagious among dogs kept together in a kennel situation. It is evidenced by harsh and persistent cough accompanied by gagging. The slightest bit of pressure on a collar will set off the coughing reflex.

Quiet and rest are necessary as the cough may hang on for as long as three weeks. While it is not usually serious in the adult Vizsla unless complicated by pneumonia, kennel cough is a potential danger to young puppies. The best protection seems to be from a modified live combination product of parainfluenza and bordetella that is given intranasally. The intranasal product begins protecting within four days by stimulating local immunity in the nasal cavity. The injectable form of vaccine is not as effective as the intranasal vaccine due to the mucosal nature of the disease. Two doses are required for protection.

Parvovirus

Every dog in the country, no matter where he lives, should be vaccinated for this disease. It is a highly contagious gastrointestinal virus which strikes without much warning and can cause death within twelve hours. It is especially dangerous, and most often fatal, to young puppies. It can easily be carried home on your shoes or clothes since the virus can persist in a kennel area, soil, or elsewhere for six months or more. Maternal antibodies can interfere with active immunization so there is a critical period of susceptibility.

The first sign of parvo is a high temperature accompanied by severe vomiting. Diarrhea starts with grayish or yellow-gray stools, often foul-smelling and streaked with blood. Other symptoms are loss of appetite, depression, and rapid dehydration with sunken eyes and dry, inelastic skin. Without immediate professional help, the survival rate is low, and collapse is possible within a few hours. Due to its sudden onset, this is probably the most serious gastrointestinal virus there is.

If you have had a Vizsla ill from parvo, do not bring another dog into your house unless he has had sufficient vaccinations against this disease.

Coronavirus

Coronavirus is primarily a disease of puppies and is self-limiting. Although similar to parvovirus, coronavirus is usually not as severe or deadly if the diarrhea is brought under control. Carried in the feces of an infected animal that may shed the virus for three weeks or more, coronavirus may cause repeated illnesses. Fever is mild or absent, and the virus brings about a sudden onset of diarrhea, vomiting, and mental depression. Vomiting usually decreases in frequency after the first day or two, but diarrhea may continue as an oozing of frothy yellow-orange, semi-solid material with an offensive odor. It may be projectile and often bloody.

Good supportive care is necessary to prevent dehydration, especially in a puppy, and effective sanitation and hygiene are essential, as the virus is highly contagious. Vaccination should be considered in a kennel situation with confirmed coronavirus illness in young puppies.

Rabies

Rabies is a deadly viral disease that is transmitted in the saliva of an infected animal by way of a bite or break in the skin. Infection may not be evident for at least two weeks or up to six months, but when the symptoms show, death is usually within five days. The virus travels to the spinal cord and then spreads to the brain, invades the salivary glands, and rapidly becomes infectious. It can be transmitted even though no obvious signs are showing. Symptoms are first evident in the way an animal starts behaving. He becomes excitable and aggressive, and from there, goes to being withdrawn and seeking solitude. Within three days he will show signs of becoming vicious and attack anything at the slightest move.

The disease rapidly progresses to the onset of paralysis, causing the mouth to hang open and drool from the inability to swallow. The paralysis spreads rapidly, and coma and death follow in a short time.

Rabies is a tragic disease. A Vizsla working in the field can be exposed to a rabid animal, but it can also happen in any suburban or rural yard. An unvaccinated dog bitten by a rabid animal has to be destroyed. Rabies vaccine is a killed product and highly allergenic, but animals can be protected with one dose. Rabies vaccination is required by law and the requirements for revaccinating vary from one to three years.

Lyme Disease

Ninety-nine percent of Lyme disease cases occur in the northeast and mid-Atlantic coast, the upper Midwest near the Great Lakes and the Pacific northwest. Vaccines should be given in these "at risk" areas, beginning with puppies at nine to twelve weeks, repeated in three weeks and then repeated annually. The tiny deer tick, no larger than a flea, is a carrier of this arthritic type of illness. The disease has spread across the United States by ticks carried by migrating birds, mice and squirrels.

Lime disease is not usually fatal, but it can be debilitating. Early signs in your dog may be fever, rash, lethargy, and pain with lameness in more than one limb, involving the large joints. If you have had your Vizsla in an area known to have ticks and observe any of these symptoms and can eliminate joint trauma or stress as the reason, ask your veterinarian to do a blood panel for Lyme disease. A course of antibiotic treatment usually is prescribed. Unless you live in a tick-infested area, you probably will not need the vaccine for protection.

INTERNAL PARASITES

Continuous monitoring of your Vizsla for any intestinal parasites is vital for his health and well-being. Worms rob a puppy's growing body of the nutrition it needs and are debilitating to the older dog. They drain the tissues of blood and moisture, and cause diarrhea, appetite loss, and a dry, dull coat. Since the cycle of most canine parasites allows for easy reinfestation, you must keep your yard scrupulously clean and adhere to a routine schedule of fecal checks.

Unnecessary or indiscriminatory worming can be detrimental to the health of your Vizsla, since positive identification of the parasite must be made first to determine the type of medication required. Stool samples should be checked by your veterinarian several times a year, especially if your dog has a history of worm infection.

Roundworms

Roundworms are the most common parasite that a dog owner has to deal with. Once they have infested your yard, they are almost impossible to get rid of. Do not allow children to play barefooted in an area where dog feces lie, as children are susceptible to migrating larvae from the worms, which can cause lesions in the eyes, liver, and kidneys.

A litter of puppies can be born with roundworms due to transplacental passage of larvae from the infected dam into the unborn fetus, where the larvae develop in the lungs. The larvae crawl into the trachea, are

Good sanitation practices are an absolute necessity for healthy dogs. A pooper-scooper makes it easy.

swallowed, and enter the small intestines where they mature. This method of infection is so common that most puppies are born with roundworms.

A Vizsla puppy so infected will be potbellied and thin, will have a dull coat, diarrhea, and vomiting, and will look poor. The worms can cause anemia and interfere with the absorption of food. Roundworms in your older Vizsla will not cause much difficulty since only a few of the larvae return to the intestines but, rather, encyst in the tissues and remain dormant.

Hookworms

Hookworms are tiny, thin, and thread-like, only getting as long as half an inch. Your Vizsla can become infected by larvae entering the skin or mouth, where they wander through the body tissues until they enter a blood vessel. The larvae travel to the lungs, crawl up the windpipe, and are swallowed. When they reach the small intestines, they attach themselves to the wall of the intestines, suck blood, and lay up to 20,000 eggs per day.

The amount of blood loss in a day to a single hookworm has been estimated to be as much as a milliliter, which can cause chronic anemia, weakness, emaciation, and fatality in a small puppy. Because hookworm larvae cross the placenta wall, a puppy can display the infection as young as ten days of age.

Typical symptoms in both a puppy and an adult dog are bloody and tarry diarrhea, pale gums, anemia, and impaired food absorption. A fecal check should be done several times a year if your Vizsla has a history of hookworm infections.

Whipworms

Although whipworms are the least common of the intestinal worms, they can be an obstinate problem if your Vizsla has them. Unless he is heavily infested, your dog may not show any external signs. With a heavy infestation he will have intermittent bloody and mucousy diarrhea and a dry coat, and will be undernourished.

Since the female whipworm lays fewer eggs than other worms, infestation is lighter and harder to detect in a single stool sample. Several collections may have to be taken before any diagnosis is reached.

Tapeworms

The least dangerous to your dog's health, tapeworms usually cause only a dry coat, occasional weight loss, and intermittent diarrhea. However, in the case of a heavy infestation, your Vizsla may seem nervous and hyper, and he may drag his rear on the ground because of the irritation from the worms.

Tapeworm eggs are passed through an infected dog's feces where they are ingested by flea larvae. Inside the flea, the egg segments soon develop into tapeworm larvae. The infected flea jumps onto a dog and the dog, in biting at the flea, ingests it. The tapeworm larvae then start to develop inside the dog's intestines.

Tapeworms can grow to a length of several feet and are divided into separate sections which break off and are passed in the stool. Easily visible, the segments are a quarter of an inch in size and look like pale-colored grains of rice or cucumber seeds.

Special medication is needed to rid your dog of a tapeworm since the worm has a head, or scolex, which stays firmly attached to the lining of the small intestines. If this head is not removed during treatment, it will regrow another body.

You will have a never-ending battle against tapeworms unless your Vizsla's environment is treated for flea infestation.

Coccidia

Older dogs are mostly resistant to coccidiosis but can be carriers, infecting a young puppy that has just been weaned and is possibly under stress. The Coccidia parasite lives in feces of infected animals, reproducing rapidly and causing such severe illness in a young puppy as to be fatal if correct treatment is delayed. The first signs are a mild diarrhea which will soon show mucous and blood. This progresses to weight loss, anemia, dehydration, abdominal pain, weakness, and loss of appetite. Further symptoms confuse the diagnosis as they are the same as those of distemper, such as eye discharge, cough, and a runny nose.

Good sanitation is a must and all feces should be cleaned up immediately to prevent possible contamination.

Heartworm

Previously only found in the warm and moist areas with a mosquito problem, heartworm has now spread throughout most of the United States. Without preventative care, the infection rate would be many times greater than it is now. Being a "house dog" is no guarantee that your Vizsla will not become infected.

The heartworm parasite lives in the heart and pulmonary artery of an infected dog, and can grow as long as twelve inches. The female parasite produces microfilariae, or young ones, which are released into the bloodstream. These can remain active for as long as two years, and if during that time a mosquito ingests the infected blood through a bite, the baby heartworms will develop into infective larvae in that mosquito. The mosquito will go on to feed on a new dog, releasing the larvae to develop under the skin and to migrate to the bloodstream. From the blood, the larvae go to the right ventricle of the dog's heart, arriving two to four months after being released by the mosquito. In the heart, the worms mature and reproduce, and the cycle starts again with another infected dog.

Symptoms of heartworm are a gradual weight loss, less tolerance for exercise, a cough, pale mucous membranes, lethargy, and collapse. The growth of the worms in the heart causes increased pulmonary blood pressure and impaired circulation. Your dog may cough up fresh blood, have difficulty breathing, consume more water, and have frequent bloody urination.

The treatment for heartworm disease is serious and not without risk. Injection of an arsenic-form drug is used over a period of two days and your dog must have complete rest for several weeks. As the adult worms die, they pass from the heart into the lungs and can lodge in the arteries where there is a chance of an embolism.

Several weeks after the treatment to rid your dog of the adult heartworms, treatment must be started to get the microfilariae out of the bloodstream. If the ten-day treatment is successful, your dog will be able to take a heartworm preventative drug.

A blood test will determine if a dog is clear of heartworm infestation. Prevention is accomplished by giving a heartworm preventative as a daily dose. Or, if you prefer, a once-a-month dose will kill any microfilariae that may be present in the bloodstream. Both preventative medications are available from your veterinarian and are given according to weight.

EXTERNAL PARASITES

Many a dog's coat has been ruined by his scratching to get rid of fleas and ticks. The parasites are a common problem in every part of the country and your dog does not have to leave his own yard to be exposed to them.

Fleas

Fleas spend only ten percent of their lives on your dog. The other ninety is spent in carpeting, bedding, crevices, and cracks of floors, furniture, and the yard. Ten producing female fleas will result in 1,800 new fleas in only one month, so it is important to kill all the eggs before they hatch in your dog's environment.

Fleas not only carry tapeworm, but a great percentage of Vizslas are allergic to flea saliva and break out in bumps and a rash. Constant biting, digging, and scratching break the coat and skin down into erupting sores and "hot spots," and your dog will look and feel miserable.

Medication prescribed by your veterinarian will alleviate a lot of the discomfort caused by any severe allergic reactions. Going through your Vizsla's coat daily with a fine-toothed flea comb will bring any parasites to the surface to be killed by hand or with a flea spray. Do not use a flea collar. Not only are they ineffectual, but they are also extremely toxic, and can be dangerous to young children who may handle the dogs and their collars.

Ticks

Ticks cling to bushes and shrubs, attach themselves firmly to a dog's skin as he runs through the woods, and feed on blood for several days before dropping off. Increases in the deer population, along with home development near to woodlands, have brought about an increase in Lyme disease, carried by the tiny tick that feeds on the wild animals and that deposits the bacteria for this disease to their digestive tracts. White-footed mice and wild deer are the primary animals associated with transmitting the disease to ticks. Adult ticks feed and mate on deer, then drop off to look for a new host such as a dog, which can become lame and ill from the disease.

It is important to get the tick off your dog before it has time to inject disease-carrying microbes under the skin. A safe way to remove a tick is to pull it out with tweezers or small forceps. Grasp the tick as close as possible to its mouth and then, without jerking, pull it upwards. Do not squeeze, crush, or puncture the body of the tick, or handle it with your bare hands.

Another serious disease transmitted by ticks is Rocky Mountain Spotted Fever. Carried by the female wood tick in the West and the American dog tick in the East, the disease comes to a head rapidly, bringing about very high temperatures of up to 105°F, depression, loss of appetite, lethargy, weakness, and hemorrhages under the skin.

The dog tick can also transmit a blood infection called Haemobartonellosis, which can cause anemia in your Vizsla. He may tire easily and have pale mucous membranes. The disease weakens the immune system and makes the dog susceptible to other illnesses.

Sprays, dips, and the newer products which are absorbed through the skin are usually effective for your Vizsla if you have a tick problem, but control over infestation in the environment is also essential. Labels on all pesticides now must contain explicit information about their hazardous use around the house and yard. With a large and bewildering variety of products for use, make sure you read labels carefully for any toxicity to an animal. Follow the recommendations of your local veterinarian whenever possible.

Mites

Mites are any of the numerous small to minute arachnids that often infest animals. They not only are disease carriers, but cause irritation to the skin. They are smaller than ticks and are covered with a relatively soft, often translucent skin. Their legs are provided with claw-like hooks or suction cups that either draw fluid or adhere to the dog's skin. Depending on the species, the food of parasitic mites includes blood, lymph, and living and dead epithelial cells.

Cheyletiella mites—Diagnosis depends on the identification of these mites in dandruff or skin brushings. A scaling process occurs primarily on the back, head, and neck of a dog and causes extreme itching and scratching, possibly leading to secondary skin infections.

These mite infestations in your Vizsla are highly contagious and can extend to humans. Lesions similar to ringworm appear, but they lack the inflammatory border. Treatment is successful with dips and scrubs of insecticides for your dog, and the application of topical insecticide for you.

Sarcoptic mange mites—These mites are tiny spider-like parasites which burrow in tunnels under the skin and lay eggs. Lesions appear within seventeen to twenty-one days and cause intense itching, which in turn leads to skin inflammation and secondary infections in your dog.

Preferred areas for the mites are the base of the tail and the areas around the eyes, ears, muzzle, legs, and head. The skin becomes irritated by the chemicals produced by the salivary secretions of the mites and breaks down into seeping sores from your dog's chewing and scratching. The sores crust over and scab, and the skin becomes thick and dry with hair missing in patches.

Sarcoptic mange is highly contagious and several treatments with an insecticide dip may be necessary over a period of several weeks for a complete cure, along with a cortisone medication to relieve the itching. It is very readily transmitted to humans, although of a shorter duration.

Demodectic mites—These mites are normal inhabitants of the skin and probably at least ninety percent of all short-haired dogs harbor this tiny cigar-shaped mite. Few ever exhibit clinical signs, and infestation will usually show up in a young Vizsla due to a stress factor.

There are two forms of demodectic mange. The benign form is the most common, seen as a localized condition with patches of hair loss on the face, front and rear feet, and legs. Sometimes called a "childhood disease," it will evidence itself in a young puppy during the time he is cutting teeth, going to a new home, changing diet, in need of worming, or in any other stress period which might lower his resistance. This localized condition is mild and will usually cure itself, without any problem, in just a short time.

The generalized form of demodectic mange is characterized by a vast multiplication of the mites in the hair follicles, with severe hair loss, skin lesions oozing blood and serum caused by bacterial infections, and a bad odor. The skin becomes swollen and inflamed and the dog is in a miserable state due to intense itching.

The treatment for generalized demodectic mange can be long and frustrating because it often responds poorly to treatment. New medications appear on the market every day for this debilitating problem. Antibiotics for secondary infections along with applications of a topical insecticide are used. It is important that your Vizsla be maintained on a good diet supplemented with vitamins, fatty acids, and minerals, and he must be free from intestinal parasites.

Both genetics and a depressed or altered immune system are blamed for the development of the generalized demodectic mange. Because of this critical factor, any

Toxic Plants

Dumbcane contains oxalate crystals which, on ingestion, cause immediate pain from oral, pharyngeal, and esophageal irritation; excessive salivation; anorexia, vomiting, diarrhea, and labored breathing.

Azaleas and Rhododendron cause salivation, muscle weakness, vomiting, diarrhea, and convulsions within hours of ingestion; possible coma and death.

Philodendron contains oxalate crystals which cause oral, pharyngeal, and esophageal irritation and pain, excessive salivation, swollen tongue and pharynx, labored breathing and renal failure.

Bird of Paradise causes abdominal pain, nausea, vomiting, and salivating.

Daffodils and Hyacinths contain oxalate crystals in the bulbs. Ingestion causes vomiting, diarrhea, abdominal pain, and salivating, but rarely death.

Foxglove contains digitoxin, saponins, and alkaloids, which cause vomiting, acute abdominal pain, bloody diarrhea, frequent urination, irregular slow pulse, convulsions and tremors, but rarely death.

Jasmine ingestion causes diarrhea, vomiting, pupil dilation, hyperthermia, muscle collapse, and convulsions.

Mushrooms can cause acute gastric effects, abdominal pain, nausea, salivation, vomiting, and liver and kidney damage.

Calla Lilly contains oxalate crystals which cause oral, pharyngeal and esophageal irritation, salivation, and swollen mouth.

Caladiums contain calcium oxalate crystals and ingestion causes immediate intense pain, local irritation to mucous membranes, salivation, swollen tongue and pharynx, diarrhea, and labored breathing.

Spider plants, airplane plants contain an unknown toxin which causes vomiting, salivation, retching, and anorexia.

Yews (Taxus species) ingestion of all parts except the fleshy aril will cause nervousness, gastroenteritis, trembling, labored breathing, bradycardia progressing to cardiovascular collapse, and death without a struggle. Treatment is most times useless.

Vizsla that has had this condition, even though he may be recovered, should not be used for breeding.

PUPPY-PROOFING YOUR YARD AND HOME

A Vizsla can be very much like a small child in that he explores every place and tastes and chews everything he can. Being a concerned owner means taking the time to examine your entire yard and home and remove potential dangers before your Vizsla gets into trouble.

Take a good look at the trees, bushes, and plants in your yard and be sure that you are able to identify each one. Many plants will be completely harmless, but others can cause vomiting, abdominal pains, cramps, diarrhea, and sometimes heart and respiratory failure. Some plants cause skin rashes and indirect damage due to your dog constantly digging, chewing, scratching and licking his feet or coat. Painful lesions of the mouth can result from a dog trying to remove common burdock from his body.

Preventative maintenance in your yard will keep your puppy from chewing on poisonous plants.

The greatest safety factor for your Vizsla is the fencing around his yard. It will protect him from theft, roaming loose, injury from a car, exposure to viruses, and attacks from stray dogs.

Your garage may hold some of the most toxic substances that present a danger to your Vizsla. Antifreeze contains ethylene glycol, a poisonous liquid that is attractive to a puppy due to its sweet taste and smell. Antifreeze also contains methyl alcohol, a volatile, toxic liquid used as a paint and varnish remover. It is toxic if absorbed through the skin, or, if taken internally, will cause death from respiratory failure. Clean up any spills immediately from the floor.

The same ingredients in antifreeze are found in windshield washer fluid, and brake and hydraulic fluid. An amount as little as two teaspoons can be fatal to a fifteen-pound puppy. Damage to the kidneys and the central nervous system can result in death within twelve to thirty-six hours after ingestion.

Kerosene, gasoline, mineral spirits, paint thinners, insect and rat poisons, weed killers, old batteries, putty and solder material should all be disposed of or placed in a locked cabinet. An open cabinet door under the kitchen or laundry-room sink can attract a curious puppy and result in some serious problems from the ingestion of steel wool pads, disinfectants, furniture polish, detergents, bleach, drain cleaners, soaps, and moth balls.

In the bathroom, not only can deodorant soaps, bath oils, perfume, shampoo, shaving lotions, and health and beauty aids result in toxic poisoning, but a sponge left carelessly on the side of the tub can be chewed and swallowed with disastrous results to your Vizsla's intestines.

Sleeping pills, tranquilizers, stimulants, aspirin, barbiturates, antibiotics, decongestants, and narcotics must be kept out of reach.

Electric cords used in almost every room in the house provide an attractive nuisance to a young puppy. Be sure to unplug them if your puppy is going to be unsupervised, even if only for a short period. Shock from a chewed cord can result in a burned and damaged mouth, circulatory collapse and difficulty in breathing.

Chocolate contains the alkaloid theobromine. At toxic doses it can cause vomiting, diarrhea, depression, muscle tremors, and even death. It is estimated that around four ounces of unsweetened chocolate, or thirty-two ounces of milk chocolate, is enough to kill a forty-five pound dog. Your puppy could have a toxic reaction to a four-ounce candy bar.

The active ingredient of tobacco is nicotine, a poisonous alkaloid. Make sure that ashtrays are kept empty and that packs of cigarettes are kept out of your Vizsla's reach.

Garbage cans, both indoors and out, should be securely covered. Spoiled foods can cause vomiting, abdominal pain, diarrhea, and prostration within four hours. While this condition may not be fatal, ingestion of pins, splintered bones, fruit seeds, and corn cobs can cause complications in the digestive tract.

Windows without protective screening should never be left open. A puppy has no idea of what may present a danger to him and cannot judge distance or height.

Houseplants present the same danger as outside shrubs and bushes. The only way to keep a puppy from chewing on a dangerous plant or putting a strange substance in his mouth is to completely remove the items, especially those that are toxic. Accident prevention is your responsibility. Keep your Vizsla safe, happy, and healthy by heading off trouble before it happens. A puppy can, and does, get into problems even in the most secure home.

If you suspect your pet has been poisoned, call the National Animal Poison Control Center, a division of the American Society for Prevention of Cruelty to Animals, for information at 888-426-4435 or 900-443-0000.

What Vizslas Love

Flying in a plane or on a boat . . .

A swimming pool . . .

Loafing on the bed . . .

Swimming in the pool . . .

Kissing kids . . .

Even bubble gum. Whether bursting the bubble . . .

Or making his own.

CHAPTER FOURTEEN

Breeding and Reproduction

The dog of today is the product of evolution, that complex combination of forces which includes hereditary and environment, with heredity being the inner and stronger influence and environment being the outer and weaker. Between them they mold all life. Then there is the breeder. Not just someone who breeds dog, but a *dog breeder*—the one who brings it all together and gives it balance, the one who has been using the Mendelian laws of dominance and inheritance for years.

MENDEL'S THEORY OF INHERITANCE

Johann Gregor Mendel was a Morovian monk who studied inheritance in garden peas. He wished to establish one thing—height in his plants. In so doing he proved that when two individuals, each one pure for a pair of opposite traits or characteristics such as tallness or dwarfness were crossed, the first generation of offspring would all look like the tall parent. He thus determined that tallness was a dominant characteristic, but that each of the hybrid offspring also carried recessively the factor for dwarfness. When two of the hybrids were crossed, the next generation produced an average of one tall, one short, each breeding pure for that trait, plus two hybrids like the parents. These two hybrids appeared tall but carried the factor, or gene, for dwarfness.

Mendel's work was not taken seriously until after his death when, in 1900, a Dutch-man named DeVries read Mendel's papers and rediscovered the law of inheritance. He drew up what he considered the rules for dominant and recessive traits as this applied to both plants and animals.

Dominant traits do not skip a generation. Breeding only from individuals displaying desirable traits will mean there is less danger of continuing undesirable characteristics in a line. Recessive traits may skip one or more generations. Only by test breeding can it be ascertained whether any individual carries a certain determiner, or gene. To be expressed, that gene must be carried by both of the parents involved.

An individual in which like traits, or characteristics, are paired, is known as a homozygous individual. The one in which unlike characteristics are paired is known as heterozygous. Recessive genes are always homozygous and always breed true to their own type, which is a test of their purity. An individual can be homozygous for one characteristic and heterozygous for others.

The breeder's task is to decide what kind of genes his Vizsla carries and how they will behave in combination with the genes of other individuals.

There are two kinds of cells in the body, reproduction, or germ cells, and body cells.

Ch. Taunee's Loki Santana, CD, ROM, HOF, and his dam, Ch. Cariad's Gaybine, CD.

Breeders need to be concerned with only the germ cells, which develop into sperm and eggs in the process of reproduction. Each germ cell has within it a nucleus with chromosomes, and within the chromosomes are the genes that will determine the hereditary factors. Dogs carry seventy-eight chromosomes. The chromosomes are arranged in pairs and one of the pairs, the sex chromosomes—XX (female) or XY (male)—determine the sex of the organism.

When a dog and bitch mate, the sperm cell of the male fuses with the egg cell of the female to form a new cell, which in time develops into a fetus. One-half of the male's chromosomes, along with his genes, are shed in the ripening of the cell, as are one-half of the bitch's. Thus, when we breed, we never know which genes will be discarded by nature and which ones will determine the characteristics of the offspring. All we know for sure is that one-half of each puppy's hereditary traits will be supplied by the sire and the other half by the dam.

Each puppy in a litter is different because of the random survival of different genes in the makeup of each sperm or egg. The germ cells have within their chromosomes thousands of genes. Some will be used, others discarded and lost for all time.

Not only is each puppy in a litter different, but each puppy in every subsequent litter by the same sire and dam will be different. This is something many breeders fail to understand. After getting a beautiful first litter, they repeat the breeding with the same sire and dam, only to never duplicate the quality of the first breeding. We have no control over the loss or preservation of the chromosomes or characteristics we wish to perpetuate. All we can do is breed good parents possessing all of the hereditary factors we want, and then trust to luck that these factors will be passed on to the offspring.

If not passed on in the next litter, they may be passed on in the one after that, or never at all. The point is that you *must* use a dog and bitch that are endowed with the characteristics you consider desirable and, just as important, a dog and bitch whose parents are also endowed with everything you want. Only in this manner can you ever hope to obtain the good traits in succeeding generations.

Probably the most valuable lesson taught by the study of heredity is that both faults and virtues will be inherited. This means that breeding good to poor will not result in something in between the two, but rather in good specimens and poor specimens. In other words, breeding a big Vizsla to a small Vizsla will not give you a medium-sized Vizsla. If, when selecting two dogs for breeding, one of them possesses traits that you absolutely do not want in your puppies, do not use that dog. Always remember that the individual is as important as his pedigree. Do not join the host of breeders who never manage to improve upon their original stock.

Linebreeding

The object of linebreeding is to be able to keep all the good qualities that have been attributed to one very outstanding ancestor.

Ch. Dorratz Diamond Tiara, CD, with her daughter, Ch. Dorratz-Cariad Tiara's Jewel, CD. Owned by Doris Ratzlaff.

It is the mating of two dogs that are related to that common ancestor, such as a granddaughter to a grandsire, or simply dogs that go back to a common ancestor several times in the last four generations. This joining of the related individuals narrows down the number of ancestors, and thus intensifies whatever hereditary tendencies are present.

By breeding together related individuals the breeder is concentrating on only one line. It should not be persisted in for too long without recourse to outcrosses, and should not be done at unless the breeder personally knew a lot of the Vizslas involved.

Inbreeding

Inbreeding is the fastest way to set type, but this method should never be used by an inexperienced breeder since it requires complete, personal knowledge of each Vizsla involved, even more so than linebreeding. Inbreeding does not create new or different traits—it brings out what is already in the genetic structure, both the good and the bad.

Inbreeding, in a true sense, is mating brother to sister, father to daughter, son to mother. For such a program, it is essential that you use two Vizslas with the least possible number of common faults and whose common ancestor is likewise almost faultless.

Outcrossing

Outcrossing is considered the safest procedure for the amateur and will result in satisfactory puppies provided that all of the ancestors are credible specimens. You will, however, have to accept the fact that even if a dog with this genetic background became a champion, he may never prove to be a really prepotent breeding specimen; that is, he may not have the ability to pass on his good traits.

Outbreeding is usually considered to be the mating of two individual dogs that have nothing in common for four generations. The breeder who outcrosses can unwittingly introduce many unwanted qualities into the line because he will be dealing with so many different genes.

You can successfully outcross if your bitch has been closely linebred or inbred. Look for a stud dog that has also been closely bred, but to a different ancestor. Although both dog and bitch have no common ancestor, you will cut down on the number of unrelated ancestors in their combined pedigree. This will help to eliminate a tremendous number of unknowns.

HEREDITARY PROBLEMS IN VIZSLAS

The best way to develop a line of dogs with sound genetic composition is to do your homework. Exhaustive research through the pedigrees of the dog and bitch should be the foundation for your decision to breed or not. Simply looking up the number of champions in the pedigrees is not enough; you will require much more data to ensure genetic soundness.

Make phone calls and write letters. Ask owners of dogs in the line you are considering if they have any health problems with their dogs. Some breeders may be reluctant to discuss problems or admit there even is a problem, so cooperation is essential. Explain that your reasons for researching the line are to better determine the potential quality of your own proposed breeding stock, and that your ultimate goal is to enhance the genetic soundness and quality of the breed.

Keeping in mind that birth defects can be classified as inherited, induced, or spontaneous, it will be up to you to fully research individual dogs, littermates, and offspring before reaching a conclusion. Hereditary factors are those programmed to happen because of the genetic material from both the male and the female. At the moment the egg is fertilized, the final outcome is determined as long as no mutations occur. Many congenital deformities in the developing fetus are caused by genetic mutations. These are totally unpredictable, chance deviations from the normal genetic pattern. Such a mutation is assumed to be induced or spontaneous if a careful check of the lineage reveals no tendency toward the problem and you know of a probable inducer, such as the use of vaccines or insecticide during the bitch's pregnancy. In that instance, the same bitch and dog can be bred again.

This is why it is so important to get an honest and complete accounting of all the individuals. It is as necessary for the welfare of the Vizsla breed to know who is begetting the defects as it is to exalt those producing breed and field champions. If a similar defect keeps showing up in a careful search of lines, the answer is that it is an inherited problem and the individual and parents should not be used for breeding.

The first litters of Vizslas in the United States brought numerous problems with dysplasia, bad temperaments, monorchidism, and eye faults. Many of those dogs exhibiting faults were never bred or were put down, so problems were kept to a minimum with careful, selective breeding.

Because of conscientious breeders, the Vizsla breed has fewer hereditary problems than many other sporting breeds. Canine hip dysplasia still is evident, but with the use of X-ray diagnosis and published lists of OFA certifications, anyone can look up the rating of any Vizsla and determine by careful study of different lines which ones are the cleanest. Unfortunately, the dogs that are not certified are not listed, so there is little way of tracing if a top-producing sire or dam had a littermate with dysplasia. If so, the genetic disposition will be in every breeding combination in the next generations.

Hypothyroidism is blamed for a wide range of common and uncommon symptoms. This is considered a true thyroid disease which is an actual alteration in the thyroid gland, caused by low circulating levels of thyroid hormones in the body. The majority of cases result from destruction of functioning thyroid tissue by the body's own immune system. The clinical signs of hypothyroidism can manifest very slowly, as your dog's metabolic rate gradually decreases. It is not a problem with young dogs; most dogs diagnosed are between four and ten years of age. Weight gain is common, even though the food intake and appetite remains normal. Lethargy or inactivity and loss of mental alertness are common, along with shivering and appearing cold. Hair loss over the trunk and tail is common, along with dry, flaky brittle hair coat and seborrhea. Almost every system in the body can be affected and can result in a number of secondary muscular, cardiac, gastrointestinal, reproductive, immunological, musculoskeletal, and eye problems. Diagnosis is easy with a simple blood test and treatment consists of lifelong oral supplementation with a synthetic thyroxine tablet twice a day. The prognosis of a dog with hypothyroidism on regular daily medication is excellent. The treatment restores normal metabolic activity and your dog's lifestyle does not have to be changed.

Several isolated cases of Von Willebrand's disease have been reported in the Vizsla. This is a hereditary blood disease which is characterized by excessive bleeding and slow clotting of blood. Bloody diarrhea, prolonged and excessive bleeding during estrus and whelping, dangerous hemorrhage during surgery, and occasions of bloody urine are some of the symptoms. Von Willebrand's disease has been reported in forty-nine breeds of purebred dogs. Since many drugs can interfere with normal platelet function, and certain clotting factors can be depressed by agents in dog food, or by various diseases, diagnosis is often incorrect and misleading. The collection and processing of blood samples is critical, along with a complete history of physical and physiological stresses, as well as any concomitant disease such as parvovirus, hypothyroidism, or auto-immune disease. The normal amount of Von Willebrand factor protein in your dog's blood sample should be seventy percent. Borderline range is fifty to sixty-nine percent, and carrier range is one to forty-nine percent. Learn the risks of transmitting this bleeding problem before you breed.

Seizures (epilepsy) are a common worry for breeders who are trying to research breeding stock. Seizures are the result of muscle response to an abnormal nerve-signal burst from the brain. They are a symptom of an underlying neurological dysfunction. Toxic substances and metabolic or electrolyte abnormalities and imbalances cause an uncoordinated firing of neurons in the cerebrum of the brain, creating seizures from mild ("petit mal"), to severe ("grand mal"). Medical treatment and close monitoring is usually advised for a dog having one or more seizures a month. Successful drug therapy depends on the owner's dedication to administering any drug exactly as prescribed. Epilepsy is not a death sentence but it is important that the dog, and possibly any relatives, is not used for breeding.

Hereditary problems also include cryptorchidism (neither testicle descended) or monorchidism, involving one undescended testicle. A male with one testicle can still produce but should never be used for breeding, and neutering is recommended.

Other inherited problems in the breed include incorrect bite, eye problems such as entropian and ectropian, skull defects, and allergies. None of these are classified as being major problems, but they exist and should never be included in your breeding program.

Certain characteristics that are not a problem such as hair feet, yellow eyes, light-colored coats, and "gay" tails also are inherited. These faults can be eliminated from the gene pool very easily with selective breeding. The one problem which every breeder is concerned about, however, has to do with the amount of white on their dog's chest and feet. Even with careful, thoughtful breeding, the white cannot be completely eliminated. Some white will probably always be with us in the form of recessive

Ch. Cariad's Gaybine, CD, dam of sixteen champions, including a record winning Best in Show son as well as the first Triple Champion in AKC history. Both sons are now in the VCA Hall of Fame.

genes since the early Vizslas had large amounts of white on their neck, chest, and toes.

THE BROOD BITCH

The decision to breed your Vizsla bitch and raise a litter of puppies is not one to be taken lightly. It involves time, money, energy, and a commitment to raising healthy, happy puppies able to adapt to whatever their new owners desire.

If you want to produce show specimens, and you feel that your bitch has something to contribute to the breed by way of her puppies, see how she compares to other Vizslas by entering her in the show

Ch. Firebrand's Constant Comment and her son Ch. Boelte's Brant of Penlee, both Best in Show winners.

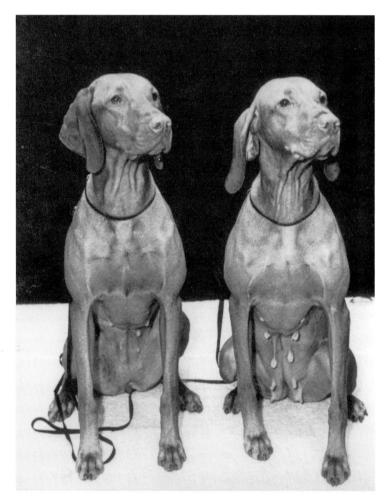

Ch. Cariad's Elkenyeztetett, foundation brood bitch for the Boelte's Vizslas, and her daughter, Ch. Boelte's Bronze Beauty, JH. As a brace, they earned a Best in Show. Owned by Pat Boelte.

ring. The dog show ring is a testing ground for breeders. The idea that if your bitch is a champion she is good enough to breed is not necessarily true. Many Vizslas hold Dual titles as well as titles in obedience and agility. It is important to keep in mind that you will want the puppies to adhere closely to the Vizsla Standard if they are to compete in any type of competition.

The brood bitch is actually a lot more important than the stud dog you will be using. She is the fixture of the strain. She will be contributing one of the two sets of chromosomes that determine the characteristics of each puppy. The stud dog is finished with the puppies at the end of the tie, but the bitch is not. Her overall health and condition can affect the puppies. So will her parasites, diet, and temperament.

Bad temperament is a genetic as well as an environmental problem, but the temperament of the puppies, from the beginning, is more dependent on the bitch than on the stud dog. Her temperament greatly affects the puppies even while she carries and nurses them, and in the early weeks of their development and training. It will have a lasting effect.

The ideal brood bitch comes from a closely linebred family with few faults. She must not have any serious faults. Her coat, eye color, body, angulation, bite, and size should be near perfect. She should have substance while still being feminine, with a lovely head and expression. She must be sound in body and mind and be everything that you would like to duplicate in your litter of Vizsla puppies.

A Vizsla bitch should not be bred before her second birthday, at which time she is both physically and mentally mature. Before that time, even though her body has developed fairly rapidly, her brain has not developed enough to take on the responsibilities of maternity and she may lack common sense when caring for her puppies.

Weeks before she is due to be in season, take the time to take a good look at her physical condition. An overweight bitch is unlikely to conceive and, if she does, may have a hard time whelping her litter. If she is underweight, she should be started on extra nourishment and supplements which will need to be continued after breeding, since the nutritional demands of the fetuses will be a drain on her body.

Stool samples must be checked early enough for treatment if necessary. Worming your bitch does not always guarantee that her puppies will be born worm-free, but it does put your bitch in better condition for the job ahead.

Every Vizsla used for breeding should be X-rayed for hip dysplasia, and none should bred unless their hips have been certified free from any degree of canine hip dysplasia. The AKC also requires that all breeding stock have a registered DNA number and certificate on file.

Your bitch should have a heartworm test. All of her vaccinations should be updated. A booster given several weeks before breeding will raise her titer level and give better passive immunity to her puppies. She should not have any vaccinations or worming medications after she has been bred.

A blood test for brucellosis should be done on both the bitch and the stud dog prior to breeding. Brucellosis is a highly contagious disease and breeding stock can become infected through sexual contact. Brucellosis causes abortions and stillborn puppies in the bitch and sterility in the male.

PICKING A STUD DOG

The stud dog should always be a good representative of the breed. Once you have established that, you can get into the finer points of what will make him a good mate for your bitch. The most prestigious winner in the show ring is no credit to the breed if he cannot pass along his excellence. Furthermore, a big winner may not be an exceptional specimen. Some judges do the breed a grave disservice by putting up dogs with major faults while playing a political game.

Csitri Mihalyi Povazia, owned by Bev Wanjon, foundation bitch for the Russet Leather Vizslas, here shown in 1962 photo. She was bred to BIS Ch. Napkeltei Vadasz Dalas and produced Ch. Jo-B Russet Leather.

A big string of wins sets the stamp of approval on a dog and does much to bring him to the attention of breeders. But a show or field record does not assure that the holder of all those laurels can pass on his good merits. Only the best among the males should be used at stud. It is a painful truth for enthusiastic owners of new champion males, but most of them should never be used at stud.

If you are interested in using a certain male for breeding to your bitch, try to see as many of his offspring as possible. Evaluate what he has produced from different bitches to see if any dominant trait comes through which you would not like to see in your litter.

Ch. Oakleaf's Dandy Dalton, SH, owned by Jan Simer, winning the Stud Dog class at the Contra Costa specialty. He was the sire of seventy-one titled get. Photo © Cook Phodography.

Ch. Taunee's Loki Santana, CD, a member of the VCA Hall of Fame for his outstanding contribution to the breed with fifty-two Champions.

Ch. Glen Cottage Loki Barat, CDX, sire of thirty-four Champions, including a record Best in Show winner and a Triple Champion. Loki and his two sons are in the VCA Hall of Fame.

From a breeding standpoint, it is better to use an average, but good, male from top breeding stock than a top-winning dog from a below-average line.

After thinking, and looking at stud dogs, go back and study Vizsla pedigrees, because that is what is going to be the most important in the final decision. Study the quality of the grandsires and granddams because your litter will be inheriting their traits or characteristics.

Make your arrangements with the stud dog owner well in advance, with an approximate date for breeding, so that you are certain he will be available. This will be very important if you decide to make arrangements for the shipping and use of chilled or frozen semen. Make sure you understand, and are in agreement with, the terms the dog's owner will want for his stud fee and veterinarian bills. Most stud fees are based on what the stud dog may have already produced or perhaps his records and titles.

CONTRACT FOR STUD SERVICE

Policy for Approved Bitches

Bitches must be approved by the stud dog's owner before being accepted for breeding. Bitch's owner must be willing and able to provide correct care for the litter and agree that no puppies from the resultant litter will be sold to pet shops or other wholesale outlets, and will be willing to accept the responsibility for placing all puppies in proper, caring homes.

Bitch must be in good health and condition at the time of breeding and must be free of hereditary defects, parasites, or infections. The bitch must be of good conformation and temperament, and must be physically suitable for breeding. She must have an OFA certificate stating GOOD or EXCELLENT hips. A recent negative brucellosis culture is required. Additional expenses incurred in the breeding will be the responsibility of the owner of the bitch.

Stud Owner's Responsibility

The stud dog is guaranteed to be in the same good health required of the bitch and free from any genetic defect. A recent brucellosis culture result will be supplied, along with the dog's OFA certificate, registration, pedigree, and DNA. The owner also guarantees that his stud dog has had experience with sperm collections and that samples done this past week show an excellent sperm count and a ___% motility.

Stud Fee and Guarantee

The stud fee for this breeding will be $1,000, with one-half to be paid at time of breeding. Three puppies living to the age of three weeks are guaranteed. Registration application is to be signed by the stud dog owner when balance of stud fee is paid. If fewer than three puppies result from the service, the balance of stud fee is not required, and the owner of the bitch is entitled to a return service, if desired.

Stud dog_____ Registration number_____

Bitch_____ Registration number_____

Owner of bitch

_____

Owner of stud

_____

While there may be a difference in the stud fee in some areas of the country based on whatever price breeders are selling their puppies for, be prepared to pay from $500 to $1,000 for the stud fee, plus any other expenses involved in the breeding. Most stud fees are paid with one-half down at time of breeding and the other half when the puppies are born.

A stud dog owner will usually guarantee a certain number of live puppies or a return service will be offered the next time your bitch is in season. Get a written agreement on a stud contract to avoid any hard feelings or a misunderstanding at a future date.

RESPONSIBILITIES OF THE STUD DOG OWNER

As the owner of a new field or show champion it is flattering to be approached about using your dog for stud. There are many good, proven Vizsla studs. Think about what your dog has to offer. Is he potentially a better stud than the others? As the owner of a stud dog, you will have the sole responsibility to breed him only to the best bitches presented. You cannot consider the possibility that if you turn a bitch down, her owner will only go to another stud. You have to refuse service and be able to give a cogent reason for it. If the bitch being presented is in poor health or condition, too old or too young, or if you have any doubts at all about what care and attention her puppies will receive, you have the responsibility to refuse stud service. It is your dog's reputation that will be ruined if the puppies do not amount to anything. If you want to safeguard that reputation, it is up to you to save him for the best. Do not let the temptation of a stud fee influence your better judgment.

A dog offered at stud should be free from any disease, but this also means free from any hereditary defects such as a poorly shaped head, yellow eyes, incorrect bite and, above everything else, a poor temperament. Your Vizsla stud must not only be in good condition, which means lean and hard, but also free from worms, skin ailments, and external parasites. He should have OFA certification of good hips and a clean bill of health with a brucellosis test and a sperm test.

If your Vizsla is going to be bred normally instead of from chilled or frozen semen, you must be prepared to cope with visiting bitches whether it is a convenient time for you or not. If a bitch is coming by air travel, you will have to pick her up at the airport, and several days later, drive her back. Her safety while she is under your care means extreme caution at all times to see that she does not panic in a strange area and escape from your home or yard.

Your basic responsibility of course, is that your dog knows what to do. Just because he is a male does not necessarily mean that he knows what the process is all about or how to handle it. If, as a puppy, your Vizsla was continually scolded or punished for incorrect behavior such as riding your leg, you may find him reluctant to breed his first bitch. A stud dog should be taught from his first service that the routine includes someone holding his bitches for him. If you are offering an inexperienced, young male for stud, it is sometimes helpful for this first mating to be with an experienced bitch that is known to be easy to breed.

Whether it is in your garage, home, yard, or kennel, take your Vizsla stud dog to the same place each time you use him for breeding. In this way he will associate that area with the act and will know that he has your permission to go ahead and breed. Once your male has been used for breeding, it is in your best interest to know the quality of the puppies he is producing. Be realistic and objective. Do not encourage owners to put his offspring in the show ring if you have to make excuses for obvious faults.

And finally, be absolutely sure that there is no misunderstanding about the stud fee, whether it will be cash or a pick puppy. Protect everyone's interest by putting the agreement in writing and having it signed by both parties involved.

REPRODUCTIVE ORGANS

The Dog

The most important of the male's sexual organs are the two testicles which produce sperm in a fluid called semen. Actually, the semen stays in ducts that run on the side of each testicle. The testicles are located outside the abdominal cavity since sperm require a lower temperature. Because sperm can tolerate cold better than heat, you may want to avoid letting your dog lie on a hot surface prior to breeding. It could lower his sperm count. However, since thousands of sperm are released and only a minute fraction used, smaller litters do not usually occur with a normally fertile male.

The external sex organ for the male is called the penis, and its function is to deliver the semen into the bitch's vagina during the mating process. The penis is enclosed and protected by a sheath of skin called the prepuce. The prepuce pushes back out of the way as the penis enlarges. A small amount of yellow discharge is normally seen leaking from the prepuce, but an excessive amount of discharge may indicate an infection.

Most of the area of the penis is a very elaborate system of blood sinuses (cavities)

Male Reproductive System

Female Reproductive System

surrounded by a lot of connective tissue. During sexual excitement these tissues fill with blood and the penis enlarges. During mating, a ball at the base of the penis, called the bulbus glandis, enlarges and keeps the two dogs joined (tied) until the blood recedes and the penis returns to normal size. A bone called the os penis gives the penis support.

The Bitch

In the bitch, cell division and growth take place within the ovaries. A bitch has two ovaries which lie behind the kidneys close to the body wall. The ovaries contain a great many ova, or eggs, each of which is contained in a small sac called a follicle. The follicle enlarges as it approaches the surface of the ovary, bursts, and releases the egg. Rupture of this follicle and release of the egg constitutes ovulation.

The empty follicles then become a new gland, the corpus luteum, which contains a hormone—progesterone. It is this hormone that is directly connected to the physiological changes which indicate when it is time for the bitch to be bred. As soon as the follicle bursts and releases the egg, the sac fills up rapidly with another mass of cells called

luteal bodies. These bodies secrete progesterone, and it is this hormone that signifies ovulation and the end of the mating cycle, and also maintains pregnancy.

When an egg is released from the ovaries, it goes into the oviduct, a long, thin, tubular organ that extends from the ovary to the uterus. There are two ovaries, so there are two tubes, each of which leads into a horn of the uterus. The eggs move along these tubes for a couple of days before they reach the uterus.

Fertilization is the uniting of a sperm and an egg. When sperm are present in the oviduct of the bitch, one will penetrate the outer covering of an egg. This covering immediately grows thicker to prevent penetration by another sperm. The egg and sperm join and a new life is created.

The new life, called a zygote, or embryo, moves into the uterus to develop into a fetus during pregnancy. The uterus is a hollow, muscular Y-shaped organ consisting of the two long horns which form the upper parts of the Y, and a shorter horn, which is the stem, going into the cervix. The cervix, a fibrous and muscular structure, is the opening connecting the uterus to the vagina, or birth canal. The vagina extends from the cervix to the vulva, the external genital organ of the bitch.

THE MATING

The perfect time for mating is, of course, as close to ovulation as possible. By approximately the tenth or eleventh day in season, your bitch's vulva will begin to swell and soften; her discharge will lighten in color and change odor. She will mount another bitch playfully but will snap and growl at a male if he attempts to mount her.

Behavior, more than anything else, is a good indication of readiness. She will become more restless and readily swing her tail to one side if you touch her rear. She will usually accept a male within two days of displaying this behavior.

Many Vizsla owners try to determine the right day to breed with the use of vaginal smears. Your veterinarian will use a microscopic examination, staining the cells that line the uterus and that are sloughed off in the vaginal discharge. Several smears should be taken over a period of a few days in order to observe the changes.

A more exact method of pinpointing the time of ovulation is with simple blood tests that measure the LH (luteinizing hormone), which actually causes ovulation. The blood tests are usually repeated every other day until ovulation is shown. These tests also detect the rise in progesterone. Normally, progesterone and LH are present in the bitch's blood in very small amounts, but just prior to ovulation there is an increase in both which continue to rise as the cycle progresses. It is this surge of progesterone and LH that starts ovulation and determines the bitch's fertile period.

The first day of the LH surge is counted as day zero and can happen anywhere from three to twenty-eight days after the first signs of heat, although the average is eight to twelve days. Ovulation occurs two days after the LH surge. The eggs will take another two to three days to mature to a stage that supports fertilization, and then will usually live for another forty-eight to seventy-two hours. This makes days five and six after the LH surge the most fertile days for the bitch to be bred. For most natural breedings, the breeding is done two to three days after the LH surge and is usually repeated for two or three days until the end of the fertile period. Knowing the date of the LH surge will help you determine the whelping date, which will be extra important if you need to plan an elective Caesarean section.

Accurate ovulation timing is extremely critical to the success of pregnancy from both chilled and frozen semen. It is no longer necessary to ship a bitch across the country for a natural breeding to a desirable stud. Airlines now have numerous restrictions which make the process of shipping a bitch almost obsolete.

If you are using chilled or frozen semen for breeding, contact both your veterinarian and your stud owner immediately after the bitch comes in season to arrange for the collections of chilled, or transfer of frozen semen. Again, critical timing is necessary. If you are using chilled semen it will be the responsibility of the stud dog owner to get to a fertilization specialist and have the dog's semen collected and prepared for overnight shipping in time to coincide with the bitch's insemination. Two separate collections, shipping, and inseminations are usually recommended to effectively cover the fertile period of the bitch.

The stress of the chilling and shipping decreases the life-span of the dog's sperm cells from the normal five to seven days to only two to four days. With one day taken up by shipping, this makes it even more important to determine the correct days for insemination.

If you have important qualities in your stud dog that you would like to see preserved for future use in your breeding program, freezing and storing semen is the way to guarantee future generations. The semen is collected from the stud dog by manual stimulation, with the different factions collected separately, so that only sperm-rich semen is frozen and saved. The semen is evaluated for motility and count before it is extended with a buffer solution and then diluted to fifty million sperm in individual straws for storage at a freezing center. The number of straws obtained from the semen depends on your dog's sperm count, so it is important to consider your dog's health, age, and even experience.

The veterinarian you use must be AKC approved, qualified, and experienced in using frozen semen, not only for the collection but also for thawing and inseminating the bitch. There is a lot of paperwork connected with this method, plus a special litter registration form. The stud dog's owner is responsible for notifying the storage location to release the straws needed for shipping and insemination. Frozen semen lives twelve to twenty-four hours after it is thawed, so it must be used during the short two- to three-day fertile period for conception. Accurate ovulation timing is even more essential because of the shortened lifespan of the sperm cells. It is the bitch owner's responsibility to begin ovulation timing procedures when the bitch shows the first signs of being in season.

The most common method of inseminating the bitch, other than the long-used artificial insemination, is a procedure called surgical intrauterine implantation, in which the sperm is placed directly into the uterus through an outer incision in the abdominal wall. Another procedure which is gaining popularity is called transcervical insemination and involves passing a catheter through the cervix and into the uterus. Vaginal inseminations are used only if the motility of the thawed semen is at least forty percent and of good quality.

When the stud dog is within traveling possibilities, the old fashioned "natural" way is still the surest way used by many breeders, especially if the stud is experienced. He will merely sniff at the bitch's rear and walk away if the correct odor isn't present or if he gets a positive rejection from the bitch. But as the bitch gets closer to ovulation, the male may refuse to eat, will moan, groan and howl, and he may even attempt to chew his way through a door to get to the bitch in his desire to mate. It is almost impossible at this time to console him or reason with him.

When the bitch is ready, she will let the male mount her. An inexperienced male may try to mount her head, but the bitch will usually swing her body around and present her rear to him until he gets the idea. Both dogs may spend several minutes going through a time of "courtship." If this continues to the point of tiring either of them, they should be separated for a short time.

When the male mounts the female, he will grab her around her body and feel around with his penis for her vulva. Upon penetration he will thrust intensely until the penis swells and locks or "ties" the two of them together. A few seconds later you will see the male's body relax over her back. At this point he can be helped to dismount by placing both his front feet on the ground, lifting a rear leg over the back of the bitch so that he can turn, putting both dogs in a tail-to-tail position.

If there are two people assisting in the mating, each one can kneel on one knee beside a dog and place the other knee under that dog to give support. If only one person is supervising the mating, either sit on a chair or kneel alongside the dogs. Encircle both dogs completely under the flanks. Join your hands, and hold them in place.

It is important that dogs being mated are supervised to prevent injury to either one. Even if it is hard on your back, do not allow a dog to sit or lie down. Most Vizslas are easy breeders, but if you have one that is restless, you can use a leash tied to a stationary object as a restraint.

There is no way of estimating how long a tie will last. It could be fifteen minutes or an hour. When the blood recedes from the tissues, the bulb and penis will shrink and the dogs will part. Place the bitch quickly in a crate. Do not let her urinate.

Regardless of when the breeding takes place, the sperm will not join the egg until it is the right time for the egg to be fertilized. Nourished by secretions from uterine glands in the bitch, the sperm can live forty-eight hours waiting for fertilization. Rather than miss the right timing, a second and even a third mating should be completed in the following days, as long as both dogs are receptive.

THE PREGNANT BITCH

From the moment your bitch is bred, until you definitely know otherwise, consider her pregnant. This means that, from the first day, she should not receive any wormings, medications, or vaccinations unless prescribed by your veterinarian.

For the first four weeks of pregnancy she will have no extra needs. If she has been on a well-balanced diet and is in good condition there is no need to increase her food supply or give her vitamin supplements, and she can continue with normal exercise as long as there is no danger of injury. However, if she has been training and working in obedience or agility that requires jumping, it is advisable to delay that or use only one board for the jumps.

Your bitch may experience some "morning sickness" or mild vomiting in her third week as the embryos attach themselves to the uterus and placentas are formed around them. Some enlargement of her breasts and nipples may be evident at this time.

If you are not sure that your bitch is pregnant, your veterinarian can palpate her abdomen between twenty-eight and thirty-one days after breeding. By this time the fetuses can be felt by an experienced person. A blood test can also be taken at this time to determine pregnancy, or a diagnosis can be made with ultrasound. X-rays are not recommended during the early stages of fetal development as their use can cause deformities in the puppies. If an X-ray is desired or necessary it can be done after the fifty-fourth day, by which time the skeleton of the fetus has been formed.

Your Vizsla bitch will sometimes show changes in her personality very early into her pregnancy by becoming more affectionate and cling, seeming to need more reassurance that you are near. If she is around other dogs she will try to stay apart so as not to be jostled or bumped. She will also be less inclined to exercise, but it is important to keep her from gaining too much weight and to keep her in good muscle tone.

The last couple of weeks of her pregnancy, her rib cage will expand and if she is carrying a large litter she will want to exercise even less. Take her for slow walks on a lead to avoid overexertion. Go only as far as she can go without returning home tired and panting. As her girth increases, the walks must be taken more slowly, and as the eighth week ends, do away with them if she looks like she is carrying a big load.

Most fetal growth occurs during the last trimester, so increase food intake by ten to fifteen percent. Because protein requirements are high during this period, you should not feed a low protein food. Diets designed for adult maintenance do not contain enough protein. Do not feed supplements. At the end of pregnancy, body weight should have increased ten to fifteen percent and intake should be forty to fifty percent more than usual. The pregnant uterus often limits intake however, so feed energy-dense (high fat) food in small frequent meals. Most of the additional body weight should then be lost when she gives birth.

During the last half of her gestation period, your Vizsla may have a clear, thick string of mucous discharge from her vagina, especially if she is carrying a large litter. If at any time there is blood or pus in this discharge, have her examined by your veterinarian immediately. Thick, dark green discharge may mean a fetus has died and separated from the uterus prematurely.

Ch. Cariad's Classic Mariah (right) is shown with nine-month-old son (left), Classic Rhymes and Reasons (Denver), and her daughter (center), Classic Call The Wind Mariah (Breeze.) Photo © Booth Photography.

When the fetuses have reached maximum size, your Vizsla will appear very fat, though a certain percentage of that will be water. In her final week of pregnancy, the litter will begin to shift and settle lower, leaving the bitch's hipbones gaunt, where before they appeared well padded with flesh. Her abdomen will sag with the weight and her backbone may look bent with the strain. Her eyes may look haggard and worn, and she will try continuously to find some way to get comfortable. When she is lying quietly, you can see the puppies moving and the bulge of a head or foot.

Now is the time to introduce your bitch to the place where she will have her puppies. Be sure the whelping box is in a quiet, draft-free area that will give her and her puppies the privacy and warmth they need. Show the box to the bitch often and try to convince her that she is having her babies in her own place—and not in the middle of your bed.

Advise your veterinarian as to the due date and stay in close touch with him to make sure you will be able to contact him for assistance if needed. It will be easier for the novice breeder if an experienced friend is available to offer advice and a helping hand. Once whelping starts, someone should stay with the bitch every minute, rather than risk losing her from complications, or losing a puppy due to an injury.

Whelping Chart

Each pair of columns gives the **Date bred** month and the **Date due to whelp** month.

Date bred (Jan)	Due to whelp (Mar)	Date bred (Feb)	Due to whelp (Apr)	Date bred (Mar)	Due to whelp (May)	Date bred (Apr)	Due to whelp (Jun)	Date bred (May)	Due to whelp (Jul)	Date bred (Jun)	Due to whelp (Aug)	Date bred (Jul)	Due to whelp (Sep)	Date bred (Aug)	Due to whelp (Oct)	Date bred (Sep)	Due to whelp (Nov)	Date bred (Oct)	Due to whelp (Dec)	Date bred (Nov)	Due to whelp (Jan)	Date bred (Dec)	Due to whelp (Feb)
1	5	1	5	1	3	1	3	1	3	1	3	1	2	1	3	1	3	1	3	1	3	1	2
2	6	2	6	2	4	2	4	2	4	2	4	2	3	2	4	2	4	2	4	2	4	2	3
3	7	3	7	3	5	3	5	3	5	3	5	3	4	3	5	3	5	3	5	3	5	3	4
4	8	4	8	4	6	4	6	4	6	4	6	4	5	4	6	4	6	4	6	4	6	4	5
5	9	5	9	5	7	5	7	5	7	5	7	5	6	5	7	5	7	5	7	5	7	5	6
6	10	6	10	6	8	6	8	6	8	6	8	6	7	6	8	6	8	6	8	6	8	6	7
7	11	7	11	7	9	7	9	7	9	7	9	7	8	7	9	7	9	7	9	7	9	7	8
8	12	8	12	8	10	8	10	8	10	8	10	8	9	8	10	8	10	8	10	8	10	8	9
9	13	9	13	9	11	9	11	9	11	9	11	9	10	9	11	9	11	9	11	9	11	9	10
10	14	10	14	10	12	10	12	10	12	10	12	10	11	10	12	10	12	10	12	10	12	10	11
11	15	11	15	11	13	11	13	11	13	11	13	11	12	11	13	11	13	11	13	11	13	11	12
12	16	12	16	12	14	12	14	12	14	12	14	12	13	12	14	12	14	12	14	12	14	12	13
13	17	13	17	13	15	13	15	13	15	13	15	13	14	13	15	13	15	13	15	13	15	13	14
14	18	14	18	14	16	14	16	14	16	14	16	14	15	14	16	14	16	14	16	14	16	14	15
15	19	15	19	15	17	15	17	15	17	15	17	15	16	15	17	15	17	15	17	15	17	15	16
16	20	16	20	16	18	16	18	16	18	16	18	16	17	16	18	16	18	16	18	16	18	16	17
17	21	17	21	17	19	17	19	17	19	17	19	17	18	17	19	17	19	17	19	17	19	17	18
18	22	18	22	18	20	18	20	18	20	18	20	18	19	18	20	18	20	18	20	18	20	18	19
19	23	19	23	19	21	19	21	19	21	19	21	19	20	19	21	19	21	19	21	19	21	19	20
20	24	20	24	20	22	20	22	20	22	20	22	20	21	20	22	20	22	20	22	20	22	20	21
21	25	21	25	21	23	21	23	21	23	21	23	21	22	21	23	21	23	21	23	21	23	21	22
22	26	22	26	22	24	22	24	22	24	22	24	22	23	22	24	22	24	22	24	22	24	22	23
23	27	23	27	23	25	23	25	23	25	23	25	23	24	23	25	23	25	23	25	23	25	23	24
24	28	24	28	24	26	24	26	24	26	24	26	24	25	24	26	24	26	24	26	24	26	24	25
25	29	25	29	25	27	25	27	25	27	25	27	25	26	25	27	25	27	25	27	25	27	25	26
26	30	26	30	26	28	26	28	26	28	26	28	26	27	26	28	26	28	26	28	26	28	26	27
27	31	27	May 1	27	29	27	29	27	29	27	29	27	28	27	29	27	29	27	29	27	29	27	28
28	Apr. 1	28	2	28	30	28	30	28	30	28	30	28	29	28	30	28	30	28	30	28	30	28	Mar. 1
29	2			29	31	29	July 1	29	31	29	31	29	30	29	31	29	Dec. 1	29	31	29	31	29	2
30	3			30	June 1	30	2	30	Aug. 1	30	Sep. 1	30	Oct. 1	30	Nov 1	30	2	30	Jan. 1	30	Feb. 1	30	3
31	4			31	2			31	2			31	2	31	2			31	2			31	4

As birth appears imminent, the birth's face takes on a worried look.

CHAPTER FIFTEEN

Whelping

An average gestation is sixty-three days, but puppies can be safely born as early as the fifty-ninth or sixtieth day from the first breeding and as late as the sixty-fifth day. Be prepared.

As her time gets closer, your bitch will become restless. She may even look for places to hide—behind a chair or in the closet. She may refuse all food, or eat very little, and go from digging a nest to sleeping deeply. As whelping becomes imminent the bitch's face will take on a worried look. She will want to go outside often because of the increasing pressure on her bladder. Do not let her out alone. If it is nighttime, use a flashlight and keep her on leash. Watch her closely for any roaching of her back and do not assume that she is only having a bowel movement. In reality, she may be having her first puppy.

Start taking your Vizsla's temperature (rectally) on her fifty-eighth day to establish what a normal temperature is for her. Take it morning, noon, and night and keep a written record. When it drops from a normal 101.5°F to almost 98.4°F you can be sure of labor starting within the next eight to ten hours. That is not to say that temperature always drops; some bitches will whelp without that warning.

As her restlessness continues, your bitch will experience excessive panting, accompanied by quivering legs or a trembling body. In between, she may stand or sit with glassy eyes. During this time, gather all your supplies, raise the room temperature to 80°F, turn the heating pad on low, put on a pot of coffee if you are afraid of falling asleep, and prepare to spend the next few hours at your bitch's side.

Supplies for the Whelping Box

The following supplies should be handy to the whelping box:

- Clean, dry cloths (cotton diapers are the perfect size and weight)
- A clean, medium-size cardboard box with a covered heating pad
- Rectal thermometer
- Clock
- Baby scales
- Hemostat(s)
- Sharp scissors with blunt ends
- Paper and pencil to chart weights and times of birth
- Rubber gloves
- KY Jelly
- Dental floss or heavy thread
- Room thermometer
- Electric space heater with temperature control
- Water bowl for the bitch
- Blankets or flannel sheets for whelping box
- Clean newspapers
- Alcohol or Merthiolate for navel cords
- Garbage bag
- Flashlight and leash for taking bitch out at night

Keep assuring your bitch that you are nearby and will help her through this. Remember, whelping is a frightening time for her, too, but do not overdo and smother her. Nature has prepared her to take care of this situation, but it is up to you to help ensure the safe arrival of her puppies.

LABOR AND DELIVERY

Labor starts with pressure from within forcing the puppy down the birth canal toward the pelvis. Abdominal contractions can be observed at this time and your bitch will roach her back as she pushes to get the puppy down the passage to the vulva.

Before the first puppy is expelled, a plug of mucus will precede him, along with a lot of fluid. Soon afterward you will see the bulge over the vulva, indicating that a puppy is pressing against it and is ready to be expelled with the next contraction. Keep your bitch calm by talking to her constantly. You may have to force her to stay in the whelping box.

The puppy will be enclosed in a membranous sac which is attached to the placenta, or afterbirth, by the umbilical cord. When a puppy begins the birthing process he is in his sac and protected by the surrounding fluid. There is enough oxygen left in his life-support system to see him through the journey down the birth canal. However, since each puppy can take a different length of time to make this passage, it is important that the newborn is removed from his sac as soon as possible after delivery. Most breeders help the bitch in this process instead of risking the chance that an overzealous, anxious, or scared bitch might unintentionally injure her puppy or might forget to remove the membrane.

You may have to help the puppy being expelled from the birth canal by gently grasping him with a cloth and easing him out. Gentle pulls should be timed with the contractions. Most of the time it is only the first puppy that will be a problem. This is also the one that may give the bitch the most pain, so be prepared for some screaming. When the puppy is out, immediately stick your finger in the sac by the puppy's head and tear the sac. It will peel back, exposing the newborn and releasing the fluids surrounding him. If the afterbirth is still connected, pinch the cord tightly about two inches from the stomach, pushing the blood supply in it towards the puppy. Quickly cut the cord, leaving at least one and a half inches attached to the puppy.

Pick the puppy up in a dry cloth. With his head facing downward, wipe the fluid from his nostrils and mouth. Then rub gently, but briskly, up and down his back to stimulate circulation. You may have to use a bulb syringe to get excess fluid from his mouth. When you hear him give his first strong yelp, quickly weigh him, note the sex, time of delivery, and if the afterbirth was expelled. Then give him to his mother (dam) to be cleaned and fed.

If the afterbirth was expelled, scoop it up in a newspaper and dispose of it. There are different opinions on whether you should allow the dam to eat it, and sometimes it can be a race to see which of you gets it first. Eating the afterbirth may give the bitch messy stools for several days.

It is however, imperative that a count of the afterbirths is done, to be sure that one arrives with each puppy. Quite often the afterbirth breaks away from the newborn and is retained. If it does not come out with subsequent births, make sure your veterinarian is told how many were retained when the whelping is over. A retained afterbirth can result in a serious infection and even the loss of the puppies or your bitch. The bitch must be given an injection to stimulate further contractions and clean out the uterus within the next twelve to sixteen hours.

The dam will get busy cleaning her new puppy. If she seems a little rough as she flips him upside down, do not be alarmed. She is actually stimulating his circulation and respiration. Check that she is also licking his rear to encourage the passage of his

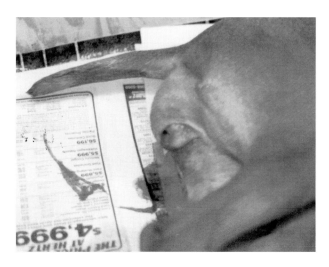

Note the bulge over the vulva, indicating that a puppy is being presented.

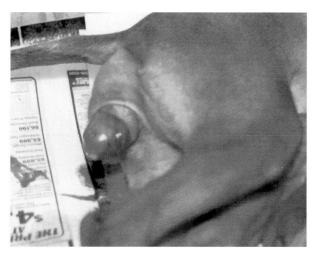

A large bubble appears first, indicating the sac with fluids.

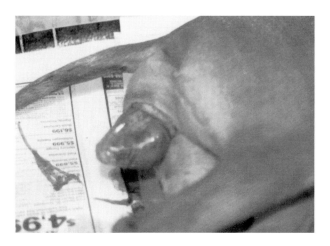

Assist the birth but do not pull the puppy out. Work with the contractions.

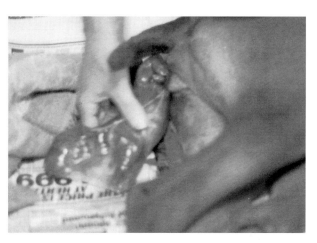

A normal delivery, with the newborn enclosed in the sac.

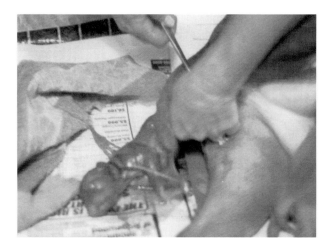

The cord is being cut. The afterbirth is still inside the dam.

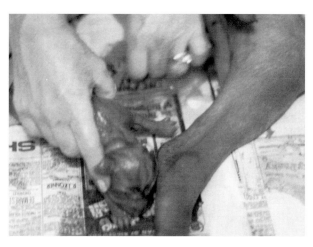

The newborn has been released from his sac so that he can breathe, and the afterbirth is gently being helped out. *Photos of the whelping by Paul Ratzlaff.*

The newborn is given to his dam to be cleaned.

Active cleaning of the newborn by his dam will stimulate breathing and circulation.

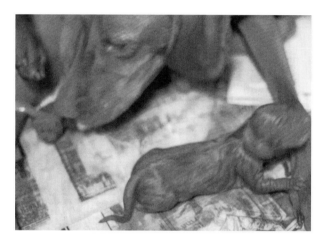

The dam turns her attention to consuming the afterbirth. It is doubtful that it offers any benefit and will give her messy stools.

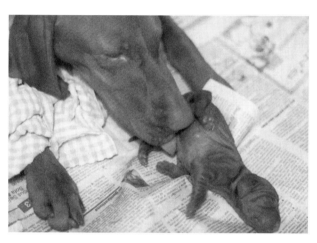

The dam will stimulate the newborn's urination by licking and washing him.

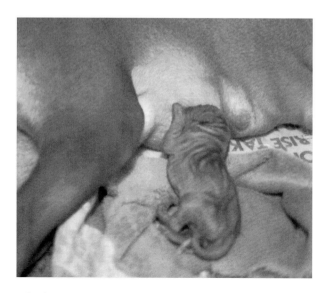

The first puppy nurses contentedly by himself.

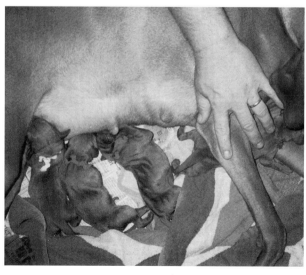

Newborns nurse as whelping continues. Photo by Lu Hart.

first stool. This will be dark in color and is called the *meconium*. Until it is passed, the puppy may suffer from constipation and may not nurse.

Guard that the dam does not chew on the umbilical cord of the newborn. If the cord is bleeding even slightly, clamp it with a hemostat for a few seconds and then tie a length of heavy thread, cord, or even dental floss, around it a good inch from the puppy's body. If the cord is still ragged and too long, trim it with scissors and put a drop of iodine on it.

If the cord was accidentally torn or cut too short, and if you have enough length left, tie it with cord as close to the end as possible, but never against the body of the puppy. If the dam licks it off again, and there is seepage, you will have to retie it. The umbilical cord will shrivel up and drop off within three days.

Most puppies are born with a tremendous instinct of where to go and how to suckle. A healthy, strong newborn with a will to live will nurse quickly. This nursing action will aid in stimulating uterine contractions and help in the delivery of subsequent puppies. If the newborn needs assistance, express a little milk from a nipple for him to smell, then gently and carefully open his mouth with a finger and insert the nipple into it while holding his body in place.

Your bitch may lie calmly feeding a puppy while having contractions or pushing another newborn out. On the other hand, she may become restless and agitated with another birth imminent and try to deliver it from a sitting or crouching position. If this is the case and you see the bulge over the vulva, quickly place the newborn puppies into the warming box so that they will not be accidentally stepped on in her distress.

You may be able to tell when your bitch has whelped her last puppy if she gives a contented sigh and calmly settles down to either take a nap or concentrate completely on her newborns. Now is the time to offer her a small bowl of food and water. That old standby of chicken soup is usually accepted.

If there have been several hours of labor, you might find her willing to go out to eliminate, especially if you take her puppies from her. Place them in the heated box, and put a leash on her.

Taking her outside will also give you the chance to see if she can pass any retained after births and to feel her abdomen for any puppies still unborn. For the next few days you may find it necessary to put a leash on your bitch and force her to go out and leave the puppies, since she will be reluctant to go on her own. Take the time to clean the whelping box before you let her back in it. Remove the wet, soiled newspapers and put down a thick, clean blanket, making sure that it fits the bottom of the box and does not leave any place for a puppy to crawl under. The puppies need the rough surface of a blanket or towel to anchor their feet and push as they nurse.

Return the new mother to her clean bed and give her puppies back to her, making sure that each one is able to nurse. It is important that the newborns are able to receive their dam's first milk, called colostrum, which contains antibodies that will protect them from disease during their first weeks of life. This first milk will change in composition about twenty-four hours after birth, so the puppies must start nursing soon. Their nursing action will help to stimulate an increase in the milk supply.

Even if the whelping was without complication and all the afterbirths are passed, it is still wise to have your bitch checked by a veterinarian within twelve hours.

PROBLEM DELIVERIES

The time between each puppy being born can vary from five minutes to over an hour in a normal whelping. Puppies are usually delivered head first, enclosed in their sac, but other types of delivery, which give some difficulty, are always a possibility. If left unaided, they could result in the loss of the newborn, or even the loss of your bitch.

A Normal Birth

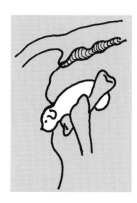

A normal birth; the puppy is head first. Note the way the birth canal curves over the pelvic bone. If you need to assist, always pull down, towards the bitch's stomach.

A Breech Birth

The puppy's rear is first. Breech births are sometimes more difficult. If possible, keep the bitch from breaking the sac until the puppy's head is out.

Weigh puppies regularly and keep charts of gain or loss.

Any delivery where a puppy is being presented rear end first is going to be more difficult. As you check the puppy in the vulva, you will be able to feel or see if he is still in the sac or if the sac has already broken under the pressure of the delivery. This is a dry delivery, and is quite common. If this is the case, it is imperative that you get the puppy into the world as quickly as possible before he asphyxiates. You must also deliver the puppy without injuring him or his dam.

Sometimes just standing your bitch on her feet and changing her position will force the puppy from her without any problems. In some cases the puppy may have a leg or two stuck inside the passage, or he may be turned sideways so that his back is presented. In either case, the dam cannot pass the puppy without him first being turned.

If you are dealing with a dry delivery and the puppy is out of the sac as you are attempting to turn him, he is in danger of drowning or suffocating. You must work quickly, but calmly. Put some lubricant on your surgical glove or scrubbed finger and carefully lubricate the inside opening of the vulva and as much of the puppy as you can reach. Determine if it is the back, rear, stomach, or a foot being presented. The puppy may be jammed against the vulva and if that is so, insert one or two fingers and push him very gently a small way up so that you are able to turn him and reposition the legs or the entire body. At no time should you attempt to pull the puppy out.

After turning the puppy, the dam should be able to expel him. As you help in any part of the delivery, if the puppy is arriving rear end first, you will have to remember to keep that end towards the dam's feet as he is being delivered. If the puppy is coming out head first, he should be brought out and downward in the direction of the dam's stomach. Never pull a puppy straight out.

If the contractions are strong and visible but no puppy is delivered after two hours, there is a chance that a puppy could have become stuck farther up in the birth canal. Puppies are carried in both horns of the uterus. If one is coming down each horn at the same time, they can become jammed at the stem of the Y.

If you are unable to feel anything within reach of your fingers, you need your veterinarian's assistance. Do not let this condition go beyond two hours. Your veterinarian will be able to determine the exact problem with an X-ray. A caesarean section may be necessary to prevent the bitch's uterus from rupturing.

Uterine Inertia

Primary inertia is the name given to the condition in which contractions and whelping do not start at all, even though early signs of whelping are present. The uterus is unable to contract, due perhaps to a large litter and the muscular wall of the uterus lacking either the room or the strength to contract. It could be that the bitch is overweight with poor muscle tone, or she may have a hormonal problem.

Whatever the cause, if your bitch's temperature has dropped to below 99°F, stayed there without fluctuating for twenty-four hours, and there are no signs of the hard contractions of the second stage of labor, take her to your veterinarian for professional help.

Secondary inertia may be the reason for a long, drawn-out whelping where your bitch does not have strong enough contractions to keep pushing a puppy down the birth canal. She may be able to whelp only part of her litter before the uterus loses strength and elasticity.

Your veterinarian may decide to give an injection of the hormone oxytocin to stimulate contractions if the inertia is due to a fatigued uterus. If the shot does not result in contractions within twenty minutes, you still may facing having the puppies removed surgically.

Caesarean Section

Surgical delivery of the litter is the only solution in some cases, and the chances of

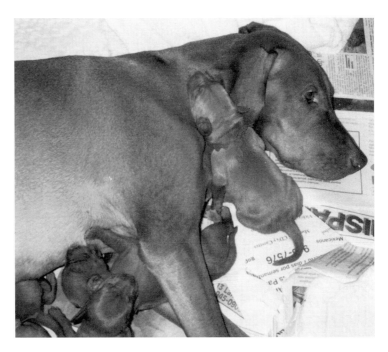

This twelve-hour-old little girl seeking the warmth of her dam grew up to become Ch. Prairie's Cobalt Blue, TD, JH.

saving both the puppies and their dam are good if the surgery is performed before your bitch becomes exhausted.

If she has already whelped several puppies, leave them in the whelping box on a warm—not hot—heating pad. Take the warming box, lined with cloths and another heating pad or hot water bottle, with you to the veterinary clinic. It is also wise to take along the stack of clean cloths used for whelping as your veterinarian may not have anything to dry the newborns with except paper towels.

Your vet will probably be glad to have an extra hand in getting the newborns rubbed down and breathing as he removes them from the uterus. If you are able to help, it will be an exciting and interesting experience for you as a breeder.

The newborn puppy may be limp, blue, and slow to breathe, and you will not have very much time to stimulate one before the next one is handed to you. Try to get that first strong cry before placing each puppy in the warm box. As your veterinarian is completing the surgery, keep working with the puppies if they are still limp and weak. Do

not give up until warmth and pink color comes back into the pads of their feet, nose and mouth.

When the veterinarian is finished, he will give your bitch a shot to reverse the analgesic, and she should be able to walk out of his door for the trip home. However, once back in the whelping box, it is possible that she will go into a deep sleep, leaving you to care for the newborns. It will be up to you to encourage their urination and passing of the meconium and to get each one nursing to stimulate milk production. Stroke each puppy's stomach and genital and anal area gently with a warm, wet cotton ball to stimulate urination and defecation. This must be repeated after each feeding until the dam takes over.

If the puppies are weak and without a healthy pink color to their skin and feet, it may be necessary to tube-feed them to get them over the trauma of their birth. Each puppy should receive almost 2 cc of a commercial bitch's milk formula for their first feeding. It may be that this one time is all that is needed to give them the strength to nurse. Your veterinarian can show you how to tube-feed and give you the necessary equipment and formula.

Your bitch may wake from her sleep and not even recognize that the newborns are hers. She may need reassuring to accept them at first, but gradually her maternal instinct will take over. Rubbing some of the discharge from her vulva onto the puppies may help her to accept them.

Take your bitch's temperature twice a day for a week following surgery and watch the incision carefully for any signs of infection. Use small manicure scissors to keep the puppies' nails cut short so they will not injure the incision.

CHAPTER SIXTEEN

Care of the Newborn Puppy

Many times an exceptionally good puppy has been saved by the extra attention given at the time when he really needed it. The inconvenience of almost constant supervision of the litter is more than worthwhile.

For the first week of the newborn's life he will look at though he is nursing incessantly, and although it looks like the dam does not have very much milk, the nursing action at her breasts will stimulate milk production. However, while a newborn may be able to exist for several hours without that milk, he cannot live long without warmth. Make sure that a weaker puppy is not being pushed away from the warmth of his dam's body.

THE HEALTHY NEWBORN VIZSLA

The newborn puppy arrives with the instinct to seek warmth and food. You will be amazed at the strength and energy shown when, barely out of the sac, he struggles so much it will be hard to get an accurate reading of his weight. Place him anywhere in the whelping box and he will rapidly propel himself to the warmth of the dam's mammary glands. He will immediately react to touch by looking for a nipple to suck.

While you may think that each puppy is constantly nursing, one may be lying there with the nipple in his mouth, too weak or tired to suck. Check often to make sure the smallest or weakest one is not being pushed out of the way while the strongest get all the milk. Hold that puppy in place at a nipple if necessary.

For careful monitoring, each puppy should be weighed daily until a week old, then every three days until two weeks of age. From then on, weighing only once a week will be fine. Making a mark on different ears or toes with a marking pencil or finger-nail polish will help you keep an identification system for each puppy and is safer than colored ribbons around their neck. Keep an accurate weight chart for each puppy.

Normal Vizsla puppies will gain weight steadily, although there is an initial loss of up to ten percent during the first two days of life. They should double their birth weight by seven to nine days and from then on steadily gain a pound a week. The average birth weight of a Vizsla newborn will be ten to fourteen ounces, and gaining steadily, he will probably weigh around five pounds at four weeks of age. A puppy weighing only eight ounces at birth will gain weight at a slower pace for the first three weeks, and will need extra attention to make sure he is getting a place on a nipple without being pushed aside by larger littermates. He may also benefit from supplemental bottle feeding.

Five days old. Each puppy should be monitored by handling and weighing often.

This small puppy is being cradled in a lap very carefully.

A healthy, happy puppy is generally quiet, but sometimes makes a singing sound as he nurses. He may fuss and get angry if his nipple is out of milk, but you will learn by the tone of his voice what is wrong. While sleeping, his body will twitch and jerk. This pattern is called activated sleep, and is necessary in the development of the neuromuscular system. A puppy that is ill will not show this movement, so watch your litter carefully. A puppy lying by himself away from his dam is not necessarily ill as long as he shows this activity. Even tiny newborns will crawl away from their heat source if too warm. If all the puppies cry and heap together in a pile, it is usually because they are cold.

A puppy that is thin or weak, does not nurse, or is continually being pushed away from a nipple needs attention. Puppies quickly dehydrate if they are not nursing. You can check on a puppy's condition by feeling inside his mouth. If it is slimy and moist, the puppy is okay; if it is dry and tacky, the puppy is dehydrated. He can also be checked by lifting the skin on his neck. In a healthy animal, the skin will rapidly fall back into place. The skin of a dehydrated puppy will remain away from the body for several seconds. Dehydrated puppies need immediate veterinarian attention and will probably require supplemental feeding by tube or bottle. During the first one to three days, a healthy neonatal puppy will suckle at least forty times a day for a total of ten to fifteen hours a day. By day four the suckling is more efficient, so only eight hours a day is necessary.

Do not be overly concerned if a puppy shuffles around and cries a little. He might have some gas or, in the case of a large litter, the dam may not have gotten around to stimulating him to urinate or defecate. Pick him up to massage or burp him, stroking the stomach with a warm, wet cotton ball to stimulate elimination. You should then be able to return him to his dam.

DEWCLAW REMOVAL AND TAIL DOCKING

If the puppies all are born healthy and in good weight, the tails and dewclaws should be cut by their second day. Dewclaws are what the Hungarians call "bastard toes." Located on the inner part of the pastern area on front legs, they are removed from many of the sporting breeds to keep them from being torn when working in the fields.

The dam will fret and tear her bed apart if left behind, so take her along on the trip to the veterinarian. Do leave her in a crate in the car, however, so that she does not hear the puppy's cries.

Make sure your veterinarian understands that the Vizsla standard calls for two thirds of the tail to be *left on*. Eyeball or measure each puppy individually before he cuts so as to be satisfied with the decision.

There are several methods used for docking and your veterinarian will usually go along with your choice. A single suture can be put across the cut of each of the tail and the dewclaw area, but the easiest and fastest way is to just have the areas cauterized after cutting, with medication designed to stop any bleeding. With the use of stitches, the dam may worry at them and lick them off, irritating the areas.

Until healed, check the sites daily for any signs of infection. Vizsla puppies are very determined as they climb over littermates on the way to a nipple. They can easily tear the scabs off dewclaw areas with their

Young puppies will sleep together in a bunch.

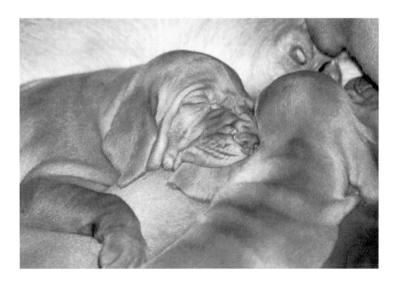

Warm, full, and happy.

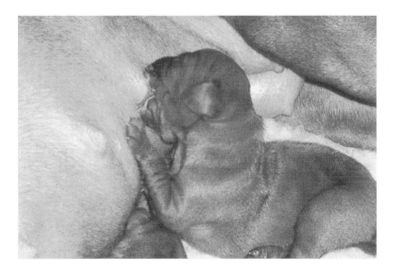

This healthy four-day-old puppy is actively sucking.

sharp nails. If an infection does develop, clean the area with hydrogen peroxide or Betadine.

ORPHAN PUPPIES

In a case where the dam is unable to feed her litter because of surgery or illness, or when a dam is lost through death, the entire job of raising orphan puppies will take over your life for several weeks. There is nothing difficult about hand rearing a litter, but it is very time-consuming.

You must keep the puppies warm, clean, and fed. A smaller size than that of a normal whelping box should be used for the first couple of weeks, since the puppies will not have the warmth of their dam's body to lie against and they will want to stay bunched up close together. It is important that the box be in a draft-free area where you can control the temperature. Place a thermometer on the floor to get the correct reading at the level of the puppies.

Since a newborn is unable to control his body temperature for the first couple of weeks of life, the area should be main-

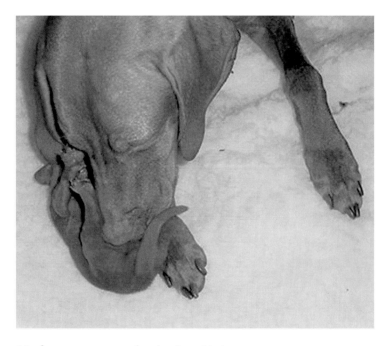

Newborn puppy gets a cleaning from his dam.

tained at a constant 85°F. Humidity is very important and, if too low, the puppies will tend to dehydrate. A pan of water near the heat source will help to balance the environment.

Cleanliness is essential since the puppies have not received colostrum from the dam to protect them from viruses. Bedding must be changed daily and all feeding utensils, nipples, and bottles should be sterilized. Be aware that your clothes and shoes can carry infectious diseases home with you from dog shows. More importantly, do not allow visitors.

The milk formula you will feed is available in most pet supply stores, or if you wish, you can mix your own. To a can of evaporated milk, add an equal amount of water, one tablespoon of honey, an egg yolk, baby vitamin drops and one teaspoon of di-calcium phosphate. For the first week, the amount being fed each day should be about fifteen percent of body weight, then twenty-five percent during the next week. Monitor body weight daily as the puppies must not lose weight. Feed every two to four hours the first day, but do not wake to feed. Gradually reduce the frequency to four times daily.

The easiest way to bottle feed a puppy is to place him, stomach down, on your lap with a rolled towel in front of him. A puppy will push and knead at his dam's breast as he nurses and the towel will enable him to simulate his normal behavior.

If you squeeze a drop of milk from the nipple first to give him a smell, a hungry puppy will wrap his tongue around the nipple with a strong sucking action. The formula *must be the right temperature*. Too hot or too cold and he will refuse it. Squeeze a little onto the back of your hand first to test it—if it is uncomfortably hot or cold for you, do not attempt to feed it to the puppy until the temperature is right. Feed enough that his stomach becomes just slightly distended, and keep a slight pull on the bottle to encourage strong sucking.

For the first two weeks of life a young puppy relies on being stimulated in order to urinate or pass a stool. In the case of the orphan, these functions will have to be aided by you, so gently rub his abdomen and rear with a warm, wet cotton ball.

After you feed and clean the puppies, burp each one as you would a baby. Hold him against your shoulder and rub his back. This will relieve him of any air taken in from the bottle.

A puppy with a loose stool could be either overfed or ill. At the first sign of diarrhea, dilute your formula with some additional water. If the condition persists, have your veterinarian check for any bacterial infection. A healthy puppy fed six times a day will have from six to seven bowel movements.

At two weeks of age, the puppies will be able to eliminate on their own and maintain their own body temperature. If your puppies are gaining weight daily and seem reasonably happy and quiet, you can be sure that they are adequately fed. They should actually be at the same stage in their development as a normal litter, so by eighteen days of age you should consider feeding them partially solid food from a pan. Do not eliminate the bottle completely for several days until you are sure each puppy is eating well and still gaining weight.

Puppies raised without their dam will associate you with the food supply within a couple of days after birth and will have a very close attachment to you, so continue to give them a lot of attention even when the bottle feeding has been discontinued.

Tube-Feeding

The formula for the feeding should be freshly prepared for each feeding. All items to be used should be freshly sanitized by washing in good hot detergent and rinsed in clear water to remove all residue. Proper sanitation practices play a very important part in the development of healthy puppies.

Withdraw the amount of formula to be used by sucking the desired amount up through the syringe with a needle or tube affixed. A clean tube should be used for each puppy, making sure of the measurement prior to insertion. Stretch the tube along the side of the puppy's body from the tip of his nose to the last rib. A mark at this point on the tube is the maximum depth that is to be inserted into the puppy.

With the palm of your hand over the forehead of the puppy; apply gently pressure between the jaws to aid in spreading open his mouth. Keep him on a level surface that is a convenient height for working. With the other hand, gently insert the tube into the mouth, back over the tongue, and permit the puppy to swallow the tube. If a cough is evoked, remove the tube and reinsert again. Wetting the tube with water prior to insertion makes it easier to pass. As the tube goes down the esophagus, watch your mark to aid in judging the amount of tube to be inserted. Although the tube is soft enough to bend in the stomach if too much is passed, it is wiser to pass only the minimum amount of tube to permit room for milk.

After the tube is passed, then attach the syringe and slowly press the plunger to permit flow into the tube. The average

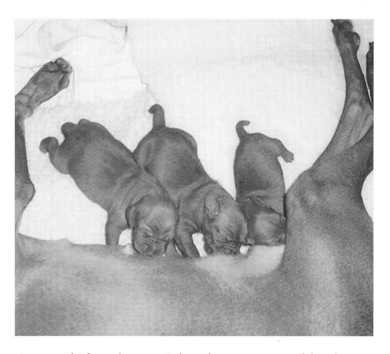

At one week of age, these puppies' eyes have not yet opened, but they know where the food is.

newborn puppy should get 3-4 cc at four-hour intervals. If at any time the puppy acts extremely uncomfortable, coughs or gags, or permits milk to come out of the mouth or nostrils, immediately stop feeding and disconnect the syringe and carefully withdraw the tube from his stomach. In some instances, you may have overfed. Wipe any excess milk from the mouth and nostrils and lower his head to permit any excess to run out of the nose and mouth. Give less formula at the next feeding.

After the first week, the amount to be fed may be increased, and the number of feedings decreased.

ILLNESS IN NEWBORNS

The most frequent time of death for a newborn is between twenty-four and forty-eight hours after birth. General signs of illness include poor reflexes when stimulated, the puppy straying from his dam and not nursing, weight loss, high-pitched screaming, crying and restlessness even in a warm environment, diarrhea, and labored breathing accompanied by blue coloration of pads and membranes. A healthy puppy does little crying and will sleep relaxed with occasional muscle twitching.

"Fading puppy" is a term used to describe a death that occurs in the first few days of life, not including death caused by birth defects or any anatomical malformations. Changes in newborns can occur suddenly. Where just a few hours ago you had a happy, healthy puppy, you could suddenly have one that is quiet, listless, cold, and lying away from the rest of the litter.

The normal temperature of a newborn is 94 to 97°F during the first week of life. Born soaking wet from his dam, his body temperature is 101°F, but within minutes it will drop to 94°F. By the time he is twenty-four hours old, his temperature will stabilize if he is getting heat from his dam.

By the end of his first week of life, his body temperature will rise to 99°F and by the end of his fourth week the puppy will maintain a temperature of 101°F.

If at any time his rectal temperature falls below 94°F, his digestive system becomes paralyzed and nursing becomes ineffectual. The puppy will die unless he quickly receives help for his low energy. At this point dehydration is a very serious development, but giving any milk formula may be the surest way to guarantee the puppy's death. It is essential that the puppy be warmed gradually and this may take two to three hours.

Mix a solution of one teaspoon of Karo syrup or honey to one ounce of warm water. Give some to the puppy by dropper every half-hour until he is warm and responsive. It will be absorbed immediately into the stomach, raising his blood sugar and halting the hypoglycemic condition.

Try to keep him close to his dam's body for extra warmth, or on a warm—never hot—heating pad. Examine him closely as he is being warmed, as his condition may warrant a specific treatment.

Toxic Milk

If there are toxins in the dam's system, symptoms will appear in the puppies around the end of their first week of life. These toxins usually result from debris or a retained placenta in the dam's uterus breaking down into toxic substances that are excreted in her milk.

After the first stools, which will be dark, have been passed, the dam will be cleaning up after the puppies so fast it will be hard to find any evidence of their condition. However, there may be signs of fecal material left on the bedding when diarrhea is present.

The color of a normal bowel movement should be brownish yellow and the consistency fairly firm. If a case of diarrhea shows up as only a temporary problem, it may be the result of overeating. If the color progresses to a dark green stool and you have a puppy with a red, sore anus, the problem may have been caused by toxic milk.

The entire litter will have to be bottle or tube fed formula and treated with both

The Healthy Versus the Sick Puppy: What to Look For

The Healthy Puppy	The Sick Puppy
gains weight	doesn't gain weight
sleek, smooth coat	rough, dull coat
cries infrequently	cries frequently
good muscle and skin tone	limp, wrinkled skin
round, plump, firm body	flat, tucked up appearance
pink mucous membranes	pot-bellied
activated sleep	reddish-purple or blue mucous membranes
yawns frequently	scattered around the nest
nurses strongly	cries or mews
	diarrhea
	can't or won't suck

Careful observation will warn you of any complication. If your bitch seems abnormally depressed, anxious, or upset, it would be wise to have her checked. It is in whelping and caring for puppies and their mother, more than at any other time, that you and your vet will need to work as a team. Be sure to have a veterinarian you can trust and work with; then consult him regularly.

an antibiotic and an antidiarrheal medication while the dam is also under treatment. Puppies may possibly be able to be returned to their nursing after twenty-four hours.

It is wise to give puppies yogurt or lactobacillus acidophilus any time they are under treatment for diarrhea in order to restore the normal bacteria level to their intestines. Two teaspoons every twelve hours should be sufficient.

Septicemia

Septicemia is a bacterial infection in a puppy's bloodstream which either enters the body through infected milk or from the site of an infected umbilical cord. It is essential to find the cause as one puppy can infect the entire litter and death may occur.

Inspect the umbilical cord for any pus, redness, or swelling. If such is the case, clean the area with hydrogen peroxide or Betadine and swab it with iodine. Antibiotic therapy must be started immediately. A clean whelping box is a necessity. Blankets must be changed several times a day and any infected

puppy must be isolated. Also check the site of tail docking and dewclaw removal daily.

Another site of contamination that can rapidly spread bacterial infection through the entire litter may be the dam's mammary

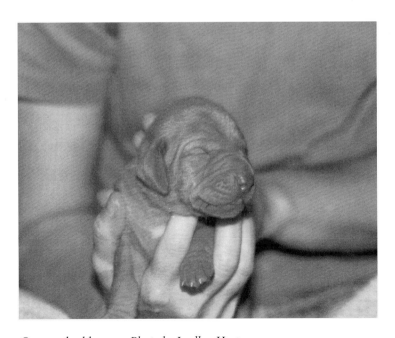

One-week-old puppy. Photo by Luellen Hart.

glands. It may be necessary to remove the puppies from her and hand feed them while she is under treatment for an abscess or infection.

Herpes

Herpes is a virus that may be acquired by the newborns as they pass through an infected vaginal tract at birth. The symptoms appear suddenly in previously healthy puppies. Starting with constant crying from abdominal swelling and pain, the puppies soon refuse to nurse and become chilled. Their stools are soft, green diarrhea. Hemorrhages of the liver and kidneys follow and it is almost impossible to save a puppy at this stage. Death could occur within twenty-four hours of the first signs.

Herpes usually affects a puppy under the age of three weeks while his body temperature is still at a low level. The virus will reproduce rapidly at body temperatures of 95°F. If a puppy's temperature can be raised and maintained closer to 100°F by increasing the temperature and humidity in the box, and he is treated with antibiotics and fluids, there is a slight chance of saving him, providing the treatment is started early.

Handle the puppies daily and get them used to the sound of your voice.

CHAPTER SEVENTEEN

The Growing Vizsla Puppy

Puppies are living, breathing creatures that require more than just a clean bed, food, and medical care. Unlike Topsy, they do not "just grow." After the whelping is over and the puppies are nursing on their own, do not make the mistake of spending less time with them, depriving them of the individual attention which each one needs to guarantee he will accept a human relationship. Socialization is the responsibility of the breeder from the minute the puppies are born.

SOCIALIZATION AND CARE

During the neonatal period, or the first two weeks of life, the dam will provide optimal care for her puppies, and your attention should be concentrated upon making sure the mother is well nourished and allowed to care for her litter quietly, undisturbed by strangers or commotion.

Inspect each puppy once a day for possible illness or injury, and put down clean bedding for them. Even puppies this young will benefit from handling. They will react strongly to touch and will fuss and struggle. If picked up suddenly they may give a yelp of sudden fear as if in pain. Hold them close to your body so they can get used to your smell. Their nails should be trimmed regularly to keep them from scratching littermates and their dam as they climb and scramble for a nipple.

As your Vizsla puppies go into their second week of life, they will have deeper, less activated sleep until their ears open at thirteen to fifteen days, when sudden noises will startle them.

Eyes should open at the same time if the puppies were born at approximately the full term of sixty-three days. Puppies born early will rarely open their eyes before their sixteenth day, while puppies born late may start to open their eyes as early as twelve days of age. Watch their eyes carefully during this time for any swelling or pus from irritation or infections.

During this time you should keep the puppies out of direct sunlight and reduce the constant glare of overhead lighting until their eyes are completely open. Eye color will be bluish for several weeks, but should darken by the time the puppies are eight weeks old.

By twelve days of age, the puppies will be making awkward, comical efforts to get up on their feet, and will stand for a few seconds at a time. From now on their development will be rapid. Handle and talk to them often so that they can get used to the sound of your voice and your smell.

At seventeen days of age, the puppies will be more active on their legs and will mouth each other and growl. They will be very much aware of their surroundings and their littermates, and they will no longer need the stimulation from their dam to urinate or

Ouch! These puppies have teeth.

Coby at five weeks of age already has his favorite toys.
Photo courtesy Luellen Hart.

defecate, although she will still clean up after them.

The eruption of their first teeth through the gums can be felt at approximately eighteen days, and soon the mother is glad to be away from them, returning only when she knows they have to be fed. Normal room temperature should be maintained now, without drafts. The dam's body will keep the puppies warm at night if it gets cool. Make sure their bedding is clean and dry.

Suddenly when they are twenty-one days old, it may seem as if a light bulb goes on inside your puppies' heads as they start to put it all together. Every day becomes a new experience. This is called the "socialization period," and the puppies become very much aware of any changes in their environment. They may not start to explore or relax outside their whelping box until they have been out several times. The bolder ones will be the most inquisitive and the others will follow. They will generally react as a group and even a timid puppy will not want to be left behind.

This period is the most critical time of their development. How you handle them will determine their adult life. Your Vizsla puppies have started to become independent of their dam, capable of knowing different people and voices. They should exhibit no fear of people as long as care is taken to prevent them from being injured or unnecessarily frightened.

Only by daily observation, talking, playing, and personal contact with your puppies can you prevent fear behavior. The things that a Vizsla breeder should offer to each buyer of his puppies are dependability and a well-adjusted, happy dog that will readily accept the new owner as his leader.

Between the third and fourth week there is an amazingly rapid development in the puppies' senses. This is the time to give them safe toys to play with and encourage their natural retrieving instinct. Soft, washable stuffed animals, which are safe for small children, are the most fun for them to carry and will also encourage a soft bite.

Do not allow anyone to hold a struggling puppy. He may jump out of their arms and be injured. Ask visitors, especially children, to sit on the floor and allow the puppies to approach them on their own.

During this socialization period your puppies will start to go to one side of their whelping box to eliminate instead of soiling their sleeping area. Put a blanket on only one-half of the box and newspapers on the other half. The dam will clean up after the puppies only until they start getting meat in their diet. Even so, you will find that the box will stay clean except for urination once you have started to let them out to play after each meal. Cover an area on the floor with newspapers and wait until each puppy has a bowel movement before

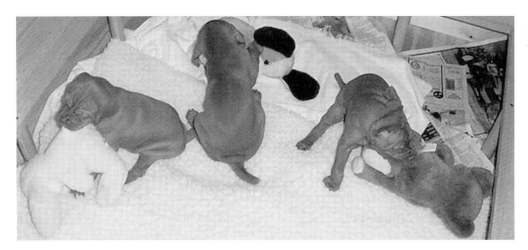

Even puppies this young enjoy stuffed toys to wrestle with.

It only takes a couple of days for puppies to master eating from a dish and graduate to solid foods.

A round feeding dish makes it easier to feed Lori Salb's litter of nine.

placing him back into the box. Do this early in the morning and after each meal and there will be very little soiling in the whelping box.

The puppies can start to eat out of a pan as early as eighteen days of age if they are fairly steady on their legs. Keep them away from their dam for several hours so that they are hungry and they will be eager to lap up their first meal. Puppies have to be taught to eat and how they get their start may easily determine eating habits later on.

Mix baby cereal with either a commercial bitch's milk formula or mix your own, using the same directions for tube or bottle feedings. Keep the formula refrigerated and use only what is needed for each meal.

Warm the milk first and mix it with human baby cereal, making it fairly sloppy and thin.

The first few meals will be messy as the puppies plaster themselves with the sticky cereal, standing with their feet in the dish or even lying in it. You may have to push their mouths into the food to give them a taste and start them off. Let their dam clean them—she will enjoy the extra food.

After they have mastered eating the soft, sloppy gruel, gradually combine it with soaked and softened puppy meal. You need to get your pups on an established feeding program, so try to feed them each day at the same time. Soak the meal in warm water until it has softened and then mash it well before adding it to the cereal and milk mix.

Confining a litter of young puppies behind a baby gate or a pen helps keep cleaning and feeding easier.

One-month-old litter of Luellen Hart's is active and healthy.

Feed the puppies three times a day and allow their dam to spending time with them between meals and at night.

By the time the puppies are four weeks of age, add boiled hamburger and the broth from it to the meal, eliminating the baby cereal. A little bit of cottage cheese or cooked egg can also be added occasionally.

By the time the puppies are five and a half weeks old, they should be completely weaned from their dam. They will need four meals a day, with the last one given in the late evening to carry them through the night. Their teeth will be stronger and they will be a great deal rougher. As a result, there will be a rapid change in their relationship with the dam. She may return to them only to regurgitate her food for them to eat. The puppies will have become completely independent of her. They will be active and happy and fun to watch. They will chew on everything they come into contact with, and show rapid development of intelligence.

They may growl and fight among themselves, establishing a dominance pattern. In a litter of both sexes, the most dominant puppy is usually a very active, outgoing female. Give special attention to any puppy which is not joining the play group.

By seven weeks of age, your puppies are going to be ready for their first vaccinations. Follow your veterinarian's protocol. There have been many changes in the vaccine combinations, so carefully consider what will work the best not only with this first shot but also with subsequent ones. Vaccinations will carry the puppies from the passive immunity provided by their dam to their own active immunity against those diseases.

When you take your puppies in for their vaccinations, take a stool sample for a final test before they go to their new homes. Also ask your veterinarian to do a complete physical on each puppy. This examination should also include listening to the puppy's heart, or cardiac auscultation, with a stethoscope. Each time the puppy goes to a veterinarian for his vaccinations, this cardiac auscultation should be performed with special attention to the location and size of the heart, the rhythm and intensity of the heart sounds, and the presence of abnormal sounds. If a heart murmur is detected, it is important to follow up with routine blood work.

Average Weight Chart

	Bitches				Dogs		
	1	2	3	4	1	2	3
	dark no/w	dark no/w	lighter color	small w/on/rt rear	lighter color	dark w/on chest	dark Sm. w/ on chest
Birth	.15	.15	.14	.13	1.	1.	1.2
3 Days	1.2	1.3	1.2	1.	1.4	1.3	1.6
Gain	.3	.4	.4	.3	.4	.3	.4
5 Days	1.6	1.8	1.6	1.1	1.6	1.8	1.8
Gain	.4	.5	.4	.1	.2	.5	.2
7 Days	1.14	1.14	1.10	1.4	1.12	1.14	2.2
Gain	.8	.6	.4	.3	.6	.6	.10
10 Days	2.2	2.8	2.4	2.	2.14	2.6	2.6
Gain	.4	.10	.10	.12	1.2	1.8	.4
2 Weeks	3.	3.	3.	2.10	3.14	3.	3.4
Wkly Gain	1.2	1.2	1.6	1.6	2.2	1.2	1.2
2½ Weeks	3.4	3.14	3.4	3.	4.8	3.14	3.8
Wkly Gain	1.2	1.6	1.	1.	1.10	1.8	1.2
3 Weeks	4.	4.2	4.4	3.12	5.4	4.4	4.4
Wkly Gain	1.	1.2	1.4	1.2	1.6	1.4	1.
4 Weeks	5.10	5.10	5.12	4.8	7.	5.14	6.
Wkly Gain	1.10	1.8	1.8	.12	1.12	1.10	1.12
5 Weeks	7.2	7.2	7.	5.14	8.4	7.6	7.2
Wkly Gain	1.8	1.8	1.4	1.6	1.4	1.8	1.2
6 Weeks	8.8	9.	8.6	6.14	10.8	9.6	9.6
Wkly Gain	1.6	1.14	1.6	1.	2.4	2.	2.4
7 Weeks	10.4	11.6	10.6	8.6	13.4	11.6	11.6
Wkly Gain	1.12	2.6	2.	1.8	2.12	2.	2.
8 Weeks	12.8	13.6	12.4	10.	14.8	13.12	13.14
Wkly Gain	2.4	2.	1.14	1.10	1.4	2.6	2.8
Total Gain	11.7	12.9	11.6	9.3	13.8	12.12	12.12

This five-week-old puppy of Shelley Coburn's will soon be climbing.

PROBLEMS WITH GROWING PUPPIES

Swimmers

This condition is not hereditary but environmental, and can possibly be controlled or prevented by realizing what is happening to an overweight puppy. It usually happens in a small litter of two or three puppies with a dam that has an abundance of rich milk. The "swimmer" puppy will lie there and eat, getting a constantly filled stomach until, when he is about two weeks of age and should be learning to walk, he is too heavy to pull himself up on his feet. He will lie sprawled on his stomach with the weight flattening his rib cage so that he grows sideways instead of upwards. His rear legs will spread out behind him with the feet turned inward so that he looks deformed. He will try to propel himself by pulling with his front feet and using his head and neck as leverage.

The immediate problem can be helped by always keeping a blanket in the whelping box instead of newspapers to provide better footing. Puppies need a rough surface to provide traction. At this age, the puppy's rib cage is soft and pliable. If the swimmer can be taught to use his rear legs and walk normally, his rib cage will eventually round out and be normal.

Several times a day take the puppy to a carpeted area. Place one hand under the rear and the other hand under his chest with his feet barely touching the carpet. Gradually let the weight come down on the feet until he learns to move all four legs. Keep your hand under his rear to support most of the weight.

It will take several days of following this procedure before he learns to straighten his rear legs enough to support himself, but from then on the progress is rapid. While you are teaching him to walk, you can also control his weight gain by keeping him away from his dam for longer periods of time so that he is not constantly nursing.

Do not get discouraged by this condition. If you keep at it during the early stage, by eight to ten weeks of age the swimmer puppy's rib cage and legs will be normal.

Umbilical Hernia

If there is a great deal of strain and pulling on a puppy's umbilical cord during whelping,

Puppies will wrestle with each other but a playmate is a lot more fun.

Six-week-old puppies love the attention and learn socialization.

a tear can develop in the abdominal wall, allowing a portion of the skin to protrude and hindering the normal closing of the umbilical ring. Quite often this hernia, or protrusion, can be pushed into the opening and tape placed over it to hold it in place. However, most hernias have to be corrected with surgery when the puppy gets older, especially on a female puppy that may eventually be used for breeding. On rare occasions a hernia will get smaller and disappear by the time a puppy is six months old without any treatment.

A litter of six-week-old puppies at meal time.

Conjunctivitis

The eyes of Vizsla puppies usually start to open about eleven days after their birth, but will stay mere slits for a couple of days until fully opened. During this time of being only partially open, the eyes must be examined daily for any swelling or pus.

As young puppies push and scramble for a nipple, a toenail can scratch an eyelid and cause a bacterial infection which could rapidly multiply behind the eyelid.

Untreated, this can cause permanent damage. Pus must be drained out by gently opening the eyelid a little and pressing carefully to express the pus. Obtain antibiotic ointment or drops from your veterinary and kept the eyelid from sealing over, trapping the infection.

Skin Problems

Even under the cleanest conditions, problems can arise, especially skin conditions that require an expert diagnosis. These conditions can be caused by staphylococcus, fungus, or even allergies.

The dam's discharge after whelping may contain the microorganisms responsible for a staphylococcus infection erupting on the face and feet of puppies. Sores erupt rapidly when the Vizsla puppy is around five weeks of age, with the symptoms starting as inflamed, swollen areas of the feet, then opening up into sores, and finally infecting the muzzle area as the puppy lays his head down on his feet to sleep.

Coby at six weeks trying to figure out how to carry his chukar.

Never too young to start thinking of all those obedience titles. Six-week-old Scarlett. Photo by Luellen Hart.

The affected area will have to be treated locally with a shampoo and internally with an antibiotic. It will take at least three weeks of consistent care to bring a staphylococcus infection under control. There will be hair loss in the affected areas, but this should start to fill in as soon as the sores heal.

In the case of a fungal infection, the sores may not be as penetrating and may only show up as red areas with hair loss. A veterinarian may prescribe a good betadine shampoo combined with an antibiotic treatment. In cases that do not respond, he may decide to do a skin scraping and culture.

One problem that can be readily identified is juvenile pyoderma (strangles). Along with pus-filled sores, the lymph glands in the neck are enlarged, the face and lips are swollen, the temperature is elevated and the puppy becomes very ill. The lesions must be handled very gently as they are painful. They must be cleaned with a mild antiseptic solution. As they crust, mineral oil can be used to soften them so that the crusts can be removed without leaving any scars. In the case of a very young puppy, liquid antibiotics can be given with a medicine dropper.

Another skin problem among very young puppies has been called "Vizsla rash," although it is common in many breeds. Small pimples or pustules appear on the puppy's head and sometimes his entire body. These pustules break and scab over, leaving a very scruffy look to the coat.

There is no clear evidence that attributes the condition to a dirty whelping box, but rather the dam's tongue may be infecting the puppy after she has cleaned up her vaginal discharge. Whatever the cause, the condition should be brought to the attention of your veterinarian and treatment started immediately with scrubs and medication. Blankets and newspapers in the whelping box must be kept clean at all times.

Internal Parasites

Keeping a litter of puppies worm-free is a primary concern for every breeder. Even worming your bitch before breeding does not guarantee that her puppies will not be born already infested. If at any time in her life your bitch harbored hookworms or roundworms, the parasites can live in a dormant stage until she becomes pregnant. At that point they migrate through the placenta and into the puppy in utero.

As early as two weeks of age the puppies may start having a dark stool with a mucous

Shelley Coburn's puppies have a strange playmate.

At seven weeks, alert, healthy, and active.

What a nice masculine head on this boy!

These puppies of Peggy Schmidt's are comfort seekers.

These seven-week-old puppies must be tired to be able to get this shot of them. Owned by Steve Shlyen.

Let me at that bird!!

Crate training these young puppies will make it easier for their new owners.

These puppies belonging to Lori Salb are ready to explore a bigger world.

A seven-week-old puppy being taught to "stack."

Tired puppies. Owned by Steve Shlyen.

coating. You will have to monitor the box fairly closely in order to get a stool sample before the dam cleans it up. You can identify roundworms passed in the stool, as they are visible as small, skinny, spaghetti-shaped worms, usually wound into a coil. Hookworms must be identified under a microscope. These are the most debilitating of the parasites. The worm attaches itself to the lining of the small intestines and nourishes itself by sucking the puppy's blood. If left untreated, hookworms can cause anemia and prove fatal to your puppy. Hookworm eggs can be seen in the stool as early as ten days after your litter's birth, and early diagnosis and treatment is necessary. A puppy with hookworm infestation will have a dark, tarry stool and fail to gain weight.

Several liquid worming medications can be used safely on puppies even as young as two to three weeks of age. One worming treatment is not sufficient to completely rid a puppy of the worms; a second treatment will be necessary two weeks later. Continue having stool checks done at two- or three-week intervals.

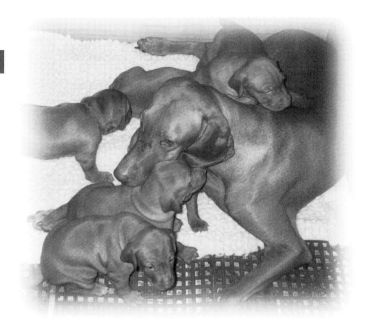

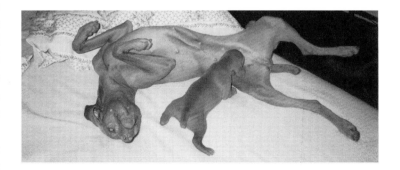

CHAPTER EIGHTEEN

Care of the Vizsla Dam

A Vizsla bitch is usually a very good mother. Even the one that still acts like a puppy most of the time and that you are sure will never know how to care for a litter, will surprise you with "instant motherhood." She will constantly push, clean, and count her newborns. She will be reluctant to leave them for the first few days and you will have to put her on leash and forcibly make her go out to eliminate.

A new mother will be possessive and overprotective of her babies. It is best not to allow any visitors for at least two weeks as any emotional upset or stress could cause her to step or lie on a small puppy. Most of your focus has to be on keeping her and the whelping box clean, the room temperature correct, and the newborns contented.

PROBLEMS AFTER WHELPING

After your bitch has had some rest and fed her newborns, you should take her to your veterinarian to be checked over for any retained afterbirths or even a retained puppy. Make sure you have kept an accurate count of any afterbirths that were missing and inform your veterinarian of the problem. He or she will administer a shot of oxytocin which will cause the bitch's uterus to contract and expel any debris left, perhaps saving your puppies from a serious case of toxic milk syndrome. A shot of oxytocin also helps to increase milk supply if it has been slow in developing.

In the case of a caesarean section, if your veterinarian has recommended antibiotic treatment, both the bitch and her puppies should be given daily doses of lactobacillus acidophilus to restore the natural flora in the intestinal tract that is destroyed by the medication. You can buy a package of granules from the pharmacy and mix it according to directions, or purchase it in liquid from from a health food store. The dosage for each puppy should be 300 milligrams (two teaspoons) every twelve hours and can be given by eyedropper. Yogurt with active culture also contains the same ingredients.

Acute Metritis

Your bitch will have a discharge for as long as four to five weeks following whelping. The normal color will be reddish-brown at the start with blood clots, or it could be a greenish-black discharge for the first few days as the uterus continues its cleaning-out

I'm not getting any milk. Is this really my mother?

Two week old puppies from Elgin's Sarah Rhiannon are active and eating well.

process. It will change to a light-brown, mucoid discharge by the third week. Any foul odor, yellowish discharge, vomiting, fever, loss of appetite, or listlessness with no interest in her puppies could be a sign of an infection called acute metritis, which may be associated with fetal infection, abortions, and retained placentas. Escherichia coli is the most common bacterium found in the infected uterus.

The infection may run its course in less than a week with the uterus becoming swollen and the abdomen tender and painful. If the problem is diagnosed early, the prognosis for your bitch's recovery is good, but if she is not given immediate professional care, she may have to be spayed to save her life. The infection must be brought under control with antibiotics, but unfortunately, if she is extremely ill, a hysterectomy may have to be performed.

Either way, her puppies must be raised as orphans because her milk will be toxic. If your bitch has a history that includes any abnormal vaginal discharges, pyometra, vaginitis, or has been given mismating shots, all of these should be taken into account as contributing causes in a case of acute metritis.

Eclampsia

Eclampsia (milk fever) usually occurs two to four weeks after delivery when the dam's milk supply is at its highest demand from the growing puppies. Eclampsia occurs when there is more calcium leaving the dam's body through her milk than she can replace from her bones and food. It is a critical condition with symptoms including nervousness, excessive panting, extremely high temperature, whining, disorientation, stiffening of the leg muscles, tensing, quivering, and staring wildly. Saliva will accumulate in her mouth, clogging her throat and causing a rattling sound. Finally, she will have convulsions. This is an emergency and you must act fast to save your bitch. Your veterinarian will give her a slow IV administration of calcium gluconate which usually results in rapid improvement, with muscle relaxation in fifteen minutes.

It is best not to let the puppies nurse for twelve to twenty-four hours after treatment to let the dam recover from the shock and correct the imbalance of calcium in her body. A bitch can have a recurrence of eclampsia in the next one to three weeks. She will need an appropriate increase in calcium-rich food for the duration of nursing. Supplementing the litter with bottled formula and early weaning onto solid food is recommended.

Large doses of calcium supplements during pregnancy are thought to be one of the causes of eclampsia, as over supplimentation can suppress the hormone responsible for mobilizing calcium stores from the body. Instead of supplementing with calcium, feed a high quality, nutritionally balanced, and appropriate diet during pregnancy and lactation.

Mastitis

Mastitis is an acute inflammation of, or abscess formation in, the dam's breast. The breast will be very swollen, reddish blue, and be extremely painful. The milk may have some streaks of blood or pus in it and your bitch will run a high temperature, lose her appetite, and in most cases will appear ill and listless. In some cases, the dam may not show signs of illness. Mastitis can involve one or more mammary glands.

Inflammation can be caused by an over-production of milk combined with

Fat, healthy puppies almost ready for weaning.

the puppies not draining each breast adequately, resulting in the milk glands becoming caked. If caught early before an abscess forms, the breast can be milked by hand and, if the milk looks normal, the condition may possibly be halted. However, if the inflammation is caused by a bacterial infection in the glands, the puppies must be prevented from getting any of the infected milk.

The affected gland (breast) can be covered and the puppies can still nurse on the other ones while treatment is started. Hot packs on the affected gland will bring the abscess to a head, where it will burst and drain. If it doesn't, it must be lanced, drained, flushed and treated as an open wound. If antibiotics are required, any broad-spectrum antibiotic must be chosen with the realization that it will be passed in the milk to the young.

Mastitis possibly can be prevented by keeping puppies' nails short to avoid scratching the dam's breasts and introducing bacteria into the scratches. Also you should be sure that your bitch changes position often so that her puppies use all of the nipples and keep each breast drained. If you have a small litter that cannot keep all the breasts drained, reduce the dam's food intake to slow her milk production.

Ch. Reilloc's CMF Zeiss, JH, playing with her puppy. Photo by Freitag.

FEEDING AND CARE OF THE DAM

If you expect to have healthy Vizsla puppies, then you must have a bitch that can give them a good supply of milk. This is only possible if she is fed a well-balanced, adequate diet. Food intake increases with milk production to a peak three to four weeks after whelping. Water intake increases proportionately, so free access to water is essential. The amount you need to increase the bitch's food and water intake varies with the size of the litter to as much as three or four times normal. Frequent meals of an energy-dense (high fat), high

A litter of five week olds are watched over carefully by their dam.

protein food is recommended. The diet should also contain some carbohydrates for optimal milk production.

Your new mother may be fussy about eating for a few days following whelping, which can contribute to a slowly developing milk supply in her breasts. Make sure that she is getting a lot of liquids. Use soup, broths, and cottage cheese to tempt her. Within a couple of days, the natural demand for her body to supply food for her newborns will take over and she will begin eating her regular meals.

As her puppies grow, they will require more nourishment. Increase her meals gradually to keep up with the demand for a larger milk supply. If she has an average-sized litter of eight, for the first ten days feed her three large meals a day of at least two cups of meal plus added meat. Add a fourth meal if necessary.

More and more breeders are having larger litters of ten or more puppies. In that case, by the time your litter is seven days old the dam should be eating a minimum of four large meals a day with smaller snacks in between.

As the puppies go into their fourth week of life and are eating solid food from a pan, begin to decrease the dam's food intake in preparation for completely weaning the litter

and drying up her milk supply. By the litter's fifth week, your bitch should receive only two meals a day. Decrease the amount of food considerably with each meal. Watch her carefully during this period for any congestion of the breasts. If she is uncomfortable with swollen breasts you will have to put her with the puppies in order for them to drain each breast fully. Otherwise, keep her completely away from her puppies as their continued nursing will stimulate the glands to keep producing milk.

During weaning, remember that your bitch's food intake helps to produce milk, so you must not allow any snacks, treats or extra food, no matter how hard she begs, and she must not be allowed to play with the puppies until she is no longer producing milk.

From the time her puppies are three weeks old, your bitch will be willing to spend time away from them, returning to the box several times a day to feed and clean them. She should have only controlled exercise and not be allowed to run and play, because her engorged breasts can easily be damaged. Even as the weaning process is going on, the breasts will still be hanging down until the muscles surrounding the glands regain their elasticity. It will usually take only a few weeks for all the muscles to tighten up, but until then the breasts will be flapping in the breeze every time she moves, and she must be restrained from hard running and jumping.

While it is not advisable to give the dam a complete bath while she is nursing, keep her rear cleaned to get rid of the discharge that occurs after whelping. A clean cloth with warm water and a mild soap should be used several times a day. Pay particular attention to the underside of her tail and include that area when washing her. Try to keep the puppies out of the discharge.

Because of the higher temperature in the whelping room, combined with the hormonal changes in her body, the dam will have shed most of her coat by the time the puppies are eight weeks old. Brush it out often and the new coat will soon grow in. Until it does, she will look a little moth-eaten.

CHAPTER NINETEEN

The Aging Process

There is a nobility in the aging Vizsla that is unequaled at any other stage of his life. Getting old is not a disease, nor should a dog that has shown nothing but love and devotion to his owners be treated like a pariah just because he is well into advanced age.

The Vizsla is a healthy, long-lived breed that is able to enjoy life well into old age. The foundation bitch for the Cariad line, Ch. Balatoni Sassy Olca, lived to seventeen and a half years with fairly good eyesight and health to the very end.

A dog may be considered "old" when he has trouble functioning with dimmer eyesight, his steps begin to falter and slow, and he is not as continent as he was as an adult in his prime. His hearing starts to go and you have to speak louder or use hand signals. Physiological aging is just a part of the natural order of things and neither man nor beast dies merely from "old age." Aging is a generalized condition, or multiple conditions, where one or more organs start to malfunction and fail. Aging is inevitable, but aging well is not. Providing good nutrition and regular preventative care, plus accepting that most older dogs cope quite well with the normal changes that come with aging, can help dispel your worries about your Vizsla getting old.

CARE FOR THE AGING DOG

As the older dog ages, he undergoes both physical and metabolic changes that affect your interaction with him. These changes can often manifest themselves as behavior changes, and understanding them can help increase the comfort of your dog and maintain your enjoyment in him. When he was younger, he learned just how much deafness you would tolerate; now the reason he does not respond will make you go to him and gently lead him back into the house.

Preventative medicine and early diagnosis of any changes can help save your aging dog from unnecessary suffering and can increase the quality and length of your Vizsla's life. It is also a wise investment since it will cost less in the long run than treating a health problem.

It is extremely important that your veterinarian do a urinalysis and also a complete blood panel at least once a year as your dog advances in age. These tests should include a BUN (blood urea nitrogen) test to make sure that your dog's kidneys are functioning normally. An annual CBC (complete blood count) will show infections, anemia, and whether blood cells are normal. If your Vizsla increases his water intake and the frequency of urination, do not try to cut back on his water supply so that he will urinate less frequently. Instead, bring it to the attention of your veterinarian. The best form

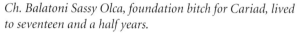

Ch. Balatoni Sassy Olca, foundation bitch for Cariad, lived to seventeen and a half years.

The aged dog needs a soft bed out of drafts.

of preventative medicine is early detection so that, as soon as a problem is seen, it can be controlled to a point where your Vizsla can be reasonably comfortable. Good care coupled with careful feeding and exercise, plus a happy and interesting existence, can slow the hands of time a bit and help keep your old friend with you for a while longer. When an elderly dog has given you years of love and devotion, it is important that, in the brief time he may have left, you give him comfort and security.

The skin glands and hair go through a number of changes in old age, the most noticeable of these being graying of the face and legs. Grooming is very important to the older dog. Brush him weekly to remove the dead hairs and stimulate the skin. This will also give you the chance to find any lumps or growths that are just beginning. Do not neglect your dog's nails just because he gets cranky about being handled. Nails that are too long will give added strain to weakened legs and poor traction on smooth floors. Ears should be examined on a daily basis to keep any yeast or infection from getting a firm start.

Eyes go through drastic changes and cataracts, which must be accepted as a normal part of the aging process, occur. Check the eyes daily since they do tend to need mucus collections cleaned from them.

Vaccinations should not be neglected or ignored just because your Vizsla never leaves the yard. Get yearly titers that will show the level of immunity, and give booster shots if warranted. Any virus in an older dog can have devastating results since he is without the strength and vitality of youth to pull him through. It is also important not to neglect an annual blood test for heartworm and regular fecal tests.

One of the most important concerns with your older Vizsla will be his weight. A dog that has a tendency to thinness in his advanced years will be far healthier than an obese one. Obesity in a dog is the direct result of consuming more food than he can properly burn, so it is stored as fat, or fatty tissue, in his body. A "couch potato" is more inclined to become obese than a dog working in the field, but obesity is a concern for every dog as he gets older or as his exercise is curtailed.

The life-span of an obese dog is decreased for several reasons. Excess weight puts undue stress on the heart as well as the joints. The

Ch. Oakleaf's Dandy Dalton, SH, owned by Jan Simer, is twelve years old and aging gracefully.

Older Vizslas, like Lark, love the extra attention and hugs.

dog becomes a poor anesthesia risk, and has less resistance to viral or bacterial infections.

An aging dog experiences metabolic changes, and as a result he will need a lower volume or fat in his diet to keep him at his proper weight. If you have been providing him with an adequate diet and he is in moderately good physical condition, there will be no need to change his protein intake. Rather than changing the total dietary aspect, corrections can be made to bring it into better balance by adding prescribed nutrients like glucosamine and chondroitin for aching bones and muscles.

Most older dogs are a poor risk for surgery. Their system does not have the ability to tolerate anesthesia and they have slower recuperative powers. For this reason, in spite of the advances in the anesthesia field, surgery should be avoided unless absolute-

ly necessary. Treatment of any kind should only be undertaken with the most serious problems, as the older dog eliminates medications a lot slower and the drugs can have an accumulative effect.

CHANGES WITH AGE

Since one of the systems subject to senile changes is the digestive system, which starts with bad teeth, have your veterinarian check for tartar accumulation. It is not only unsightly, but can lead to serious problems. Dirty teeth affect the gums, cause roots to decay, and can lead to heart problems or arthritis by releasing bacteria into the blood stream.

An older dog can also suffer a loss of muscle tone and decrease in secretion of the

Ch. Cariad's Classic Mariah, ROM, with owner Marcia Folley. Photo © Booth Photography.

Ch. Cariad's Cricket'Nak Hivnak still showing beauty and grace in the Veterans class. Owned by Bonnie and Mark Goodwein. Photo © Cook.

digestive juices of the stomach. Slow emptying of the stomach can lead to bloat or indigestion. He will experience constipation due to weakness of his abdominal muscles, which results in lessened bowel activity. A special diet may have to be given. Giving him his food soaked and softened in water may help relieve this problem. Frequent cleaning of the teeth will be necessary. Locate a veterinarian or canine dental specialist who will clean the teeth without anesthesia if at all possible.

Older dogs sleep a lot and, probably because of the hearing loss, sleep more deeply. A safe and comfortable bed out of drafts is a must because an aged dog is not as capable of keeping warm as he once was. Most older Vizslas do not adjust well to any change in their environment, so keep your dog's favorite chair in the same place, and if he has always slept on your bed, do not exclude him now unless he has become badly incontinent. He may have to be helped onto the bed if he can no longer make the jump.

The nervous system undergoes changes as your Vizsla ages. Atrophy of the brain is manifested by a lessened response to, and decreased ability to obey, commands. Irritability, and, sadly, the forgetting of habits or training also may be evident. Sometimes a dog can become so disoriented as to stand with his head in a corner, not knowing how to get out.

For these reasons, an aged Vizsla does not do well if he needs to be boarded at a kennel. However, if there is no way it can be avoided, duplicate his home surroundings by taking his favorite blanket and toys to help his mental outlook. Changes in environment or feeding routine will add stress to your older dog.

Probably the one sign of old age that every owner recognizes is the change that bones, joints and muscles undergo. The muscles suffer from atrophy and a reduction in their size. Joint lesions result in spondylosis deformans, a degenerative condition

Swimming is the best form of exercise for older dogs.

Ch. Dorratz Double Trouble, owned by Doris Ratzlaff, bringing in the daily newspaper.

that involves the spinal column and its discs. Most dogs do not reveal any clinical signs of this progressive, chronic disease until pain becomes evident and they become reluctant to move or are paralyzed.

ACTIVITIES AND EXERCISE

Very few Vizsla owners have attended a National Specialty and not had tears in their eyes watching the Veterans' class. This is the class where we honor the "retired" oldsters, aged eight years and up. They may be champions or not, they may be gray-haired and slow moving or still active and in their prime. But it gives each dog a chance to remember the companionship, fun, and applause as he is moved and judged. It also gives the novice Vizsla owner a chance to see the dogs they might only have heard about and that influenced and shaped the generations behind the youngsters in competition now.

A Vizsla running in the bird field may keep going until he drops, and a wise owner

Even an older Vizsla can enjoy dressing up for Halloween.

will curtail the older dog's activities to short sessions. Moderate exercise will keep the flexibility in your dog's joints and he will make an excellent companion gundog as long as he is not arthritic or ill. Field work will also make life more interesting for him, especially if he has been put aside in favor of a younger, more active dog.

No older dog should be subjected to strenuous exercise if he invariably winds up appearing physically sore. It is only common sense to treat old age with some consideration, and any dog should not be exercised beyond his comfort level of activity. With his failing eyesight and hearing, an older Vizsla may lack the self-confidence of his youth, so it is essential that he gets extra reassurance that his owner is nearby at all times. Getting the aged dog off the sofa and out for a slow, easy walk will be beneficial to both the dog and his owner.

The aging dog needs extra care and attention.

Swimming is the exercise with the most beneficial effects, as it strengthens the body in the same way as running but without putting any pressure on muscles or joints. If your dog tends to sink, hold him up by placing your arms under his body for support. A dog with partial paralysis from back problems will have to be handled gently, but he will benefit from massage of his back and legs, along with the passive movement of the limbs while swimming. Special care should be taken with an older dog to prevent chilling, and he should be toweled dry and kept out of drafts. Always remember to dry the inside of his ears.

An aging dog should never be placed in circumstances which are genuinely dangerous. That means that special treatment, consideration, patience, and thoughtfulness will demand more of the owner's time, and also time from family children. The entire family should share the responsibility of their dog's exercise and health. Unless a dog is weak or has a bad heart, half an hour of activity at a time is a good rule of thumb.

PROBLEMS OF OLDER DOGS

Bladder Problems

Bladder problems are common in an older dog. The aging Vizsla that becomes incontinent and dribbles urine as he walks or sleeps may have a deficiency of sex hormones if he or she has been neutered or spayed. A female may have cystitis, a bacterial infection in the lining of the bladder. A urine culture will determine the problem and treatment.

Pain, a sudden suppression of urine with frequent attempts to urinate, depression, thirst, vomiting, and a weakness in the hind legs could be signs of a condition called retroflexion, common to older males.

Your Vizsla may not show any obvious signs of kidney problems until he starts to consume a lot more water than usual, combined with excessive and frequent urination. The kidneys are bean-shaped organs which

Ch. Dorratz Double Trouble, UD, MH, NA, VC, ROM, at twelve years of age. Owned by Doris Ratzlaff.

are located behind and below the last ribs, near the spinal cord. No dog can survive without at least one of them functioning properly because they eliminate metabolic wastes. If the kidneys are not working these poisonous wastes will accumulate in the body and death will result if the condition is not treated and arrested. In addition to treatment, your dog may need a special diet. It is highly important to keep a fresh supply of water available at all times.

Tumors

The incidence of tumors is greatest in dogs over nine years of age, and clinical signs may not be noticed if the tumors are small. Unfortunately, when they reach a large size they become an emergency. Vizslas are no more prone to cancer than any other breed, it all being a matter of chance involving genetic predisposition and inheritance, just as it is with the human population.

Neutering and spaying are important steps in promoting longevity in your Vizsla. Studies show that unsprayed females reaching the age of ten years have more than a sixty percent chance of developing mamma-

ry tumors. Mammary tumors have a fifty-fifty chance of being malignant, and it is recommended that you examine your older bitch's breasts regularly between annual check-ups. The two hind pairs of mammary glands (towards the tail) develop tumors more frequently than the front pair, and tumors may occur in one gland or in several.

A common condition in an older male is senile atrophy of, and tumors in, the testes. In an advanced case, his organs will become considerably smaller, and either hard, or soft and flabby. The effects are sterility and an endocrine imbalance. Castrating your older male will help to avoid some of these problems, and can possibly rejuvenate his life. If your male is still being used for breeding, one of the first signs of problems could be a drop in the motility and sperm count. If there is a tumor only on one of the testicles, that testicle can be removed. The other testicle can take over the job of producing healthy sperm and get the count up to ninety percent of normal within two months.

A tumor of the kidneys has a greater tendency to develop in the older dog, and

Ch. Dorratz Double Trouble in the foreground, with his son Ch. Dorratz Bebop of Birdland, backing.

this is frequently a renal carcinoma located at one of the kidney's poles. If it goes undetected, it will metastasize in the lungs, glands, and liver. Blood in the urine, anemia, and a drastic weight loss may be associated with kidney tumors.

A large tumor in your Vizsla's spleen will produce an abdominal enlargement which can be felt on the left side behind the stomach. Symptoms will include weakness, weight loss, digestive problems and, quite often, a disinclination to move. Your dog may have a tendency to remain sitting due to pressure from fluid in the abdominal cavity.

Sneezing, snorting, and breathing through the mouth can be a sign of a tumor in your dog's nasal cavity. Discharge or bleeding from the nose are also early signs.

Heart Failure

Heart disease must be distinguished from heart failure. Heart disease is a condition in which there is an abnormality of the heart, whereas heart failure exists when the heart is unable to meet the circulatory demands of the body.

The chances of heart failure in an older Vizsla are quite high. Failure of the blood circulation, due to the inability of his heart muscles to function adequately, will affect his kidney, lungs, and liver, causing a multiple organ problem.

Symptoms of heart failure may be a cough, edema, labored breathing, and a weak, irregular pulse. With an active dog with higher circulatory demands, the signs may be more pronounced; in sedentary dogs, the signs of heart failure may be delayed.

Initially, rest and diuretics to increase urination are essential since the kidneys slow down their function and retain fluid. With early treatment, your dog can be put on a special salt-free diet along with vasodilator drugs to control and stabilize the condition. Limiting exercise will help reduce stress on the heart.

Pancreatitis

Pancreatic disorders occur frequently in the older dog. The pancreas, a gland located on the upper part of the small intestines, provides not only the enzymes to the digestive system but also insulin to regulate your dog's blood sugar level.

Pancreatitis, an inflammation of the gland, occurs when these digestive enzymes become activated within the pancreas before they are released, and begin to digest the pancreas itself. This self-destruction causes severe inflammation and pain in the abdomen.

There are two forms of pancreatitis, chronic and acute. Chronic pancreatitis is an ongoing condition, usually in the form of repeated episodes, with clinical signs generally resembling those of acute pancreatitis. In both cases, the signs of pancreatitis occur suddenly with a lack of appetite, frequent vomiting, diarrhea which may contain blood, extreme thirst and higher temperature. Veterinarian treatment as soon as possible will be necessary.

If diagnosed as chronic pancreatitis, there will be repeated bouts of abdominal pain and gastrointestinal upset. Between episodes, the dog will seem normal and have a good appetite, but each episode causes additional destruction to the pancreas. Careful dietary management with a diet low in fat can alter these repeat episodes, but the continued mild episodes may result in your dog losing weight or condition because of the lack of sufficient enzymes to digest his food sufficiently. He may have foul-smelling, clay-colored, voluminous stools containing undigested food. After enough of these repeated episodes, the endocrine function of the gland is lost, insulin is not produced, and diabetes mellitus will occur, causing the dog's blood sugar to rise to excessively high levels.

Chronic pancreatitis, without acute flare-ups, is best treated by controlling your older dog's diet carefully, preventing obesity, and providing him with exercise. A high blood fat content in his blood may mean your dog has a metabolic problem which prevents the proper clearing of the fat from the blood stream, contributing to the development of the pancreatitis.

Ch. Koppertone's Cariad Baratom, CDX, gets a hug from owner Marion Coffman after placing first in Veterans obedience. Photo © Christina M. Freitag.

Acute pancreatitis can be sudden, severe, and appear without warning. Your dog will stop eating, be depressed, have abdominal pain, weakness, inability to walk, sunken eyes, dehydration and severe shock. Your dog needs immediate veterinary attention. Some cases of acute pancreatitis may improve spontaneously in a day or two since the refusal of the dog to eat reduces the need for his pancreas to work. Any food that is eaten will stimulate the release of digestive enzymes and the pancreas is extremely sensitive at this time.

Nutritional imbalances from indiscriminate feeding practices of giving table scraps with a high fat content to older dogs that

Ch. Cariad's Classic Mariah celebrating her sixteenth birthday.

are overweight and inactive play an important role in most cases of pancreatitis. Additional episodes may be prevented with a special diet.

Diabetes Mellitus

Sugar diabetes results from inadequate insulin production by the pancreas, causing faulty metabolism of sugars and starches. This results in an abnormal rise in the amount of sugar in the dog's urine and blood.

A diabetic dog will eat and drink a lot but still lose weight. His breath may have an odor of acetone due to the formation of acids in the blood. Ulceration of the cornea, or cataracts, are common. In extreme cases, diabetic coma may occur. Overweight, older bitches are most commonly affected. A strict, high-fiber diet is necessary to control the blood glucose levels. Diabetes cannot be cured, but it can be kept under control by routine testing, diet supervision, and daily injections of insulin if needed.

Canine Dysfunction Syndrome

Your old dog's mental health may be more important than his physical health. With dogs, as with people, "If your mind is in the right place, your health is likely to be better." It is difficult to watch your dog age, especially if he begins to lose interest in his family and his everyday routine and starts to require a lot more care.

Some of the signs you may be taking for just the normal "old age" may actually be signs of a medical condition called canine cognitive dysfunction (CCD). What has been classified as Alzheimer's-like senility includes behavior changes that are not due to primary failure of any organ system.

Researchers now believe that CCD is caused by physical and chemical changes that affect the brain function in an older dog. Early signs of the syndrome include confusion, aimless wandering, staring into space, endless barking for no reason, not responding to commands or calls, having difficulty finding the correct opening for the door, and even standing with his face in a corner or behind furniture, not able to find his way out. He may sleep a lot more during the day, but be restless at night, wandering and pacing the floor in circles. He forgets his housebreaking and urinates inside instead of asking to go out.

All of this confusion on the part of the older dog does not come on all at once, but occurs so gradually that you don't even notice until your Vizsla looks at you with no sign of recognition and no longer seeks your company but goes off into his own isolation. All of this can be as hard on the dog as on family members. Your Vizsla needs your attention and care more now than at any other time, and this period in his life is the time for you to be especially understanding and patient.

The main method of evaluating cognitive dysfunction in people, like being assessed through their performance of tasks and the solving of problems, is not applicable to our dogs and until recently very little research had been done to help. But there are now new drugs that can offer relief to dogs suffering from these behavioral changes. It is up to the owners to resist telling themselves that their dog is just "getting old." Since there may be other age-related conditions that can cause the behavior changes, impairment of memory or previously learned behavior is sufficient to indicate CCD.

EUTHANASIA

We all wish that one day we could just find our beloved old Vizsla "asleep" without him ever having known any of the painful infirmities which advancing age can bring. We have a loving, incredibly strong bond with our older dog—strongest when near the end.

The pain of having to part with a beloved pet is the hardest thing for a dog owner to cope with. Your Vizsla's death will not exist as an isolated occurrence, because when his life comes to an end, so will a part of yours. It will not be just an "old dog" that is buried; a very real part of you will go into the grave to keep him company.

Making a decision about euthanasia is the greatest act of love you can show your dog, and the most difficult. If your old Vizsla is suffering and can no longer enjoy his life, you have to accept death as being in his best interest. When the weight of time makes him weary, he will be content to have it over. Give him peace for his tired old heart, head, and limbs.

Do not abandon him to strange hands in his final last minutes. No matter how bad your pain, hold him and gently ease him out of his world. It only takes a few seconds before his head grows heavy in your hand, his breathing stops, and his eyes close in sleep.

The pain over losing a "special" old Vizsla never really goes away. It is just that, with time, it is a little easier to bear. And, if you're fortunate, you will meet a new Vizsla friend and begin the experience of discovering a special, unique companion once again.

Ch. Taunee's Loki Santana, CD, ROM, HOF, winning the Veterans class at the VCGNY specialty, his last show. Owned by Marion Coffman, handled by Bobby Barlow. Photo © Ashbey.

VCA Hall of Fame

Ch. Oakleaf's Dandy Dalton, SH. Owned by Jan Simer. Photo © Cook Phodography.

In 1978 the VCA drew up the procedures and requirements for nominating a dog to its Hall of Fame in order to give recognition to Vizslas whose outstanding achievements have brought honor to the breed. The requirements for nomination were that the Vizsla be deemed to have made a significant contribution to the breed through exceptional merit in his own right. The Vizsla had to have been dead for two years before the nomination. Two Vizslas are voted into the Hall of Fame each year.

1978
DCh. Futaki Darocz
FCh./AFCh. Jodi of Czuki Barat

1979
DCh. Behi Csinos Csiny, CD
DCh. Weedy Creek Lobo

1980
Ch. Csinos V Hunt
FCh. Weedy Creek Dutchess

1981
FCh. Ripp Barat
Dual/AFCh. Sir Lancelot

1982
Dual/AFCh. Brook's Amber Mist
DCh. Szekeres Kis Szereto

1983
Ch. Nikki's Arco
DCh. Rebel Rouser Duke

1984
Broc Olca
Haans V Selle

1985
Dual/AFCh. Amber's Windy Autumn
Dual/AFCh. Rothan's Rozsda Kisanya, CD

1986
Ch. Glen Cottage Loki Barat, CDX
Rebel Rouser Bandieto

1987
Ch. Johnson's Titan Charger
Ch. Miklos Schloss Loosdorf

1988
FCh./AFCh. Randy Duke

1989, 1990, 1991, 1992
no nominations

1993
Triple Ch. Cariad's Kutya Kai Costa, VC
Dual/AFCh. Brook's Willie Wompum

1994
Ch. Rotkopf's Super Charger, CD, JH, VC
Ch. Valhi's Stick to Your Guns, CD, VC

1995
Ch. Firebrand's Constant Comment
Ch. Taunee's Cariann

1996
Ch. Sandor Barat
Ch. Harann's Tulipann

1997
Dual/AFCh. Mehagian's Peppy Paloma
Dual/AFCh. FK's Rivendell Reaghan,
CDX, MH, VC

1998
Dual/AFCh. Askim, MH
DCh. Rebel Rouser ET, MH

1999
Ch. Penlee's Cutter, UD
Dual/AFCh. Golden Empire's Doctor T,
MH

2000
Ch. Joshua Melto
Ch. Oakleaf's Whistlin Dixie, CD, SH, VC

2001
Ch. Russet Leather Indian Giver
Ch. Sandyacre Poquito Chili Bean, UDX,
MH, MX, VC

2002
Ch./AFCh. Hodag's Kirby, CD, MH, VC
Ch. Oakleaf's Dandy Dalton, SH

2003
Ch. Taunee's Loki Santana, CD
Ch. Lyon's Skipjack of Harann

Dual Champions

1965
Dual Ch. Futaki Darocz

1969
Dual Ch. Weedy Creek Lobo

1970
Dual Ch. Bobo Buck Selle
Dual Ch. Szekeres Kis Szereto

1971
Dual Ch./AFC Brook's Amber Mist
Dual Ch. Behi's Csinos Csiny, CD

1972
Dual Ch./AFC Sir Lancelot
Dual Ch./AFC Amber's Windy Autumn

1973
Dual Ch./AFC Pirolin
Dual Ch./ Chip Odyddeus

1974
Dual Ch. Rippi of Webster Woodlands
Dual Ch. Rebel Rouser Duke

1975
Dual Ch. Sir Amber Sam
Dual Ch./AFC Jodi's Jump'N Bing Bang
    Bucz
Dual Ch./AFC Csibesz Rotkopt
Dual Ch./AFC Arco's Arco

1976
Dual Ch./AFC Rothan's Rozsda Kisany, CD
Dual Ch./AFC Brook's Willie Whompum

1977
Dual Ch./AFC Janos VW Come Lately

1978
Dual Ch./AFC Victor of Holtzworth Farm

1979
Dual Ch./AFC Mehagian's Peppy Paloma
Dual Ch. Cline's Olympia Blitz
Dual Ch. W D Regina
Dual Ch./AFC Valhi's Liberty Valence

1980
Dual Ch./AFC Fieldstone's Hey Duke
Dual Ch./AFC Behi Csecse Gyors Lab
Dual Ch./AFC Bratt's FK Gippen
Dual Ch. Cariad's Kutya Kai Costa, UD

1982
Dual Ch. Bry-Lynn's Golden Taurus
Dual Ch./AFC Fieldstone's Tip Top Timmy
Dual Ch. Rotkopf's Minor Miracle
Dual Ch./AFC Cazador's Ripp Van Winkle

1983
DualCh/AFC Sage Richards
Dual Ch. Cody's Dark Star
Dual Ch. Redef's Hellza Poppin
Dual Ch. Fieldstone's Tip Top Chester

1984
Dual Ch./AFC FK's Rivendell Reaghan,
   CDX
Dual Ch. Pride's Joy
Dual Ch./AFC Willie's Cedar Chip
Dual Ch. My T Hi Thunderstorm
Dual Ch./AFC Bo Sassy Delibab

1985
Dual Ch. Popple Dungeon Super Star
Dual Ch./AFC Boyd's JR of Futaki
Dual Ch./AFC Papago Samsson, MH
Dual Ch./AFC Caesar's Image Bargin Buck

1986
Dual Ch./AFC Upwind Selkie
Dual Ch../AFC Askim
Dual Ch./AFC Popple Dungeon Trillium
Dual Ch./AFC Camarily Sandman
Dual Ch./AFC Randy Bee's Rambling Man
   MH
Dual Ch. Futaki Marci
Dual Ch. Pleasant Run Gunner
Dual Ch./AFC Popple Dungeon What a
Dickens, CD

1987
Dual Ch. Paradox Title Chase of Behi
Dual Ch. Golden Empire's Beauregard, CD
Dual Ch. Behi's Gyros Vonat PD Carla
Dual Ch./AFC Semper Fi Chesty Puller,
   MH
Dual Ch. Rebel Rouser ET
Dual Ch. Masha's Best Flash Dancer

1988
Dual Ch. Russet Leather Pretty Pawnee
Dual Ch./AFC Berry's Mason Dixon Lover

1989
Dual Ch. Riverbend's Deacon's Dandy
Dual Ch./AFC Golden Empire's Doctor T
Dual Ch. Viesso's Prodical Son

1990
Dual Ch./AFC Askim's Diamond Reo
Dual Ch. Oakleaf's Screamin Demon
Dual Ch. Oakleaf's Whiskey Pete

1991
Dual Ch./AFC Melto-N-Futaki's Rapstone
   Red, MH
Dual Ch./AFC Camelot's Capricious Caper
Dual Ch./AFC Greffin's Ha'Penny MH
Dual Ch./AFC Mehagian's KRC's Phoenix
   Fridge
Dual Ch./AFC Paradox Remarqueable Jake
Dual Ch./AFC Semper Fi Montezuma

1992
Dual Ch. Mehagian's Firestarter
Dual Ch./AFC Lakeside Luke Skywalker,
   MH
Dual Ch./AFC Mudsville Lorac Makk
Dual Ch./AFC Triad's XXIV Karat Oakleaf,
   CD
Dual Ch./AFC Corky

1993
Dual Ch. JJ Kedves Vadasz, SH
Dual Ch. Sir Kis Janos of Shipping
Dual Ch./AFC Coleto Cheyanne
Dual Ch./AFC Viesoo's X-factor Konya,
   MH
Dual Ch./AFC Hodag's Hunter, UDX, MH

1994
Dual Ch. Camarily Mesquite
Dual Ch. Mattapex Winsome Girl
Dual Ch./AFC Fourwinds Rebel Rouser
   Gator
Dual Ch./AFC Golden Empire's Texas
   Topaz, MH
Dual Ch./AFC Linden's Belle Starr, CD, MH
Dual Ch./AFC Behi Red Chief, JH
Dual Ch./AFC Reckless Ballofire, MH
Dual Ch./AFC Morning Sky Mista Bone

1995
Dual Ch./AFC Legacy's DeChartay, UDX,
   MH
Dual Ch./AFC Sun Up Magnum Forty
   Four, MH
Dual Ch./AFC Sierra's Wooden Nickel,
   CDX, MH
Dual Ch./AFC Masha's Sinfully Wild
   Cheri, CD

1996
Dual Ch. Rebel Rouser Diamondback
Dual Ch. Rebel Rouser Cal
Dual Ch./AFC Mar-Ed's Ask'm He Knoz, SH

1997
Dual Ch. Zekiel Regel of Kent
Dual Ch. Paradise Master of the Hunt, MH

1998
Dual Ch./AFC Snow Ridge Nokomis
Dual Ch./AFC Desert Storm's Jet Tripper

1999
Dual Ch./AFC Red Oak's Stormin Norman, MH
Dual Ch./AFC Rebel Rouser N Lynden's Cyote, SH
Dual Ch./AFC Sienna Gold Tidal Victory, SH
Dual Ch. Krackerjack's Bela Bartalk, UDX, MH
Dual Ch. Barben's Rapacious Rascal, Mh
Dual Ch. Oakleaf's Everwhen Chances R, CDX, MH

2000
Dual Ch./AFC Triad's Dry Martini, CD
Dual./AFC Valley Hunter's Divine Penlee, CDX, MH
Dual Ch./AFC Berry's Borne to be Wilde, JH
Dual Ch./AFC Maximum Strider, SH

2001
Dual Ch./AFC Upwind's Chas'n My Jason
Dual Ch./AFC Copperfield's High Roller, SH
Dual Ch. Tonka's Rebel Rouser Maniitou
Dual Ch./AFC Keystone Upwind Doubledipity
Dual Ch./AFC Outbound Ike, SH
Dual Ch. Piper's Upwind of Bunker Hill
Dual Ch./AFC Onpoint's Tuff Stuff

2002
Dual Ch./AFC Fieldstone Lord Fox of Linden, SH
Dual Ch. Winsong's Cinnabar Hannah, MH
Dual Ch. Csardas Lakeside Zephyr, SH

2003
Dual Ch. Rebel Rouser Orion, JH
Dual Ch./AFC Wildwood's Back With Zach, SH

Ch. Balltis Brant of Penlee. Photo © Ashbey.

Regional Vizsla Clubs

Central California VC
Michele Coburn
7740 Cobb Rd.
Bakersfield, CA 93313
661-831-5049

Central Wisconsin VC
Janet Silverman
1825 W. Woodbury Lane
Milwaukee, WI 53209
414-352-5908

Conestoga VC
Terry Luca
3387 Midland Rd.
Midland, VA 22728
504-788-3383

Connecticut Valley VC
Sandy Jacobus
44 Trailsend Dr.
Canton, CT 06019
860-693-2158

Gateway VC
Debbie Baker
11592 Joslyn
St. Louis, MO 63138
314-355-6754

Hawkeye VC
LeLoie Dutemple
523 Gear St.
Prole, IA 50229
515-981-0050

Lone Cypress VC
Arline Lovett
330 San Benancia Rd.
Salinas, CA 93908
831-484-2777

Miami Valley VC
Margaret Schaefer
811 Bunty Station Rd.
Delaware, OH 43015
740-363-6164

Nebraska VC
Andy Bailey
10900 Rocky Ridge Rd.
Lincoln, NE 68526
402-486-4121

Old Dominion VC
Gerald Garnsey
P.O. Box 429
Hughesville, MD 20637
301-274-4456

Puget Sound VC
Jill Isaak Brennan
19023 172nd Pl. SE
Renton, WA 98058
425-235-1140

Rio Salado VC
Marla Molvin
1985 E. Hillary Dr.
Phoenix, AZ 85022
602-971-7491

Show Me VC of Kansas City
Lin Kozlowski
66 SE 1040
Deepwater, MO 64740
417-644-7425

South Coast VC
Rick Demolina
256 W. Eighth St.
Claremont, CA 91711

South Louisiana VC
Adele Neupert
105 Southwood Dr.
Lafayette, LA 70503
337-981-4566

Tampa Bay VC
Kathy Helmuth
160 30th Ave. N
St. Petersburg, FL 33704
727-822-7829

Trails End VC of Oregon
Linda Kenyon
4515 NE 141st Ct.
Vancouver, WA 98682
360-883-3949

Texas Gulf Coast VC
Peggy Ross
20825 Karen Switch Rd.
Magnolia, TX 77354
281-356-7350

Twin Cities VC
Stella Lang
11520 Holdridge Rd. E.
Wayzata, MN 55391
952-473-8931

VC of Central New England
Wendy Russell
1503 Bear Hill Rd.
Dover-Foxcroft, ME 04426
207-564-7926

VC of Eastern Iowa
Steve Laughlin

110 Glen Dr.
Iowa City, IA 52240

VC of Greater New York
Tony Smid
110 Hiawatha Blvd.
Oakland, NJ 07436
201-337-5646

VC of Illinois
Linda Bush
2643 Keith Rd.
Winnebago, IL 61088
815-335-7673

VC of Metro Atlanta
Barbara Zahn
5314 River Mill Circle
Marietta, GA 30068
770-992-0869

VC of Michigan
Sue Jagoda
8441 Five Point Highway
Eaton Rapids, MI 48843
517-663-4943

VC of Northern California
Catherine Pokorny
1807 Holland Dr.
Walnut Creek, CA 94596
510-933-4110

VC of Northern New Jersey
Georgia Zambas
215 Low's Hollow Rd.
Stewartsville, NJ 08886

VC of Southern California
Darlene Anthony
13144 Bromont Ave.
Sylmar, CA 91342
818-362-5026

VC of the Carolinas
Paula Murphy
5319 Stephens Lane
Durham, NC 27712
919-471-6363

VC of Utah
William Hart
1172 Lost Eden Dr.
Sandy, UT 84094

Sources of Information

ORGANIZATIONS

The American Kennel Club
5580 Centerview Dr.
Raleigh, NC 27606-3390
www.AKC.org

ASPCA Poison Control
888-426-4435

Canine Health Foundation
P.O. Box 37941
Raleigh, NC 27627
888-682-9696
www.AKCCHF

Delta Society
Pet Partners Program
580 Naches Ave. SW Suite 101
Renton, WA 98055
425-226-7357

HOPE Crisis
14145 NW Evergreen
Portland, OR 97229
503-645-4649

National Dog Registry
Box 116, Dept. AK2
Woodstock, NY 12498
800-637-3647
www.info@natldogregistry.com

North American Versatile Hunting Dog
Association
1700 Skyline Dr.
Burnsville, MN 55337

847-253-6488
www.navhda.org
E-mail: NAVoffice@AOL.com

Orthopedic Foundation for Animals
2300 E. Nifong Blvd.
Columbia, MO 65201
573-442-0418
www.offa.org
E-mail: OFA@offa.org

Therapy Dogs, Inc.
P.O. Box 5868
Cheyenne, WY 82003
877-843-7364
www.therapydogs.com

Coming off the A-frame. Photo © Christina M. Freitag.

Therapy Dogs International
88 Bartley Rd.
Flanders, NJ 07836
973-252-9800
www.tdi-dog.org

United Kennel Club
100 East Kilgore Rd.
Kalamazoo, MI 49001
269-343-9020
www.UKCdogs.com

Vizsla Rescue
Stephen Shlyen
134 Mt. Airy Rd.
Pipersville, PA 18947
610-294-8020
E-mail: rheing@epix.net

SHOW SUPERINTENDENTS

Bob Peters Dog Shows
P.O. Box 579
Wake Forest, NC 27588

Jack Bradshaw Dog Shows
Jack Bradshaw
P.O. Box 227303
Los Angeles, CA 90022

Jack Onofrio Dog Shows
P.O. Box 25764
Oklahoma City, OK 73125

Kevin Rogers Dog Shows
P.O. Box 230
Hattiesburg, MS 39403

MB-F, Inc
P.O. Box 22107
Greensboro, NC 27420

Roy Jones Dog Shows
Kenneth Sleeper
P.O. Box 828
Auburn, IN 46706

Rau Dog Shows
P.O. Box 6898
Reading, PA 19610

Recommended Reading

VIZSLA BREED BOOKS

Boggs, Bernard. *The Vizsla*. Greenbriar, 1982.

Cunningham, J., and Strauz, J. *Your Vizsla*. Denlinger, 1973.

Gottlieb, Gay. *The Complete Vizsla*. Howell, 1992.

———. *The Hungarian Vizsla*. Nimrod, 1985.

Hart, Ernest. *Vizslas*. TFH, 1990.

Pinney, Chris. *Vizslas—Barron's Complete Pet Owner's Manual*. Barron's Educational Series, 1998.

Stott, Winnie. *Not Your Average Dog*. Canadian, 1998.

MEDICAL AND NUTRITIONAL REFERENCE

Allegretti, Jan, and Katy Sommers, DVM. *The Complete Holistic Dog Book*. Celestial Arts, 2003.

Bamberger, Michelle, DVM. *Help! The Quick Guide to First Aid for Your Dog*. Howell, 1993.

Blood, D. C., OBE, and Virginia P. Studdert, DVM. *Saunders Comprehensive Veterinary Dictionary*. Saunders, 2000.

Carlson, Delbert, DVM, and James Griffin, MD. *Dog Owner's Home Veterinary Handbook*. Howell, 1992.

Fogle, Bruce DVM. *Caring For Your Dog*. DK Publishing, 2002.

———, and Amanda Williams. *First Aid for Dogs: What to Do When Emergencies Happen*. DK Publishing, 1997.

Guthrie, Sue, BA. *Ultimate Dog Care: A Complete Veterinary Guide*. Howell, 2001.

James, Ruth, DVM. *The Dog Repair Book*, Alpine Press, 1990.

Merck Veterinary Manual. 8th ed. Merck, 1998.

Padgett, George. *Control of Canine Genetic Diseases*. Howell, 1998.

Pitcairn, Richard, DVM, and Susan Pitcairn. *Dr. Pitcairn's Complete Guide to Natural Health for Dogs and Cats*. Rodale, 1995.

Zucker, Martin. *Veterinarian's Guide to Natural Remedies for Dogs*. Random House, 2000.

BREEDING AND GENETICS

Beauchamp, Richard. *Breeding Dogs, for Dummies*. Hungry Minds, 2002.

England, Gary. *Allen's Fertility and Obstetrics in the Dog*. Blackwell Science, 1998.

Evans, J. M., and Kay White. *Book of the Bitch*. Howell, 1997.

Fernandez, Amy. *Dog Breeding as a Fine Art*. Self-published, 2002.

Harris, Beth J. Finder. *Breeding a Litter: The Complete Book of Prenatal and Postnatal Care*. Howell, 1993.

Holst, Phyllis, DVM. *Canine Reproduction*. Alpine Publications, 1985.

Isabell, Jackie. *Genetics—An Introduction for Dog Breeders*. Alpine Publications, 2003.

Jackson, Frank. *Dog Breeding—The Theory and the Practice*. Trafalgar Square, 2000.

Lee, Muriel, *Whelping and Rearing of Puppies*. TFH, 1997.

Richards, Herbert, DVM. *Dog Breeding for Professionals*. TFH, 1981.

Serranne, Ann. *The Joy of Breeding Your Own Show Dog*. Howell, 1980.

Walkowicz, Chris, and Bonnie Wilcox, DVM. *Successful Dog Breeding*. Howell, 1994.

CANINE BEHAVIOR

Benjamin, Carol, and Stephen Lennard. *Mother Knows Best*. Howell, 1985.

Dodman, Nicholas, DVM. *Dogs Behaving Badly: An A-to-Z Guide to Understanding and Curing Behavioral Problems in Dogs*. Bantam, 1999.

Donaldson, Jean. *Culture Clash*. James & Kenneth, 1997.

Dunbar, Ian, DVM. *Dog Behavior: An Owner's Guide to a Happy Healthy Pet*. Howell, 1996.

Fisher, John. *Think Dog: An Owner's Guide to Canine Psychology*. Tralfagar Square, 1995.

Monks of New Skete. *How to Be Your Dog's Best Friend—The Classic Training Manual for Dog Owners*. Little, Brown & Co., 2002.

Pryor, Karen. *Don't Shoot the Dog: The New Art of Teaching and Training*. Simon & Shuster, 1999.

Rutherford, Clarice, and David Neil. *How to Raise a Puppy You Can Live With*. Alpine Publications, 1989.

Siegal, Mordecai, and Matthew Margolis. *I Just Got a Puppy; What Do I Do?* Fireside, 1992.

Spadafori, Gina. *Dogs for Dummies*. For Dummies, 1996.

Volhard, Joachim. *The Canine Good Citizen: Every Dog Can Be One*. Wiley, John & Sons, 1997.

FIELD TRAINING

Brander, Michael. *Training the Pointer Retriever Gundog*. Voyageur, 2002.

Crangle, Earl. *Pointing Dogs: Their Handling and Training*. Androscoggin, 2000.

Falk, John. *Gun Dogs*. Voyageur, 1997.

Long, Paul. *Training Pointing Dogs*. Globe Pequot, 1986.

Mueller, Larry. *Speed Train Your Own Bird Dog*. Stackpole, 1990.

Robinson, Jerome. *Ultimate Guide to Bird Dog Training*. Lyons, 2000.

Smith, Jason. *Dog Training: Retrievers and Pointers, at Home and in the Field*. Creative Publishing International, 2003.

Spartas, Dale, and Tom Davis. *To the Point*. Stackpole, 2003.

Tarrant, Bill. *How to Hunt Birds With Gun Dogs*. Stackpole, 2003.

OBEDIENCE TRAINING

Bauman, Diane. *Beyond Basic Dog Training*. Howell, 2003.

Benjamin, Gail Lea. *Mother Knows Best*. Howell, 1985.

Byron, Judy, and Adele Yunck. *Competition Obedience: A Balancing Act*. Jabby, 1998.

Handler, Barbara. *Successful Obedience Handling*. Alpine Publications, 2003.

Koehler, William. *The Koehler Method of Dog Training—Classic Edition*. Wiley, John & Sons, 2003.

Miller, Pat. *The Power of Positive Dog Training*. Howell, 2001.

Reid, Pamela, PhD. *Excel-Erated Learning, Explaining How Dogs Learn and How Best to Teach Them*. James & Kenneth, 1996.

Tucker, Michael. *Dog Training for Children and Parents*. 1998.

Volhard, Jack. *Dog Training for Dummies.* For Dummies, 2001.

Volhard, Joachim, and Gail Fisher. *Training Your Dog: The Step-by-Step Manual.* Howell, 1988.

Woodman, Barbara. *Dog Training My Way.* Berkley Pub. Group, 1997.

SHOW RING TRAINING

Alston, George. *The Winning Edge: Show Ring Secrets.* Howell, 1992.

Beauchamp, Richard. *The Simple Guide to Showing Your Dog.* TFH, 2003.

Caras, Roger. *Going for the Blue.* Warner, 2001.

Craige, Patricia. *Born to Win—Breed to Succeed.* Doral, 1997.

Grossman, Alvin, and Beverly Grossman. *Winning With Pure Bred Dogs: Success by Design.* Doral, 1997.

Hall, Lynne. *Dog Showing for Beginners.* Howell, 1994.

Smith, Cheryl. *The Absolute Beginner's Guide to Showing Your Dog.* Prima Lifestyles, 2001.

AGILITY TRAINING

Bonham, Margaret. *Introduction to Dog Agility.* Barrons Educational Series, 2000.

Daniels, Julie, and Bardi McLennan. *Enjoying Dog Agility.* Doral, 2001.

O'Neil, Jacqueline. *All About Agility.* Howell, 1999.

Simmons-Moake, Jane. *Agility Training: The Fun Sport for All Dogs.* Howell, 1992.

———. *Excelling at Dog Agility—Book 1, Obstacle Training.* FlashPaws Productions, 1999.

———. *Excelling at Dog Agility—Book 2, Sequence Training.* FlashPaws Productions, 2000.

———. *Excelling at Dog Agility—Book 3, Advanced Skills.* FlashPaws Productions, 2003.

STRUCTURE AND MOVEMENT

Elliot, Rachel Page. *The New Dog Steps.* Howell, 1983.

Gilbert, Edward, and Thelma Brown. *K-9 Structure and Terminology.* Howell, 1995.

Lyon, McDowell. *The Dog in Action.* Howell, 1966.

SEARCH AND RESCUE

American Rescue Dog Association. *Search and Rescue Dogs: Training the K-9 Hero.* Wiley, John & Sons, 2002.

Bulanda, Susan. *Ready—A Step-by-Step Guide for Training the Search and Rescue Dog.* Doral, 1995.

———. *Ready to Serve, Ready to Save.* Doral, 1999.

Button, Lue. *Practical Scent Dog Training.* Alpine Publications, 1998.

George, Charles. *Search and Rescue Dogs.* Capstone, 1998.

Rebmann, Andrew, Marcia Koenig, Edward David, and Marcella Sorg. *Cadaver Dog Handbook.* CRC Press, 2000.

Robicheaux, Jack, and John Jons. *Basic Narcotic Detection Dog Training.* K 9 Concepts, 1991.

Syrotuck. William. *Scent and the Scenting Dog: Search and Rescue.* Barleigh, 2000.

THERAPY DOGS

Beck, Alan. *Between Pets and People: The Importance of Animal Companionship.* Purdue, 1996.

Becker, Marty, and D. Morton. *Healing Powers of Dogs: Harnessing the Amazing Ability of Pets to Make and Keep People Healthy.* Hyperion, 2003.

Davis, Kathy. *Therapy Dogs: Training Your Dog to Reach Others.* Dogwise Publishing, 2002.

Fine, Audrey. *Handbook on Animal-Assisted Therapy.* Elsevier Science, 1999.

Graham, Bernie. *Creature Comfort: Animals that Heal.* Charnwood Pub., 2003.

Kent, Deborah. *Animal Helpers for the Disabled.* Scholastic Library, 2003.

Wilson, Cindy, and Dennis Turner. *Companion Animals in Human Health.* Sage, 1997.

TRACKING

Gantz, Sandy, and Susan Boyd. *Tracking From the Ground Up.* Show-Me Publications, 1992.

Johnson, Glen. *Tracking Dog: Theory and Methods.* Barleigh, 1975.

MAGAZINES

AKC Gazette: The Official Journal for the Sport of Purebred Dogs
American Kennel Club, Customer Service
558 Centerview Dr.
Raleigh, NC 27606

Animal Fair Media
P.O. Box 966
New York, NY 10018

Canine Chronicle
4727 NW 80th Ave.
Ocala, FL 34482

Dog & Handler
234 Butternut Hill Rd.
Guilford, VT 05301

Dog Fancy
P.O. Box 53264
Boulder, CO 80322

Dog World
P.O. Box 56244
Boulder, CO 80323

Dogs in Canada
Apex Publishing Limited
89 Skyway Ave., Suite 200
Etobicoke, Ontario MW96R4

Dogs in Review
3 Burroughs
Irvine, CA 92618

Gun Dog
7 Dundas Circle, Suite L
Greensboro, NC 27499

Wildbird
P.O. Box 52898
Boulder, CO 80323

About the Author

Marion Coffman began her career with dogs in 1963 with a Golden Retriever that she trained in obedience and tracking. A year later, she began instructing obedience classes and went on to judge at match shows.

Coffman obtained her first Vizsla in 1967, training him for both obedience and the conformation ring. This dog, Glen Cottage Loki Barat, soon gained his championship title and several years later was accepted into the Vizsla Club of America's Hall of Fame for his outstanding contribution to the breed. He was the sire of thirty-four champions, including the first Triple champion in AKC history and also the first Vizsla to gain seven Best in Shows.

Coffman began breeding Vizslas in 1969, in limited numbers, but always line-bred in order to establish a head type that is predominant in the breed even today, and always with the betterment of the breed foremost in mind. Since then she has bred over ninety champion Vizslas under the Cariad name. Cariad has provided foundation stock for numerous successful Vizsla breeders and exhibitors in the United States and Canada.

Coffman has personally owned over twenty Vizslas through the years, finished championship titles on over forty dogs, and also put more than twenty-five different obedience titles on Vizslas. She is still active in obedience training, presently with a young bitch in Utility.

She has been active in a number of all-breed and Vizsla clubs, serving as a board member, treasurer, secretary, and breed and obedience instructor. A member of the Vizsla Club of America since 1968, she has served as their historian for the past seven years. She has authored pamphlets on whelping, puppy rearing, showing, canine diseases, and early history of the Vizsla breed. She resides in Ocala, Florida, with her husband and four Vizslas and a Petit Basset Griffon Vendeen.

The author with Ch. Koppertone's Cariad Baratom, CDX. Photo © Jim Jernigan.

Index